RUTH GRAHAM

FEAR NOT TOMORROW, GOD IS ALREADY THERE

TRUSTING HIM IN UNCERTAIN TIMES

HOWARD BOOKS
A DIVISION OF SIMON & SCHUSTER
New York   London   Toronto   Sydney

Our purpose at Howard Books is to:
• *Increase faith* in the hearts of growing Christians
• *Inspire holiness* in the lives of believers
• *Instill hope* in the hearts of struggling people everywhere
Because He's coming again!

Published by Howard Books, a division of Simon & Schuster, Inc.
1230 Avenue of the Americas, New York, NY 10020
www.howardpublishing.com

ISBN 978-1-4165-5843-9
ISBN 978-1-4391-6060-2 (ebook)

1 3 5 7 9 10 8 6 4 2

HOWARD and colophon are registered trademarks of Simon & Schuster, Inc.

Manufactured in the United States of America

For information regarding special discounts for bulk purchases,
please contact: Simon & Schuster Special Sales at 1-866-506-1949
or business@simonandschuster.com.

The Simon & Schuster Speakers Bureau can bring authors to your live event. For more
information or to book an event contact the Simon & Schuster Speakers Bureau at
1-866-248-3049 or visit our website at www.simonspeakers.com.

Edited by Cindy Lambert
Cover design by Lucas Art & Design
Interior design by Davina Mock-Maniscalco

To my father, who has shown me what God is like

To Greg, who has illustrated a life lived in trust

Contents

Foreword

WHAT DO YOU do when you are afraid to face the realities of tomorrow? How do you hold things together when everything looks so uncertain? Where do you go when doubts assail you? Sooner or later all of us face uncertainty, fear, and doubt. It is important for us to have a place where uncertainities are faced, fears are conquered, and doubts expressed. But where is that place?

In today's uncertain times many people are hampered by fear—not only fear of circumstances and the future, but even fear of God. And not in the reverential sense. People are uncomfortable with God, thinking He is out to get them if they mess up. They think that He is looking for ways to exclude rather than include them. Ruth Graham takes us to God's unchanging character and examines its relevancy to the fears and anxieties we face every day.

The Bible tells us that Jesus is the exact representation of God. So in *Fear Not Tomorrow, God Is Already There,* Ruth Graham examines the encounters Jesus had with people in the Gospels. Walk with Ruth as she writes about the everyday fears and struggles we all face, and look over Jesus' shoulder as He met people where they were. A fallen woman met by forgiveness . . . frightened disciples met with power . . . grieving sisters met with comfort . . . two disillusioned men met with peace. As Ruth Graham demonstrates, this is the same Jesus whose presence we can know in our own uncertain times.

Since our ability to maintain hope in uncertain times depends upon the One in whom we put our trust, this book is primarily about drilling down to the bedrock of God's character as revealed in Jesus and placing our focus there rather than on uncertainty or short-term remedies the world has to offer.

If you are weary of the packaged, trite answers that are carelessly handed off to those who face life's questions and uncertainties, you owe it to yourself to read these pages. I encourage you to carefully and prayerfully read every word so that you, too, will encounter the living God as He reveals His character to you. We need not fear tomorrow, for God indeed is already there.

David Jeremiah
Senior Pastor, Shadow Mountain Community Church
Founder & CEO, Turning Point Ministries

Acknowledgments

NO BOOK IS the effort of one person. There are many people behind the scenes who help a book go to press, and I am fortunate to have worked with some of the best in the business:

Cindy Lambert, my editor and dear friend. Her belief in me through the years has inspired me to reach further than I thought possible. She has enthusiastically embraced this project. She shares my heart and vision and helped shape the book you now hold in your hands.

Sara Horn, a talented collaborative writer who came to the material first and organized my notes, thoughts, and scribbles, making sense of them so that they could be made into book material. She is a remarkable young woman. I am truly grateful to her.

Stacy Mattingly, with whom I have now collaboratively written four books, including this one. She is a true craftsperson who has an eye for detail and pursues excellence. She draws out of me that which God has placed in me and helps me define and craft the message. She contributed invaluable insights and depth, for which I am grateful.

Dr. James Flynn, Regent University School of Divinity, who, like an angel, looked over our shoulders to make sure we were biblically and theologically correct. I learned so much from his comments and scholarly insights.

Wes Yoder, who is more than just an agent. He is my friend and adviser. I can depend on him to always give me sound, thoughtful counsel. His integrity gives me great security. I have deep appreciation and admiration for him, his staff at Ambassador Speakers Bureau & Literary Agency, and his wonderful wife, Linda.

All those in my new publishing family at Howard Books, an imprint of Simon & Schuster: John Howard, Susan Wilson, Greg Petree, Gary Myers, and the teams that worked so diligently on production, marketing, and sales.

Texas Reardon, the executive director of Ruth Graham & Friends, who is my friend, confidant, mentor, and adviser. Everyone should have a Tex Reardon in their lives. He and his delightful wife, Sandra, are dedicated and tireless. They speak the truth into my life. I love them. Ruth Graham & Friends would not be where it is today without them. They, along with my board of directors, chaired by Dr. Tom Crow, shared my vision, took a fledgling, struggling ministry, and shaped it into the viable ministry it is today. My heart is eternally grateful.

The Ruth Graham & Friends presenters, who have illustrated God's amazing penchant for using broken, flawed people to pour out His grace and goodness to others.

My dear friends, who bless me on a daily basis by cheering me on while listening to me moan about deadlines and a too-full schedule. They love me anyway and appreciate the ministry I have. They have illustrated God's ways to me by demonstrating God's acceptance, love, and grace poured out.

My church family at First Presbyterian Church of Waynesboro. They encourage me, accept my sporadic attendance, and consider me one of their ambassadors. They cannot know how they bless me by their support and kindness.

Those who keep me organized and on track: Anne Frank, who continues to bring joy and support and who adds to every life she touches—especially mine! Michelle Fitzgerald is steady and calm when I tend to be running around in circles.

My beloved children and their spouses and all my grandchildren. I love them more dearly than they can know and am appreciative of their support and pride in what I do.

Trust at My Doorstep

chapter one

IT HAD BEEN a difficult few months. One of my children was struggling, and I didn't know how things would play out. I was anxious, frightened, and continually preoccupied. I could imagine what might be ahead. The questions were relentless: What could I have done differently? Was it my fault? What could I do to change it? How could I protect my child? Was there another step I could take? I felt as if I were being sucked under by a whirlpool of scenes, conversations, and hypothetical outcomes. I lost weight. I battled headaches. I felt like I was constantly vibrating. The fear was overwhelming.

This particular day, the postman arrived at my door with a padded envelope. It was addressed to me in familiar back-slanted handwriting—something from Mother. Feeling the envelope, I knew it was too light to contain a book. What could it be? My birthday was still a long way off. As I tore at the flap and reached inside, I took hold of what felt like a long, narrow picture frame. Pulling it out, I stopped for a moment and stared. It was the framed print from the wall in front of Mother's desk. In black calligraphy bordered by a flowering vine I read the familiar words: "Fear not tomorrow, God is already there."

Instantly, I was transported back to the mountain home of my childhood in Montreat, North Carolina. My mother's plain wooden desk flanked by a tall chest of drawers and a bookcase took up much of one wall in her room. Always lying open on the desk, surrounded by various reference materials, was her well-marked, dog-eared Bible. On the wall above the desk hung a collection of precious photographs and artifacts: a crown of thorns woven for Mother by the head of the Jerusalem police, a slave collar given to her by Johnny Cash, a rude wooden cross fashioned by my brother Franklin, photographs of loved ones and of those for whom she was praying. Centered above these mementoes was the print I now held. I'm not sure where Mother got it or who gave it to her, only that I cannot remember a time when it wasn't hanging there like a banner.

I imagined my mother standing on a chair in front of the desk, reaching to take the print off the wall. Sending me such a gift was just like Mother. All my life, since I left home for boarding school in the ninth grade, she had been sending me letters filled with encouragement from the Scriptures—bits of what she was learning in her own study time or wisdom for some situation I might be facing. Now here she was identifying with my mother's heart, sending me a poignant reassurance. We had not talked much about the circumstances of my struggle. Mother just intuitively knew I might need something like this—a reminder that God was working in our lives and that He cared about our future. I appreciated her sensitivity. She didn't blame or condemn me; she didn't unload a lot of advice. She just sent me something that had been of value to her, something that had reassured her, no doubt, as she had mothered us. Standing on my doorstep, holding that print, I felt the words penetrate my heart and mind, almost as if I had never seen them before, as if they were a message written directly to me. I read them again slowly: "Fear not tomorrow, God is already there."

Little Foxes

Since that day on my doorstep, I have faced quite a few threatening tomorrows, and I have battled fear and anxiety as resilient foes. Perhaps you have fought this same battle. We may experience moments of clarity, as I did reading my mother's framed print, but then we return to daily life and to the struggle. We wonder how we're supposed to "fear not tomorrow" in the worst-case scenarios of our lives: a frightening diagnosis, betrayal, separation from a child who has gone off to war, the loss of a job, the evaporation of our retirement fund, the drug addiction of a loved one, abandonment by a spouse, failure at our workplace, the loss of a home, a legal verdict that changes our lives, the death of a loved one, the exposure of a secret, the loss of our possessions to flood, earthquake, tornado, or financial disaster.

Fear not tomorrow? It is easy to say it but another thing to live it out. We drown in our questions: But what about . . . ? How will I . . . ? What if . . . ? But if I can't even . . . ? Who will . . . ? And what does it mean that God is already there? Where? In our crises, God can seem silent, remote, or, worse, even imaginary. You may feel as I have at times. I have real problems, and they are too big, too hard, too painful for me to solve. I don't have time for theology. I'm in trouble here! I'm inadequate, and I need something real. Something practical. Something secure. Give me some solutions, some guarantees. Can't you see that I'm terrified of tomorrow?

Fear and anxiety can exhaust us. King Solomon writes about the "little foxes that spoil the vines" (Song of Solomon 2:15 NKJV). Fear and anxiety are like that. Fear can wipe us out, burn up whatever energy we have, and hinder us from entering into the full experience of life that God desires for us. Certainly, fear and anxiety can become so severe they incapacitate us. But the majority of us live with fear and still function. I have heard fear compared to a jackhammer buzzing just outside the window. The noise is constantly there. When you sleep, the jackhammer quits, but when you wake up, it starts again, sapping your strength and attention until you're no longer really living—just enduring.

Fear takes the air out of life. When we live with fear, we lose our capacity for fun and spontaneity. We struggle to love others wholeheartedly. During the difficult period with my child that I described above, I

experienced fear in different ways. At times, I would have trouble func-
tioning; at other times, I would be able to get up in the morning and do
what was necessary. Up and down. Fear was that steady buzz or hum. I
wasn't able to hear the music of life clearly. Everything was filtered
through that fear.

My mother was a master at finding ways to enjoy life despite the intense pressures she faced. She knew how to move fear out of the way
and keep joy alive. Stories of her antics and pranks have become the
stuff of legend in our family. As a young parent, for instance, I would
tell my children, "Now don't draw on yourselves." Then I would leave
the kids with Mother, only to find them covered in inky smiley faces
that Mother herself had drawn! Once Mother made a mudslide for the
grandchildren on the side of a steep embankment near our Montreat
house. She turned on the hose and then promptly took her turn as the
first one down. When much older, she accidently drove her car down
that same steep embankment. Thinking she was stepping on the brake,
she had stepped on the accelerator instead. She and her friend escaped
unscathed, but afterward Mother arranged for a stop sign to be staked
at the bottom of the incline, lest other wayward drivers be tempted to
take the same route!

Life is a gift from God to be enjoyed. Fear suffocates our spirits and
robs us of that gift. It is human to experience the emotion of fear. Fear
entered the human experience in the garden of Eden when Adam and
Eve rebelled against God and hid themselves from Him. But Peter describes Satan as a "roaring lion, seeking someone to devour," and I believe fear is also Satan's paw print (1 Peter 5:8). It is true that some
kinds of fear can help us—the kind that keeps us from stepping into
oncoming traffic, for instance, or putting our hand on a hot stove. At
times, God may use fear to keep us from making wrong choices or
wrong decisions in life. But these moments of fear are different from
what the Bible calls the "spirit of fear," which I might describe as the
condition or attitude that takes hold when our emotion of fear con-

sumes us, cripples us (2 Timothy 1:7 NKJV). As Paul writes, the spirit of fear does not come from God.

·

Shifting Our Focus

God is concerned about the way fear affects our lives. The Bible says, "There is no fear in love; but perfect love casts out fear, because fear involves torment" (1 John 4:18 NKJV). Sometimes we experience fear as torment. Torment is not God's will for us. God is committed to our peace. Jesus said, "Peace I leave with you" (John 14:27 NKJV). We read of Jesus, "He Himself is our peace" (Ephesians 2:14 NKJV). God has ordained peace for us (Isaiah 26:12). He did not design us to live in fear and anxiety but in peace. In Scripture, we find God repeatedly urging, commanding, people not to be afraid. God is not condemning us for feeling the emotion of fear, but He doesn't want us to get stuck there or to set up camp in torment. The question is when we are at our wit's end, how do we "fear not"? At such moments, peace can seem nothing more than an abstraction. We struggle even to imagine the experience.

Often, when we experience fear, we have allowed our circumstances to overwhelm or alter our perspective. Our perspective has become skewed. I have discovered that defeating fear in my life begins with shifting my focus. I take my eyes off the circumstances, off the source of my fear, and put my focus on God. Instead of mulling over the "what ifs" in my future—instead of looking ahead with anxiety, trepidation, dread, or even horror—I make the choice to look at God, to consider His character, and to trust that the One who loves me is "already there." The message on Mother's framed print helped me to make that kind of shift as I faced uncertainty with my child. I had been focusing on tomorrow; the words on the print brought my focus back to God.

Shifting our focus is first a decision, then a process. When we turn to God, our decision opens a door for peace and reassurance to enter our hearts. The Bible says of God, "You will keep him in perfect peace, *whose mind is stayed on You*" (Isaiah 26:3 NKJV, emphasis added). When we focus on God, peace follows. I find that as I concentrate on God, as I examine facets of His character, as I spend time with Him in prayer, sharing my heart and quieting myself to listen, as I meditate on what the Bible says about Him, as I read about Jesus and observe the way He handled life—as I "stay" my mind on God— my problems begin to lose their power over me. Instead, I recognize the power, the beauty, and the love of God. He is my focus now. I am learning about Him and getting to know Him. And the more I learn, the more I discover I can trust Him.

In the coming chapters, we will be doing just what the verse above from Isaiah says—staying, or fixing, our minds on God. We will examine some of God's attributes and consider His ways. We will study the character of Jesus, for in learning about Jesus, we learn about God. Scripture calls Jesus the "express image" of God (Hebrews 1:3 NKJV). Jesus Himself told His disciples, "He who has seen Me has seen the Father" (John 14:9 NKJV). If we want to know what God is like, we can look at Jesus. We can ask: How did Jesus deal with people? What were His relationships like? How did He respond to people's distress? As we focus on God this way, we can expect God's peace to crowd out the fear in our hearts.

For some of us, focusing on God, or considering that He is "already there" in our tomorrow, is not exactly a comfort. We may be afraid of God. What little we know of Him, or what we don't know of Him, frightens us. We fear He is out to lower the boom on us, that He is looking for our faults and eager to point out our failings. We are afraid of His power. Afraid of His judgment. Afraid of being overwhelmed by Him. It is our human nature to fear what we don't understand, and we don't understand God. He is unfathomable. He is so much more than we can imagine—far more. He is not accountable to us. He is mysterious, and mystery can be frightening. On seeing the Lord on the throne, Isaiah said, "Woe is me, for I am undone!" (Isaiah 6:5 NKJV). Isaiah saw his frailty in light of God's almightiness; he was awed by God's holiness and glory.

But Scripture also calls God "Abba," an intimate word for Father that we would translate "Daddy" (Romans 8:15). While God is over-whelming, He is also tender with us. In the New Testament, we see Jesus touching, healing, and relating intimately with people. Bette Midler recorded a song about God watching us from a distance. That line is only half-true. God is watching us. But not from a distance. Jesus said, "If anyone loves Me, he will keep My word; and My Father will love him, and We will come to him and make Our home with him" (John 14:23 NKJV). God comes close. He makes His home with us. He longs for us as a lover for his bride. We take God for granted, we don't develop the relationship, we ignore Him, we don't spend time with Him; and yet He stays with us, longing for that intimacy. God makes a covenant with us, and He keeps it. To me, that is one of the most reas-suring truths about God. He will never give me up. Never desert me. Never leave me alone. Never (Hebrews 13:5).

As we learn more about God in these pages and spend time focus-ing our attention on Him, our relationship with Him will deepen. The Bible promises that when we draw near to God, he will draw near to us (James 4:8). As our relationship with God grows, so will our trust in Him. We will discover His constancy. When everything around us is unstable, God is stable. His character is consistent, unchanging. His love is secure. My prayer is that the more you learn of God and the closer you get to Him, the more you will be able not only to trust Him with your tomorrow but also to take comfort in the fact that He is the One who is already there.

Overcoming Our Misperceptions

Part of our challenge in learning to trust God involves overcoming misperceptions we may have of Him. If my view of God is not accurate, then my trust in Him will be more hesitant than hopeful. Often our picture of God is colored by our experiences with our own fathers or with other figures of authority in our lives. If your father was cold and demanding, then you may see God that way. If your father was gone, as mine often was, then you may see God as far away or busy with other things. If an authority figure was angry or abusive, then you may see God the same way and want nothing to do with Him. We are relational beings, and as such, we are hardwired to measure God by our relationships with significant people.

I did not always view God as someone with whom I could be comfortable. As I shared, my father was gone much of the time, fulfilling his calling to preach the gospel. I knew my father loved me; I knew I was important to him. But I also knew the world needed him, and for many years, I saw God as being similarly occupied with others and unreachable. I have since learned that God is not like that.

In my book *In Every Pew Sits a Broken Heart*, I share in detail about my life, my failures, and some of the ways God met me in my brokenness and redeemed it. I tell the story of what it was like to go home to Montreat after a major personal failure. Driving up the mountain to my parents' home was one of the most difficult things I have ever done. I had no idea what they would say to me or how they would respond. I had gone against everyone's advice. As I saw it, I had failed myself, my family, my children, and God. I felt deserving of condemnation and rejection. What would my parents do? Would they say they had told me so? That I had made my bed and now would have to lie in it?

As I approached the house, I saw my father standing there in the driveway. I parked the car and opened the door to get out, but before I could as much as set my feet on the asphalt, my father was at my side.

He wrapped his arms around me, and I heard him say, "Welcome home." His acceptance instantly silenced my shame. I was broken, but I no longer feared. My father had embraced me at my worst and loved me anyway. I experienced grace. I would not compare my father with God, but that day my father showed me in a very practical, gracious way what God is like.

Through that experience, I was able to get a glimpse of the unconditional love God has for me. It has taken me awhile to get to a point where I finally see God as "Abba," as Daddy. Learning to know God intimately has been a process. But through the fog of doubt, anxiety, and fear, I do see Him now as warm and embracing. He loves me, enjoys me, and wishes I would laugh more. He will do anything to draw me in. He wants my heart. He wants my trust.

Many years ago I taught a Bible study titled "Enjoying God" for the women at my home church. I was convinced most of us did not enjoy God. Even the title of the study made us a bit uncomfortable. Was it sacrilegious to "enjoy" God? Wasn't He austere and stern? Holy and unapproachable? I wanted to explore the possibilities.

The first week's homework was to imagine crawling into God's lap and calling him Daddy. I think many were slightly put off by the assignment. Some had to deal with the damaged image of an earthly father. Some had difficulty seeing God in such an intimate way. Each week the assignment was the same. Gradually, I began to hear reports of breakthroughs. Some people took longer than others to connect with God, but we sensed God doing something profound in the group. My own life changed over the course of that study as I too began to see God intimately—as a secure place of comfort and peace. As I focused on Him, God was chipping away at my misperceptions, helping me to open my heart to His love. And He can do the same for you.

Why, God?

Our misperceptions of God can also be formed in the trials and heart-aches of life. You may have a long scar of pain running through your life—a spouse leaving, the loss of a child, bankruptcy, illness, addiction, things that take the breath out of you. Perhaps you feel that God abandoned you in those experiences. That He must not care about you. That if He loved you, He wouldn't have let you go through all that hurt. You wonder, "Why should I trust Him now?"

Why, God? This is a real question we ask when life happens and things seem to go badly. *Why are You letting my life unravel? Don't You love me? Didn't You promise to protect me? How could You let this happen?* In the valleys of life, we can feel as if God has betrayed us. That He isn't trustworthy, as we once thought. That we'll never again have a stable or secure place to stand. When devastation occurs and we can't see God anywhere, our trust in Him can crumble to dust. We may even reject Him for a time.

I've lived through personal events that have left me reeling. I have written about suffering in a broken marriage. As the marriage began to come apart, I couldn't "feel" God. I couldn't hold myself together. I described the way I felt back then: "Raw. Lonely. Exposed. Like an egg without a shell."[1] I wanted to know why those circumstances were happening to me. Perhaps you have felt this way too.

I've seen loved ones suffer through crushing experiences, and I've asked God why. Why did my friend's first grandchild die just hours after birth? Why did a young missionary couple's two-year-old child drown in the backyard? Why was my friend diagnosed with lung cancer though she never smoked a day in her life? We witness or live through destruction caused by tornadoes, hurricanes, tsunamis, and earth-quakes. We call them "acts of God," and we wonder why God would allow them. Fear not tomorrow? How can we do anything *but* fear after all the devastation we've already seen?

God is not threatened by our why. People say we can't ask why, but we can—we should. We're in good company when we ask why. Jesus, Job, David, Jeremiah, and many others we would call "heroes of the faith" have asked why. Asking why is part of the human experience. When we ask God why, we are expressing our innermost emotions, our hurt and disappointment, and God wants us to do that. He works with honesty. He is not threatened by our questions and doubts. He invites us to express our feelings. We're in a relationship with Him—He doesn't want us to shut our emotions down. While God already knows how we feel, we need to know; and often we discover what is in our hearts as we express ourselves freely to Him.

But we can also get stuck at why. While asking why can be a stimulus for further exploration, understanding, and honest grappling, sometimes it can become a defense—a way to keep God out and to keep intimacy with Him at bay. We can go round and round in circles with why, never really intending to get anywhere. We can get comfortable with why. We would rather stay where we are than do the hard work of learning how to trust God again. And if we're not careful, some people will keep us there. They will feed our why as long as we let them. At a certain point, what we actually may need is someone to pull us forward and say, "Hey, let's explore why you feel this way. Let's not give up on God."

God invites us to wrestle with our why, our questions. He wrestles *with* us, as He wrestled with Jacob (Genesis 32:24–32). But finally the angel of God touched Jacob's thigh and put it out of socket. I can hear the angel saying, "It's enough now. Let's go forward." My uncle Clayton Bell, my mother's brother, died suddenly of a heart attack at age sixty-eight. He loved God passionately and was a respected leader in his denomination. Those who loved him asked God why. Why take this dynamic man at his prime? Why not leave him here to serve You? Aunt Peggy, my uncle's wife, suffered greatly, but there came a time when I remember her saying, "I'm going to lean into the pain." Whatever her questions, she was going to "lean," trusting God and expecting Him to be there.

At some point, trusting God becomes a step of faith. No one can prove God. You will have to make the choice to trust Him for yourself. Making that choice doesn't mean you have settled your questions; you may not see those questions resolved in this life. But you can make the decision to try trusting God again. You can take a step forward with all your unresolved questions and invite God to reveal Himself. It's okay to live with what I call "unfinishedness." I think about my mother and how "finished" she looked in her relationship with God—as if everything were settled, everything clear. But when you read Mother's poetry, you discover she was anything but finished. She simply learned to live with her questions and to trust God anyway.

Walking Forward

Why not bring your questions along as you walk forward to discover more about God in this book? You can invite God to work with you as you read. Ask Him to help you in your battle with fear. Ask Him to help you overcome your misperceptions of Him so you can trust Him for tomorrow. God longs to reveal Himself to you. Jesus said about those who love God, "I too will love them and show myself to them" (John 14:21 TNIV). God wants us to see Him for who He really is.

We don't have to get it all at once. Trusting God is a process. Just as there are stages of life, there are stages of faith. Trust comes bit by bit. Our part is to be willing—willing to move, willing to try. God wants our willingness. Someone once said you can't steer a car that isn't moving. If we can just make the choice to move, God will meet us. I want to challenge you. Open yourself up to the possibility of what God can do in your life. Let Him show Himself worthy of your trust. Walk forward into these pages and decide for yourself about God. See if His intimate love is real. See for yourself. Don't let your questions or misperceptions be hindrances. They don't have to stop you from moving. Let's get to know God better. Let's discover Him. We can bring our baggage, our questions, our "why" right along with us.

POINT OF FOCUS
You will keep him in perfect peace,
Whose mind is stayed on You,
Because he trusts in You.
Isaiah 26:3 NKJV

Discover His Trustworthiness

chapter two

FOR TWO YEARS I attended college north of Boston. Behind the campus was a large pond surrounded by trees. Once winter set in and temperatures became bitterly cold, my friends and I would bundle up and go out to the pond to skate. Those of us who didn't have skates would slide around the pond on the soles of our shoes. We would step out on the ice tentatively, staying close to the shore. You could gauge the strength of the ice first by looking at the color. If the ice was filled with air bubbles, then the water was close to the surface. If the ice was clear and bluish, then you knew it was frozen solid.

We would take a step or two, then another. All of our senses would be awake. We were listening, looking, feeling for the slightest hint of a break in that ice. And thick ice does groan and creak, although those sounds don't necessarily mean it will break. We would take those first steps, wondering if the ice would hold. After a few more steps, we would become more confident and take several more, maybe in quick succession this time. The more the ice proved solid, the wider our steps would fan out and the bigger our skating area would become.

I have discovered that walking with God works this way. Each time you venture a step with God and find Him to be trustworthy, you become more willing to take another step. Then another. As He secures your steps, it becomes easier to commit. Pretty soon you realize you're on the journey. You're discovering God's trustworthiness. You're living with Him in relationship.

Joseph's Walk

Joseph, the husband of Mary, the mother of Jesus, took some big steps out on the ice of his life. Joseph was a man who trusted God. Those days of planning and preparing for the marriage to Mary must have been a thrilling time in his life. He had taken the first step, betrothal, and now he had bright hopes as he and Mary planned their future. I can imagine theirs was a young, budding love and that they sensed God had brought them together. Though a man of royal blood through the line of King David, Joseph was a poor carpenter in love with a devout young woman. As far as we know, he intended to wed Mary when the year of betrothal was complete and to live quietly with his new bride, working his modest carpenter's trade. God, however, had something else in mind.

A great barrier suddenly came between Joseph and Mary. It was discovered that Mary was pregnant (Matthew 1:18). How must Joseph have felt? Betrayed? Shamed? Did he look with suspicion at every man in the village? He loved Mary. He had trusted her. Now he saw their hopes and dreams slipping away. Joseph had been given an explanation for all this, but he couldn't completely believe the audacious story. This was unbelievable, wasn't it? Not only was Mary expecting a baby, but the baby, she said, was God's child! Mary wasn't one to lie or make up stories, so Joseph couldn't totally discount the claim. And yet, what was he to think?

It is important to recognize that in a hard situation God does not expect us to quit thinking. Can you imagine the emotions Joseph must have experienced? Talk about feeling totally overwhelmed, out of his comfort zone, inadequate, and fearful! I imagine him wracked with fear and anxiety. This was a situation in which Joseph had to think seriously and prayerfully.

The solution Joseph came up with wasn't harsh. We are told he was a righteous man and didn't want to cause Mary harm. Rather than go by the letter of the law, Joseph was tempered by mercy and compassion.

He couldn't go through with the marriage, but he would not expose Mary to further shame or even to the technical possibility of death by stoning. Instead, the Bible tells us, Joseph "planned to send her away secretly" (Matthew 1:19).

And yet Joseph's plan was not God's plan. Joseph's desire to protect Mary was right, but God was going to ask him to go further in that desire. One night an angel of the Lord appeared to Joseph in a dream and said, "Do not be afraid to take Mary as your wife; for the Child who has been conceived in her is of the Holy Spirit. She will bear a Son; and you shall call His name Jesus, for He will save His people from their sins" (Matthew 1:20–21). The angel gave Joseph detailed instructions—what to name the baby—and told him specifically what the baby's purpose would be. Those words must have helped to calm Joseph's fears, ease his anxieties, and enable him to resume the joy of his love for Mary.

But what a set of directions from God! God was saying, "Joseph, I'm asking you to do something that will require a lot of you. You don't know what the future will hold, but fear not. Do not be afraid. Just take the step." Joseph didn't seem to hesitate. His response was prompt. When he awoke from sleep, we are told, he "did as the angel of the Lord commanded him, and took Mary as his wife" (Matthew 1:24). He could've backed off, shaken the dust off his feet, and walked away, saying, "I didn't sign up for this. I didn't ask for this." But Joseph trusted God and took the risk. Satan failed that day because Joseph trusted. Joseph did the right thing in the right way. He chose to offer love and grace even when he thought he had been wronged. He shielded Mary from what must have been years of gossip and slander. He shared in the unjust shame. As I have heard my pastor say, Joseph identified with Mary's shame. He stepped into the gap and became a part of her story—part of God's story.

17

Trust and Obedience

Trusting God requires obedience. Joseph's decision to follow God and take on a marriage to a woman with child went against everything he knew—all the social mores of the day, his family values, the values of the culture in which he had been brought up. What's more, Joseph had no guarantees about the future or how he would do what God was asking. He could not provide his pregnant wife with a horse—only a donkey. When it came time for the baby's delivery, he could only offer a stable bed of hay and a crude manager. God does not necessarily meet our needs on our terms or as we might expect. Still, he calls us to trust Him and to obey.

When God gives us direction, stepping out on that ice becomes a matter of more than just our willingness. The angel "commanded" Joseph. God asks us to be willing to walk with him, but following Him out on the ice is also a matter of obedience. The Bible says, "If you are willing *and* obedient, you shall eat the good of the land" (Isaiah 1:19 NKJV, emphasis added). It takes willingness to walk forward and discover God, but to grow in relationship with God will require something more—that we trust His direction and step out. Taking the first baby steps out on the ice is one thing. But we want to get across the pond. We do that step by step. As we understand God's direction, we act on what we've discovered. We engage what we've learned.

But it was easy for Joseph—he had an angel! What if I don't understand what God is asking me to do? How can I confidently take a step? How can I obey? It is true we don't always understand God's direction. Things are not always clear. It can be difficult to see ahead in the darkness of our circumstances. In my area of Virginia there are large caverns. One summer I took my grandson to tour one of them. The guide walked us underground into the cave, which was illuminated by electric lights. At a certain point, she stopped the tour and turned the lights off. It was absolutely dark. You couldn't see your hand in front of your face. Do you ever feel that way about your life? That you can't even see an inch in front of you, let alone understand the next step you're supposed to take?

There are times in life when God keeps us in the dark, when he keeps us from moving forward, because he wants us to wait. But in many situations we actually have more light than we realize. As my grandson and I were standing in the pitch blackness of that cave, the guide suddenly lit a match. The light given off by that tiny match took on the total darkness and lit up the cavern. In life, we may have just a little bit of light, just a slight sense of direction, but we can walk in the light that we have. If you believe God is leading you in a particular direction but you are unsure, try walking through the open doors until one closes, making it clear you are to stop, or until you sense God calling you to halt. Otherwise, continue on, trusting God is showing you His way for you. Like Joseph, we can step out in obedience and do what we believe God is asking and then trust Him with the rest.

Joseph did have to trust God with the rest. After Mary gave birth, things became dangerous for the family. Herod was about to order the murder of all infant boys in the region in an effort to kill Jesus. Again God spoke to Joseph: Another dream. Another angel. Another step out on the ice required. "Take the Child and His mother and flee to Egypt, and remain there until I tell you" (Matthew 2:13).

Do you see how God was being faithful to protect the family *while* requiring them to step out and trust him? The challenge to obey was also the way to safety. It couldn't have been an easy move. The young family may have been getting settled into their rhythm of life. They were living in a house and had been paid a remarkable visit by magi from the East. Herod had not yet acted, so there was no apparent threat. Joseph had only recently brought his family to Bethlehem to register for the census. Now they were going to have to move again—to Egypt. A foreign country. The place where Israel had been enslaved for four hundred years. A symbol of bondage. It was true there was a large Jewish community there, but Joseph could have said, "Wait a minute, this doesn't make sense, God. We're settling in, and we like it here.

We've made friends with other young families. I don't want to uproot Mary and Jesus now."

By this time, however, Joseph already knew what it was like to hear from God, to trust him, and to obey. God had secured Joseph's steps to this point—the ice had not broken. Perhaps Joseph found it a little easier to obey now. He had seen God at work in his life. He had a track record with God. Committing to another step might not have seemed as daunting. In fact, as we read, Joseph didn't just wake up the next morning and obey the angel's direction. The Bible tells us Joseph got up and left with his family for Egypt "while it was still night" (Matthew 2:14).

Building a Track Record

One of the gifts of walking with God is the opportunity to build a track record with Him. This is how we discover His trustworthiness. The more we walk with Him, the more we step out and see Him secure our steps, the more touchstone experiences with God we accumulate. When fear starts to hinder us, we can look to these touchstones and find courage to take the next step.

Joseph must have spent his lifetime building a track record with God. Surely he had questions along the way, but those questions did not keep him from acting. I can imagine Joseph making this decision: "I'm going to take a chance on God, obey him, engage in this process of trust, and go as far as it takes me." Joseph went to Egypt, then back to Israel, and finally to Nazareth, all along having to trust God daily for the wisdom to parent, train, and equip Jesus for His life and purpose. Joseph must have modeled fatherhood, integrity, and righteousness for Jesus. He trained Jesus in an honorable trade. He raised Jesus in the Jewish faith and traditions. God had entrusted His only Son to Joseph's fatherly care. No doubt Joseph's track record with God was rife with instances of God proving Himself trustworthy, and that must have built Joseph's confidence.

God hasn't asked me to go to Egypt—not yet anyway—but He has asked me to do things I have found challenging to obey. In trying to locate the strength to step out, I have been able to draw on my track record with God. When I was a young mother living in Texas, for example, I heard my father preach a sermon that described what it would be like when we passed on from this life into eternity. We would see the world receding and with it all the people whom we had known but had missed telling about Jesus. I remember being disturbed as I reflected on this image. In particular, I was thinking about a lovely family who had lived near us for years but with whom I had never shared the gospel. Did they know the Lord? I decided to sit down and write them a letter. In it I explained the gospel message, telling them that I loved them and that I wanted to see them in heaven one day.

Looking at the letter, I hesitated. Should I mail it? These were wonderful people, and I feared I would offend them. But I went ahead. I wanted to be sure they had heard about Jesus, so I dropped the letter in the mail. Some time later I received the nicest letter from these neighbors in reply, assuring me they knew and loved the Lord. I was relieved and delighted by both their kindness and their response. God had gone ahead of me and prepared the way for the exchange. First, He had put it on my heart to write the letter; then He had prepared this family to receive it graciously. The experience became one of my touchstones with God.

Years later, I needed that touchstone. My memory of it gave me the courage to do what I believed God was asking at that time—to write another letter, this one to my mother-in-law. My marriage to her son had failed many years before, and she and I had become estranged through the divorce and subsequent events. One afternoon I was driving back to Virginia from Mother and Daddy's house in Montreat, listening to a sermon by my uncle Clayton. He was talking about Naomi and Ruth and mother-in-law–daughter-in-law relationships. After a while, I dismissed the message as not being pertinent to me. "I don't have a mother-in-law," I thought.

Right then, it was as if the Holy Spirit were sitting in the passenger's seat. In my heart I heard Him say, "Oh, but you do have a mother-in-law!" I knew whom He meant. I thought, "Oh, no. Let bygones be bygones. I can love her from a distance." But it was very clear to me what God was telling me to do. I needed to write to my mother-in-law and ask her forgiveness for not being the kind of daughter-in-law I should've been. That's when I remembered the correspondence with my neighbors in Texas. God had prepared the way for me then. I decided I would write this new letter to my mother-in-law, trusting God to go ahead of me and prepare her heart too.

Once I got home, I immediately sat down, wrote the letter, and sent it off before I could chicken out. My mother-in-law always used pink stationery. I feared I would get a big, thick pink envelope in return and find a letter telling me what a terrible daughter-in-law I had been and that it was about time I recognized it. In fact, a big pink envelope did arrive, but the letter was full of love and gratitude. I had written my mother-in-law at an opportune time, she explained. She forgave me and said she wanted to renew our relationship. To this day, I still get emotional remembering her gracious, loving words.

The experience with my mother-in-law reinforced what I had learned in Texas—if God tells us to do something, then He will take care of us in the endeavor. He doesn't lead us out on a limb just to saw it out from under us. To use another metaphor, if God asks us to get out of the boat, then He isn't going to let us drown. Don't misunderstand me. I like it in the boat. I feel secure and safe in the boat. Just as with stepping out on the ice, I would rather not rush out. If God asks me to get out of the boat, then I would rather ease my way out. I may start by dangling my feet over the side. Then I might slip into the water, holding on to the boat with both hands. Maybe I'll eventually venture holding on with just one hand. Then with one finger. Does God really want me to let go of all my security and trust Him?

After a while, God gently, patiently, begins to pry that last finger loose. "Okay," I reason. "I can swim." I look for a life vest or a rope—

just in case. Soon, though, I find I'm growing tired. It's getting dark. It's getting cold. I can't see the shore or touch the bottom. The wind begins to blow, and the waves get rough. I see lightning flash in the distance. I begin to question whether I heard God correctly. Maybe I misinterpreted Him. I don't know where I am or where I'm going. I fear I'm about to sink. Then I remember the Lord's promise to me: "Trust in the Lord with all your heart, and lean not on your own understanding; in all your ways acknowledge Him, and He shall direct your paths" (Proverbs 3:5–6 NKJV). God knows exactly where I am and where He wants to take me. My job is to let go.

But what if it does seem that God is going to let us drown, that He is letting the limb that holds us fall to the ground, that He has let the ice break under our feet? What if the response I got from my mother-in-law had been the one I feared? Would that have meant God had ruined His track record with me? That He had failed to direct my path? That I had trusted Him with all my heart only to have Him turn out to be untrustworthy? What happens when we step out and our step doesn't appear to hold?

This is the dilemma we live with. Some things are not neat. Sometimes God does not confirm our steps of faith in the ways we expect. The principle I have learned is to act in obedience like Joseph and leave the rest to God. I wish it could be nailed down and tucked in, but we live with unanswered questions—with unfinishedness. There will be times when it will appear as if God has let us down, but God is bigger than what we see. As we shift our focus from the circumstances back to God, He will reveal Himself even in our disappointment and disillusionment.

When my first marriage began to fail, I expected God to make the marriage new and our home peaceful. I claimed the promise in Isaiah: "Behold, I will do something new" (Isaiah 43:19). And in Haggai: "The latter glory of this house will be greater than the former . . . and in this place I will give peace" (Haggai 2:9). I expected God to make things better, but they did not get better. They got worse, and my marriage ended. I got angry with God because I felt He had failed me, but in the end, I decided to let go of my expectations. I tried to see instead where God was at work. My life had not turned out as I had hoped, but I realized God was doing a new thing in *me*. God was making *me* better. In spite of the pain, I chose to live with my questions and believe what the Bible said: "Oh, taste and see that the Lord is good; blessed is the man who trusts in Him!" (Psalm 34:8 NKJV).

Remember to Remember

Do you believe God is asking you to step out on the ice in some area of your life? Are you struggling with whether to do it? I have certainly struggled. When we're in the dark, afraid and uncertain of what might happen to us, it is difficult to lay everything down and say, "God, I trust you. I'll do whatever You ask." That is what Mary did when the angel Gabriel appeared to her and told her she would become pregnant by the Holy Spirit. She said, "Behold, the bondslave of the Lord; may it be done to me according to your word" (Luke 1:38). What a powerful response! She completely abandoned herself to God. She leapt out of the boat. She rushed out on the ice—just as Joseph, her husband, did later. You can see why God brought them together. Neither of them was afraid to trust. If only I could trust God with that kind of abandon!

I have a long way to go, but one thing that makes it easier for me to trust God is cultivating the habit of remembering what He has already done. I tap into that track record. Remembering is a God-given prescription. God tells the Israelites over and over. Remember how I delivered you from Egypt. Remember how I guided you through the desert with the fire by night and the cloud by day. Remember the manna I gave you so you wouldn't be hungry and the water I provided to quench your thirst. Remember that it was I who brought you into the Promised Land, a land overflowing with milk and honey. Remember my covenant. Remember.

As we've seen, when we remember the ways God has worked in our lives in the past, we are better able to follow His lead in the midst of our current struggle. But remembering is also a form of preparation for future struggle. When we make remembering our habit, we literally build our confidence in God ahead of time so that we can obey Him when trials come—and they will come, often unexpectedly. If we are already in the habit of reviewing our track record with God, if we are constantly focusing on the evidence of his trustworthiness, then when God requires us to step out on the ice again, we won't have to dig as deep for the faith to obey. Our minds will already be saturated with examples of God's faithfulness. We will be better prepared to act.

Keep a Journal

I don't have the best memory in the world. That's one reason I keep a journal. I write down my struggles, challenges, and prayers, and then I go back later and note the ways God has answered or led me through those difficulties. This exercise is a great faith builder. I particularly like to review my journals in January, having closed out one year and entered another. Sometimes as I look back, God's involvement with me seems fuzzy; sometimes it is quite clear. But reviewing my journals always confirms for me that God is there. I can say, "Okay God, since You were with me in that storm three months ago, I believe You can help me weather this new one right now. There must be a good purpose somewhere in this experience, and I trust You to accomplish it."

Perhaps journaling is already your practice. If so, try every so often reviewing your entries, purposefully looking to trace God's involvement with you. Spend some time meditating on the ways you believe He worked in your circumstances and relationships. Get those memories into your heart so they will be easy to recall. Perhaps you haven't kept a journal before and would like to give it a try now. I've been journaling all my life and have found it an enormous resource in my relationship with God. If the practice interests you, I encourage you to go get a notebook and begin.

Study God's Word

You can also build yourself up in "remembering" by studying God's Word. The Bible is a record of God's relationship with humanity and a portrait of His character. As we read the Scriptures, we are reminding ourselves of what God has done and who He is. If you are not doing so now, try taking time to read the Bible regularly. Soak it up, memorize it, pray as you read it, and seek to understand it.

Try praying God's Word back to Him. As I am praying for my children, I often use Paul's words found in Ephesians 1:17–19: "That the God of our Lord Jesus Christ, the Father of glory, may give to you a spirit of wisdom and of revelation in the knowledge of Him. I pray that the eyes of your heart may be enlightened, so that you will know what is the hope of His calling, what are the riches of the glory of His inheritance in the saints, and what is the surpassing greatness of His power toward us who believe."

Too many of us rely on others to interpret the Bible for us. How many books like the one you are holding have you read recently? Compare the amount of time you invest in reading books with the time you spend reading God's Word. Other resources certainly can be valuable aids to our growth in God, but we need to be studying the Bible for ourselves.

I have made a habit of reading my Bible every day. If I miss a day, I don't beat myself up over it. I just start again the next day. I prefer reading in the morning when I feel fresher. Other people take time for Bible reading over lunch or before bed. The important thing is finding the window of time that works best for you. I tend to keep this routine: Before I actually read, I spend some time journaling. I write down the events of the previous day, decisions that need to be made, my worries, anxieties, thoughts, and questions. Then I ask God to speak to those issues, or to any other issues, as I read the Scriptures.

Normally, I follow a reading plan. I might spend time reading a particular book of the Bible all the way through. My mother would also trace themes through several books. I trust God to use the passages that happen to be part of my reading on any given day to speak to my concerns. As I read along and notice some verse or principle standing out, I write it down in my journal to keep a record. Some days I feel God speaking to me strongly through my reading. Other days nothing really jumps out at me. In either case, I come away edified, and I don't give up my habit. I learned a long time ago that God honors faithfulness. If I just commit to the process every day, eventually it will bear fruit. Eventually, I will understand what God is saying to me.

You may believe that what you're facing in life right now is impossible, but God says that with Him nothing is impossible (Luke 1:37). You may say, "I can't figure things out." But God says trust Him, and He will direct your steps (Proverbs 3:5–6). You may believe you can't manage it all, but as you give yourself to God, He promises to supply all your needs (Philippians 4:19). The promises of God are there in the Scriptures. My mother used to say, "All the promises of God are on the believer's side." We just need to spend time discovering those promises.

Meditate on God's Character

God's promises are based on His character, which the Bible tells us never changes: "Jesus Christ is the same yesterday and today and forever" (Hebrews 13:8). One year, drawing on Scripture, I made a list of some of God's attributes, using the alphabet (see the ABC Praise List on page 260). God is almighty, an anchor. He is beautiful and bountiful. Compassionate, a composer, a covenant keeper, creator, and so on.

I keep the list in the back of my Bible and often spend time meditating on these attributes. This is another way I "remember" who God is and affirm for myself that I can trust Him. You might try pulling attributes of God out of the verses referenced in the paragraph above and meditating on them. If nothing is impossible for God, then He is all-powerful. If He is directing your steps, then He is a guide. If He supplies all your needs, then He is a provider. Perhaps you see other attributes of God in the verses. Or you may devise another creative way to remind yourself what the Bible says about God. Remember. As you do so, you are strengthening yourself for challenges that lie ahead.

Growing in Trust

Growing in trust is just that—growing—and we all know that growing is a process. It is different for everyone. Some people take off in faith like a rocket. I have friends who have latched on to God and have never looked back. I, on the other hand, am slow. I am not where I want to be in my faith. Daily I am reminded of how far I have to go in learning to trust God. But at least I am not where I was. Nor am I where I will be in the future. God is working on me!

Like Mary, in trusting God, we are abandoning ourselves to another, and that is a powerful act. Marriage can be an illustration of that abandon. As you stand at the altar, you don't know what life is going to bring. You are placing your trust in someone whom, in many ways, you have only begun to know. You will weave your lives together. Your trust in each other will be built and tested. You will walk through life as partners, more effective together than on your own. And marriage is a human relationship. If we can step out to discover the trustworthiness of another person, opening ourselves up to the power of that relationship, then surely we can do it with Almighty God, who knows us best and loves us most.

Discovering God's trustworthiness may not be an easy process for you. It may come slowly, step by step on that ice. But as we learn in the coming pages about experiencing God's presence, knowing His comfort, encountering His power, and other aspects of walking in relationship with Him, we will see how vital it is that we open ourselves up to the process of trusting Him in order to experience the rest. As with any relationship, our relationship with God depends on trust, and God wants to show Himself to us for who He is—trustworthy.

POINT OF FOCUS

Trust in the Lord with all your heart,
And lean not on your own understanding;
In all your ways acknowledge Him,
And He shall direct your paths.

Proverbs 3:5–6 NKJV

Experience His Presence

chapter three

OFTEN IN THE Bible, when God exhorts people to "fear not," He gives this as His reason: "I am with you." God's antidote for our fear is His presence—Himself. But what exactly is God's presence, and how do we experience it? How do we experience His "I am with you"? Is it some mystical "out of this world" encounter? How do we recognize when God is with us? Can we experience God on a daily basis in the routine of life? Do we need to be in a certain state of being? In a certain place? A certain posture? Can we experience God's presence by something we do, or does it just happen?

Experiencing God's presence is not as complicated as it may seem. In our human relationships, we cultivate intimacy with our loved ones by spending time with them. We talk with them, listen to what they have to say, learn about them, and try to do what pleases them. In these ways, we come to know them. It is the same with God. You may not always "feel" His presence, as I will share later, but the more you spend time with God and develop your relationship with Him, the more you will come to recognize His presence in your life. How do you know when you are in love? The answer often given to that question can also apply to experiencing God's presence: "You just know."

Ways We Experience His Presence

In these uncertain times, experiencing God's presence is very relevant. We find in Scripture that during uncertainty, God promised His presence. His presence was the one thing people needed above all else, the one thing that would sustain them in uncertainty. When God met Moses in the burning bush and commissioned him to lead Israel out of Egypt, He encouraged Moses, who was fearful, saying, "Certainly I will be with you" (Exodus 3:12). After Moses died, God commissioned Joshua to lead Israel into the Promised Land, charging, "Do not be afraid, nor be dismayed, for the Lord your God is with you wherever you go" (Joshua 1:9 NKJV). Again to the prophet Jeremiah, God said, "Do not be afraid of them, for I am with you to deliver you" (Jeremiah 1:8). And through the prophet Isaiah, God told Israel, "Fear not, for I am with you; be not dismayed, for I am your God. I will strengthen you, yes, I will help you, I will uphold you with My righteous right hand" (Isaiah 41:10, NJKV).

We can experience God's presence in countless ways, and many will be unique to each of us. Certainly, when we talk to God in prayer, we enter His presence. Whether silent, speaking aloud, or singing— whether alone or with others—when we pray, we are engaging in a conversation, an exchange with God. We also experience God's presence as we spend time reading and meditating on His Word, listening for what He will say to our hearts. I experience God as I journal and unburden my heart to Him that way.

We can experience, or "practice," God's presence throughout the day by simply turning to Him inwardly and cultivating an awareness of Him. My father's beloved team member T. W. Wilson, "Uncle T," used to begin his prayers with us, "And now Lord . . ." He started with "and" as if to indicate that he was just picking up where he left off in an ongoing dialogue with God. My mother had her own interpretation of Paul's instruction to "pray without ceasing" (1 Thessalonians 5:17). Hers was "pray on the hoof." Mother did not neglect those special private times with God, but she also turned to Him and prayed while she was busy raising five children and tending to the needs of those around her.

My father too has said that he tries to pray constantly during the day. He draws his strength from simple prayer. When a reporter at a press conference during my father's 2005 New York City meetings, his final crusade, asked him to share his favorite prayer, Daddy answered, "There's hardly a moment goes by that I don't pray, and I say, 'Lord, help me!' That's my favorite prayer."[1] Notice that neither Uncle T nor my parents necessarily stopped what they were doing, knelt down, and addressed God using fancy words. They entered God's presence by talking to Him where they were in the midst of whatever they were doing. Simply. Honestly.

Just as we can experience God's presence based on actions we take to cultivate intimacy with Him, so we can experience Him unexpectedly. Mary did not likely expect the angel Gabriel to appear to her and announce that she would bear God's child. Paul (or Saul, as he was then called) was knocked to the ground and blinded by a bright light while traveling to Damascus. God simply arrested him and started talking (Acts 9:3–9). Abraham didn't necessarily expect God to interrupt his life in Ur and tell him to move to Canaan or, years later, to appear to him under the oak trees and tell him through three visiting angels that the time was at hand for his elderly wife, Sarah, to bear a son (Genesis 12:1–8; 18:1–14). We do not control God. We are His creation, and He can reveal Himself in our lives as He pleases. We can enter His presence, or He can just show up and make Himself known.

Often we experience God's presence according to our need in a given moment. God meets us in our need in order to be the answer. In the Bible, God is called our Comforter, Deliverer, Advocate, Teacher, Counselor, Father. He is love, wisdom, peace, grace. He is just. He is our healer and sustainer. He is mercy. He is our rest, our light, our salvation, our strength, our help in trouble, and so much more. God meets us exactly as we need Him to be—matching our need with His fullness. In this way He woos us and draws us to Himself.

One of the ways we can gain a greater understanding of God's presence is by looking at Jesus. If Jesus is the "image of the invisible God," as the Bible teaches, then we should be able to consider what people experienced in *His* presence and learn something about what it's like to be in the presence of God (Colossians 1:15). We'll begin with a dramatic encounter in the temple court.

Set Free

We are not told her name. In the Bible she is identified only as the "woman caught in adultery" (John 8:3). We don't know how she ended up in this situation. Had she been desperately lonely and fallen for false promises of love? Was she a victim of abuse, seeking tenderness from someone else? Was she a woman "of the street"? Was she having an affair? We do not know. Just that by the time we see her, her situation has gotten much worse. Caught in the "very act" of adultery, the woman has been dragged by a mob of scribes and Pharisees into the center of the temple court where Jesus is teaching.

Interrupting Jesus, the Pharisees set the woman up in front of the crowd and start challenging Him: "In the Law, Moses commanded us to stone such women. What do you say, Teacher?"

It was an attempt to entrap Jesus. He had been teaching in Jerusalem during the Feast of Tabernacles, stirring up outrage among the scholarly class with his claims of being sent from heaven by the Father. Some of the people were starting to wonder aloud whether Jesus was the Messiah, a line of speculation the Pharisees and chief priests quickly sought to stamp out, though ineffectively. They sent officers to arrest Jesus, but even the officers were mesmerized. "No one has ever spoken like this man," they explained.

Now it is early morning. Jesus is back in the temple teaching the crowd, and here come the Pharisees with this woman, although to them she isn't so much a woman as an object. The self-proclaimed monitors of righteousness want to trap Jesus at her expense. They stand before Him in all of their self-righteousness, demanding an answer. If He says, "Don't stone her," they can accuse Him of blaspheming the Law. If He says, "Stone her," they can claim He is acting in opposition to Rome, for no Jew had the power to execute a death sentence.[2]

Try to imagine the scene: The press of the Pharisees through the rapt crowd as they drag the woman toward Jesus. The woman, perhaps half-dressed, clutching her clothes about her, groveling on the ground like an animal. Do the Pharisees strike her? Are they threatening her? Does she cry out in distress? Are onlookers shouting out her sin for everyone to hear?

How must the woman have felt? Alone? Frightened? Abandoned? Betrayed? Shamed? She knows her sins better than anyone. She knows her accusers are justified. She knows very well what she has done—and the punishment she risked. She has only herself to blame. She doesn't dare look up at the famous rabbi. What will He say? What will He do with her?

All eyes are on Jesus. "What do you say, Teacher?" The Pharisees are persistent.

The woman tries to prepare herself for the sentence that the Law says must be handed down to a woman like her. *A woman like her.* In just a word, it will come. She waits. For judgment. For misery. Still in the dirt. But the Teacher says nothing. He keeps silent, as if ignoring her accusers, as if He hasn't heard them.

Then He stoops and begins to write with His finger in the dust.

Jesus stoops. He takes the posture of the humiliated woman. He doesn't stand with her accusers. He gets low. He identifies with her. The God of the universe, this woman's Creator, comes down to her level. He is calm, self-possessed, unruffled by the chaos. He knows who He is and what He will do.

Jesus writes in the dirt. What does He write? Does He write for the woman? For the Pharisees? Perhaps He writes out the Pharisees' sins. Or words from the Law. They begin to goad Him. "Tell us, Teacher. What do you say?"

Now Jesus stands to address the woman's accusers eye to eye: "He who is without sin, throw the first stone."

It is a simple charge, but with His words Jesus turns the challenge back on the Pharisees. He calls for inward purity, which none of them can claim. His words, His actions, His very presence confront them in a powerful, convicting way. He exposes their hypocrisy, and in doing so, He covers the adulterous woman.

Again Jesus stoops and writes on the ground. Maybe now He writes for her—words like mercy, forgiveness, grace. Slowly, one by one, with the Teacher bent over His work, the Pharisees file out, leaving Jesus and the woman alone in the court.

After they leave, Jesus stands and addresses her. "Where have they gone, your accusers?" He asks. "Is no one left to condemn you?"

Jesus doesn't say, "I forgive you." The woman doesn't ask for that. She doesn't ask for anything. Rather, Jesus asks her a leading question, not for His information, but so she can articulate for herself what has just happened. He is making her aware of the power of grace. Even the Law and the religious leaders can't stand up to its power. He gives her a voice. He meets her where she is—exposed, humiliated, broken by sin—and asks her to acknowledge it, so that He can take her beyond her brokenness into healing.

In the quiet of that temple court, the woman hesitates, perhaps afraid to look at Him. Then, struggling to get out the words, she whispers her answer, "No one, Lord." *No one, Lord.* She recognizes who Jesus is and calls Him Lord.

Jesus gazes at her and says, "Then I don't condemn you, either. You are free. Go your way, and leave your life of sin."

What Is Gained in His Presence?

What did this woman experience in the presence of Jesus? Here was a woman covered in shame. Can you imagine the fear she must have felt as she stood before that mob? She was exposed before the world for what she had done, and the world condemned her—was prepared to kill her, to mete out the requirements of justice. But not Jesus. He did not condemn her. He allowed her to experience conviction. While humiliated by her accusers, she was humbled by his grace. The grace Jesus extended allowed her to see herself for who she was. Desperate. Broken by sin. Deserving of death.

But Jesus did not give her what she deserved—that's grace. Grace is unmerited or undeserved favor. It is precisely what we do *not* deserve. The Bible says, "For all have sinned and fall short of the glory of God, being justified *as a gift by His grace* through the redemption which is in Christ Jesus" (Romans 3:23–24, emphasis added). Grace is God's gift to us, and we see it here in this story. For in one way or another, we are all this nameless woman caught in adultery.

What else does she experience with Jesus? While others ridicule her, Jesus treats her with respect. He protects her human dignity. He moves down to her level—he doesn't leave her alone in her shame. His gesture says, "Fear not, for I am with you." He is with her in the dirt. Writing in it. Getting his hands in it. And then he stands up to lift her out of it. He engages her, talks to her—a woman caught in the "very act" of adultery. Yet he treats her with respect and dignity. Jesus always looks at us and sees beyond our failure. He sees us restored. He sees us whole. And that is how he treated this woman. "Woman, where have your accusers gone?"

Jesus rescues her from her accusers and gives her a second chance. That is the nature of God. He frees us from our enemies—fear, anxiety, self-loathing. He rescues us and gives us a chance to begin again. This does not absolve us of responsibility. Jesus sends the woman away with a charge: Sin no more. Leave your life of sin behind. Choose a better way. Take another road. God extends grace and then gives us a choice. But even then he doesn't leave us alone to get it right. He knows our weaknesses. The Bible says he "remembers that we are dust" (Psalm 103:14 NKJV). If we can just choose His way, then God will help us live out that choice. The Bible says, "For it is God who is at work in you, both to will and to work for His good pleasure" (Philippians 2:13).

In a chaotic environment of accusation, we see Jesus as steady, unchanged, present to the needs of the woman. Emotionally, he is with her. He is unaffected by anxiety and stress. He isn't hurried. He takes his time. He isn't changed by the environment, but the environment is changed by Him. Jesus calms the storm of emotion and accusation with His presence. His presence brings peace. The Bible calls him the "Prince of Peace" (Isaiah 9:6).

How many of us have failed, sinned, been humiliated, and judged? I have. How many of us like this woman have felt alone, abandoned, and ashamed? I have. These are common experiences. We are imperfect. We all fall short. But here in the story we see that even when we fall, we do not have to fear the future. Jesus is with us. He sees us not as we are—messy, devastated, wallowing in our filth—but as restored. He meets us where we are to bring us further.

You may be carrying the weight of a wrong you have done. You may be bearing the consequences of a past sin. Perhaps others have rejected you. Perhaps you have condemned yourself. Right where you are, know that God is not condemning you. He may be convicting you, showing you your need to seek His forgiveness, repent of what you've done, and make amends to others. But the Bible says, "There is now no condemnation for those who are in Christ Jesus" (Romans 8:1). God loves you, and by His grace, He can release you into your tomorrow.

This woman caught in adultery didn't believe she had a tomorrow. Jesus stops the train of condemnation and treats her with kindness, gentleness, patience, and love; He demonstrates what Scripture calls the "fruit of the Spirit," or the evidences of God's presence (Galatians 5:22–23). He becomes for the woman the very thing that she needs. The Bible says that "God, being rich in mercy, because of His great love with which He loved us even when we were dead in our transgressions, made us alive together with Christ" (Ephesians 2:4–5). This woman was literally marked for death because of her sin, but because of His great love for her, Jesus showed up in her life as mercy and said, "Live!"

When We Can't Feel God

The woman caught in adultery experienced a powerful emotional moment with Jesus. I have often wondered what her walk home was like that day. She would've had to pass by onlookers who had just witnessed the scene. Some may have looked askance at her, but surely others were grappling with the events. Jesus had just revolutionized her life and theirs. With His treatment of this woman, He sent a powerful message. The onlookers must have thought, "Whoa—this is a new day!"

Being in God's presence, however, is not always an emotional experience. There are times when we cannot "feel" God with us. We feel alone. We can't seem to understand what He wants us to do. We don't feel comforted or loved. We feel anxious. Isn't God supposed to be our peace? Our help in trouble? Our strength? A friend who sticks closer than a brother? Yes—and He is all those things. But at certain times, God gives us a chance to believe His promise regardless of whether our emotions are on board, and His promise is "I am with you."

I learned more about this level of trust when visiting the beach one recent summer. I love the beach. I am happiest with my feet in the warm sand and my nose in a book. Each year I try to set aside two weeks in the late summer or early fall to go to my favorite beach in

South Carolina. The first week I invite my children and grandchildren, but the second week I reserve for myself. I use the time for quiet reflection, reading, shopping, and visiting with good friends. It's a time I anticipate all year long, and I count on it as my rest time—a time to be refreshed physically, emotionally, and spiritually.

I am an early riser. Even at the beach I get up before dawn, make myself a cup of coffee, and sit on the porch waiting for the sun to come up. As dawn breaks, I go to the water and take my walk. Out on the beach alone, I enjoy the warm air and the sound of the sea. I look for special shells to add to my collection. I greet any fellow beach-walkers—those few out walking their dogs or combing for shells. I listen as the gulls call to one another and the breeze moves gently through the sea grass. In my exhilaration, I open my heart to God.

As I'm walking—the beach on one side, the sea on the other—I praise God for everything that comes to mind while taking in the beauty of His creation. Scripture tells us that God's "way was in the sea" and His "paths in the mighty waters" (Psalm 77:19). Each year during my walks I meditate on what this might mean. How is God's character reflected in the sea? He is powerful, consistent, deep, awesome, and beautiful. I never tire of thinking about God in this way—as reflected in creation. Not only do I praise Him as I walk, but I also talk to Him about the things that are on my mind. And I listen for Him, waiting expectantly to hear Him speak to my heart.

This particular summer was no different. Each morning I walked the beach. I talked with God. I praised Him. I was eager to hear from Him. It had been a difficult year. I had recently lost my mother, and I was grieving. I was going through a challenging life transition. I needed direction. I needed assurance. I needed to feel God's presence in my life.

Usually it takes me a few days of vacation to quit "vibrating" and tune in spiritually, so I was not disappointed when I didn't really feel God's presence those first few days at the beach. As I rested, though, I began to expect more. I continued my habit of Bible reading and journaling, knowing that God would break through and help me to experience Him before long. But a whole week went by, and still I hadn't heard anything in my heart from God or even sensed Him near me.

I wondered if I was blocking God in some way. Was I holding a grudge against anyone? Was there any sin in my life? Had I failed to obey God in some area? I asked Him to show me. I prayed, examined myself, and listened. But nothing. Only quiet. Stillness.

By now my second beach week was going by rapidly. I started taking my iPod with me on my walks and listening to praise music, thinking this might help me connect with God. Music opens up my emotions, and I wondered if my emotions might be the problem—maybe I was just flat. But I also began to tell God that I was not happy about His silence. My time at the beach, this special time I had set aside to be with Him, was almost over. Didn't He know how hard a year it had been? Didn't He know I needed His help grieving the loss of my mother? Didn't He know there were pressing issues to deal with and decisions to be made—and that I greatly needed to feel His reassurance?

On the next to the last morning, I was at a point of desperation. "God, I really wanted You to show up for me," I told Him. "I've done everything I can possibly think of to connect with You, and I need to hear something." I was upset, disappointed, and hurt. Here I was reading my Bible, journaling, and waiting with anticipation. I was holding up what I thought was my end of the bargain, but I felt like God was letting me down.

Finally, on the last morning, I got a big mug of coffee and headed for the beach. It was so early there was barely any light on the horizon. I sat down on the steps that lead over the dunes and quietly waited for the sun to rise. I was discouraged. I had not received what I wanted from God—no breakthrough in my spiritual life, no guidance, no special experience or insight. I had tried so hard. Now my vacation was over, and I felt alone. I resigned myself to it—that was all I could do.

When it was light enough for me to see, I began my last beach walk of the year.

I took in the scene and tried to enjoy the experience. My iPod was playing praise music, but I had tuned it out, thinking about what had to be done—packing up, driving the seven hours home, preparing for my upcoming trip to Ireland. As I headed back to the house, I decided to sit back down on those steps for one last look at the beach. That's when I heard in my earphones the words of the Brooklyn Tabernacle Choir singing "Lord I Believe in You."

> *Though I can't see*
> *Your Holy Face*
> *And Your throne in Heaven above*
> *It seems so far away*
> *Though I can't touch*
> *Can't touch your nail scarred hands*
> *I have a deep unspeakable joy*
> *That makes my faith to stand*
>
> *Lord, I believe in You*
> *I always believe in You*
> *Though I can't see You with my eyes*
> *Deep in my heart, Your presence I find*
> *Lord, I believe in you*[3]

My eyes filled with tears as I listened. As the chorus came back around, I affirmed my belief in God. Though I had not heard from Him as I expected or felt His presence as I wanted, I still believed. Nothing was going to take that away. I realized I had been putting God in a box. If I just did the right things, said the right things, gave Him the time, then He would have to show up. But sitting on those steps by the dunes, I saw that my trust in God could not rest on any experience I may or may not have. My trust, my belief in God, had to rest on *the fact* that He was with me, whether I felt Him or not.

Believing in God is a choice. I had to say, "Though I don't see You or feel You, God, I believe in You anyway." It was a choice—to trust that He had been there walking the beach with me every morning regardless of whether I had any evidence. The Bible says, "Now faith is . . . the evidence of things not seen" (Hebrews 11:1 NKJV). Faith is trust. I did not see God working. I didn't feel Him, hadn't heard from Him. But He was challenging me to trust in His presence anyway. That choice to trust was my next step out on the ice, and when I made it, when I said, "Lord, I believe You are with me no matter what I see," then the emotions came.

How are you feeling about God as you read this? Can you relate to how I felt that one summer at the beach? Are you struggling to experience God's presence in the midst of some challenge or difficulty? Do you feel lonely, exhausted, and emotionally flat, uncertain whether God even cares about you let alone that He is close by? When we suffer and have no proof that God is anywhere near us, we can still make that choice to believe in Him. We have the promise of His Word. Jesus said, "I am with you always" (Matthew 28:20). In Hebrews we read, "I will never desert you, nor will I ever forsake you" (Hebrews 13:5). That same verse in the Amplified Bible reads, "I will not in any way fail you nor give you up nor leave you without support. [I will] not, [I will] not, [I will] not in any degree leave you helpless nor forsake nor let [you] down (relax My hold on you)! [Assuredly not!]" That is such a powerful truth! God will not "in any degree" leave us helpless or without support. He will not relax His hold on us. *He will not.* Our choice is to step out and believe it. Will you make that choice? In your circumstance, in your darkness, will you step out on the ice and trust in His presence?

Seeing God's Presence in Daily Life

While we certainly can experience God in dramatic ways—as the woman caught in adultery did, or as I did at the very end of those "dry" weeks at the beach—we do not need a mountaintop experience in order to enjoy God's presence. Beyond the deep work He does in our hearts, God reveals Himself to us in many ways as we go about life. As we learn to recognize some of those ways, we come to enjoy God's presence more fully. Trust, too, comes more easily as we train ourselves to appreciate God through the simple things we experience in the world. Here are a few of the ways I experience Him.

Through His Creation

We are all wired to experience God in different ways, and for many people, getting outdoors and enjoying nature is one way to feel close to God. As I have shared, I often experience God at the beach. Others may be awestruck by the beauty God creates in a sunset at the Grand Canyon. Someone who likes to fly airplanes may experience God's presence while in the air, taking in the panorama of creation from above.

My mother often looked to nature to reveal God's character. The Bible says God's "invisible attributes" are revealed in His creation (Romans 1:20). Mother loved her mountains and drew illustrative material from what she observed. Many of her poems use God's creation as a backdrop:

> *If I lived within the sound*
> *of the sea's relentless yearning,*
> *my soul would rise and fly to seek*
> *what the soul longs for—unable to speak;*
> *aware, as I go, of Him everywhere:*

in my heart, in the clouds . . . in the cold wet air . . .
And my soul would worship in joyful prayer,
receding as the waves recede,
returning with the waves' returning,
reaching up, as for Him, feeling,
then with the waves kneeling . . .

kneeling . . .

kneeling . . . [4]

I remember some years ago driving from a speaking engagement in Crescent City, California. I had to drive down to Arcata to make my flight connection, and the route took me through the redwood forest on the sea coast. It's a wonder I didn't wreck the car! The majesty of God's creation there, the beauty, is beyond description. To have the huge, magnificent redwood trees on my left and the ocean on my right, crashing against the rocky coast, sending sea spray high into the air, was almost too much to bear. God's splendor in the scene was phenomenal. As Mother wrote, I was "unable to speak; / aware . . . of Him everywhere."

Through Other People

How many times have we experienced others coming around us to offer support or encouragement when we needed it most? We can experience God's presence through other people. When a good friend prays for you during a difficult time, when you receive a hug or a compassionate look from someone at a time you really need it, when someone for no apparent reason does you a kindness, these are God's ways of letting you know He is near.

I have a dear friend named Martha who lives in the Philadelphia area. We met in 1969 on the day Neil Armstrong landed on the moon, and she has been a friend and mentor ever since. Through her, I have felt the love and presence of God too many times to remember. My early married years in Philadelphia were difficult, and Martha understood that. She would encourage me as a wife, always calling me back to an understanding of Scripture. She was an example of a skilled and gracious homemaker. She offered hospitality, holding Bible studies in her home. After I had my first baby, she would come to check on me, always bringing something in her hand—flowers, food, a book. I can't count the number of books Martha has given me. She initiated stimulating conversation that challenged me to think more deeply. She has listened to me with empathy and concern during my times of deepest despair. She has believed in me when I didn't believe in myself. And she continues to set an example of godly womanhood. Anyone privileged to bite into a slice of her homemade Swedish bread knows the comfort and love of God's presence in a tangible way!

Through Serving Others

We experience God's presence not just at the hands of others but also as we become the hands of God for someone else. "Through love," the Bible says, "serve one another" (Galatians 5:13). When we make ourselves available to serve those around us, we are imitating Jesus, who said that He "did not come to be served, but to serve" (Matthew 20:28).

Having the opportunity to speak to groups of people about the grace of God is one of the richest blessings of my life. While I feel so inadequate, when I have the chance to talk to people one-on-one at the end of these events, I can sense God ministering in the conversations and encouraging the people. Recently, at the end of an event in Kentucky, the closing speaker asked anyone who needed prayer to stand. I was privileged to pray with a couple of women, and afterward I had such a strong sense of God's presence in the room that I walked to the back of the sanctuary to pray. In my mind's eye, I pictured the Lord Jesus going from person to person, touching each one, loving and encouraging them. This wasn't a vision or something mystical. I just had a very real experience of God's presence as people were being served and their needs met.

When we make the choice to become available to others, by our decision we invite God to get involved. A few years ago, Valentine's Day fell on a Friday. I knew I would be alone. When you are unmarried, Valentine's Day is not always the most enjoyable holiday. I thought about my options. Ignore it? Impossible with all the reminders everywhere I went. Go to a movie alone? That screams, "She is all alone!" Stay home and feel sorry for myself? I was leaning toward that option when an idea occurred to me.

I had several friends who had been widowed that year. I had a friend whose husband was due to be out of town. I had other friends who were alone due to divorce. So I got creative. I would throw a fancy dinner party! I brought out my best china and finest linens. I polished my silver, made the centerpiece and decorations, found party favors, and assigned everyone to bring a dish. Over candlelight we talked about our best and worst Valentine's Days. We had a delightful time laughing and talking until midnight. The next day when we told our married friends what we had done, they were actually jealous and wished they could have come! I do not know if I *felt* the presence of God while I was sitting at dinner enjoying time with my friends, but I know He was there having as much fun as we were. He took delight in our delight. He showed up as what we needed: Love. Joy. Friendship. Life.

The Ease of His Presence

There is an ease available to us in God's presence. His presence is comforting and reassuring; it is to be enjoyed. Learning to experience God's presence can be like falling in love. Falling in love isn't a project. It flows from your desire to be with the one you love. You look for ways to spend time and connect with your beloved—in person, by correspondence, through phone calls, in thought and imagination. You seek the one you love. You enjoy that person, and as you spend time together, your intimacy grows.

Have you ever observed an older couple married for a long time? They seem to walk in step with each other, finish each other's sentences, and understand each other at just a glance. They even seem to grow to look like each other! As we spend time developing our relationship with God, the same thing will happen. We will know God's presence, be comforted by His presence, feel secure in His presence, and over time, come to look more like Him. When fear threatens us, we will be better equipped to reach for God, for it will have become our habit to turn to Him. We will have made a practice of His presence. We will know more of Him. We will know more of His love. We will have learned more about living in the promise of His presence—His "I am with you."

POINT OF FOCUS

Fear not, for I am with you;
Be not dismayed, for I am your God.
I will strengthen you,
Yes, I will help you,
I will uphold you with My righteous right hand.

Isaiah 41:10 NKJV

Know His Comfort

chapter four

W E WERE LIVING in the Dallas area when we discovered that my son Graham, who was in second grade at the time, needed surgery on his ear. His attentive teacher had noticed that he didn't seem able to hear very well. When I took him to the specialist, I was told Graham had suffered significant hearing loss in his left ear. The little bones adjoining the eardrum—the hammer, anvil, and stirrup—were being crushed by a growth. That word caused me to shudder. Growth? What kind of growth? What did this mean?

The doctor would have to go in right away and remove the growth, so I immediately shifted gears and began to make plans for Graham's surgery. The morning of the operation, I left the two girls at home with a sitter and set out early for the hospital. My husband drove separately, and Graham sat calmly in the back seat of my car. He didn't seem overly concerned about being put to sleep or about the pain he might feel later. He just trusted that his mother was going to take care of him. Meanwhile, his mother was worried.

Once at the hospital, we were met by the surgeon. This doctor was at the top of his field and a wonderful Christian man who knew how to relate to a second-grade boy. During one visit, he taught Graham how to burp! Often he gave my children pennies so they could go to the gumball machine in his waiting room. Graham never protested these visits, which were physically unpleasant for him, and on the morning of the surgery, I was reassured when I saw the doctor enter the room.

After praying with us, the doctor carried Graham piggyback-style up to the operating room. My husband left for the office, and I sat down to wait. Anxious. To keep myself occupied, I pulled out my needlepoint. I was working on a pillow with the words "Jesus Is Lord" on it, a reminder with each stitch that Jesus was Lord over the situation. Those words were a comfort, and I tried to focus on them as I worked, hoping the truth might overrule the fear in my mother's heart.

It wasn't long before I heard the soft Southern voice of my beloved aunt Peggy Bell. She kept a full schedule as a busy pastor's wife, but she had come to the hospital just to sit with me. A little later, her son, my cousin Nelson, also dropped in to check on us. Their presence brought not only comfort but a level of distraction from the anxiety I was feeling. They were being Jesus for me that day.

Soon the doctor came to report that the growth in my son's ear was benign—it was scar tissue. The relief I felt was profound, at least for the moment. Later there would be more surgeries, more waiting rooms, and ultimately the loss of Graham's hearing in his left ear. But along the way, God would do what He had done for me that morning at the hospital—use multiple means and other people to quiet my fears. He comforted me stage by stage.

Seeking Comfort

We all need comfort. We need it when we're tired, confused, frightened, lonely, heartbroken, or worried. Sometimes we need it just because we need it. We experience comfort in different ways. Young children may turn to a bottle, pacifier, or favorite toy. We adults may turn to a favorite food, the company of a special friend, a favorite movie, or a favorite place in the house. My children and grandchildren are comforting to me. The family home in Montreat that my mother designed, Little Piney Cove, has always been a comforting place. The familiar can be comforting—things and places that remind us of good times, security, and strength.

Routine can also be a comfort. Although I travel a great deal, I am a homebody. I find comfort in things like seeing the same grocery-store clerk and the same gentleman who bags my groceries. If I go to the store on Tuesdays, I will likely run into many of my older friends from the local retirement community, and we will visit together in front of the frozen-foods case or in the produce section. These are the routine experiences that comfort me, making me feel part of my small community.

I take comfort in certain books—my Bible, for instance. It is marked up with dates, names, and special insights; and when I open it, especially after a long trip, the familiar pages, notated with all that evidence of my life's journey, are a comfort to me. My *Daily Light* is a comfort. *Daily Light on the Daily Path* is a devotional book of morning and evening readings composed completely of scriptures. I've used this devotional since I was a little girl, though the copy I use now was a gift from Mother some twenty years ago. Like my Bible, it too is marked up with notes and dates in the margins, and it is often where I turn when I am walking through a crisis or dealing with challenges or heartache.

God's Word is a comfort. When my marriage began to unravel, I opened my *Daily Light* and read, "He ever liveth to make intercession . . . we have an advocate with the Father, Jesus Christ the righteous"[1] (Hebrews 7:25, 1 John 2:1 KJV). Reading that, I took comfort that Jesus was talking to God, "making intercession," about me. I had just entered a crisis that was about to become acutely painful, but I knew Jesus was talking to God about me. While these words did not alter my situation, they did change my perspective as I was comforted by God's Word to my heart.

Some of us may turn to unhealthy or destructive habits for comfort—we self-medicate. These habits can be injurious, creating more problems and stress for us and for others. Our behavior may become a dependency; it may become an addiction. If you believe you may be trapped in certain habits or behaviors, or if you are engaging in harmful behavior, I encourage you to seek help from a good Christian counselor. Truly, any habit can become destructive when it turns into a substitute for God.

One day my older daughter, Noelle, called asking if I could keep my then-two-year-old granddaughter for part of the afternoon. I had just gotten back from a weeklong trip. My desk was stacked high with mail, and my email inbox was full, but Noelle assured me Virginia Ruth would probably sleep the whole time since it would be her naptime. I quickly agreed. I would just put my granddaughter down for a nap and get back to what I needed to do.

When Noelle arrived, she broke the news that she had left both "bear" and "blanket" at home. I knew this would pose a difficulty, but I didn't realize the seriousness of our situation until I tried putting Virginia Ruth down for her nap. She wanted bear and blanket. Trying to be innovative, I showed her the monkey that was left over from my son Graham's childhood, thinking that could substitute for bear. She looked horrified when she saw it. Then I offered her a baby blanket that had belonged to Noelle. Her big blue eyes filled with tears and she moaned, "Nooo . . ." I reached for an old doll, hoping that would comfort her. Her wailing grew more intense. I felt helpless. Finally, I scooped my granddaughter up and held her close. I sat down with her in my favorite chair as she snuggled and nested her little blond head on my shoulder. Soon she was breathing heavily and sleeping sweetly.

My granddaughter would take no substitute for her bear and blanket, but so often we try to substitute something else for God's comfort. God certainly uses our relationships and the things of this life to comfort us, as he did while comforting me through Graham's ordeal. The problem comes when we look to our comforts to stop the pain. True comfort doesn't stop the pain. It makes the situation bearable. It gets us through. We are human—we want the pain to stop. And yet, sometimes, pain is what opens the door to our experiencing God's comfort. It is when we are desperate and undone that He steps in and touches us in unusual ways. He wants to cradle us, rock us, and soothe us.

Coming Undone

We need comfort in a host of situations, experiences, and emotional states, but there is a difference between needing comfort and what I call coming undone. What is "undone"? We can come undone in our greatest moments of loss, failure, betrayal, or fear. We no longer feel in control of ourselves, others, or our situation. We are unable to find relief. When you are undone, you've exhausted your ability to get comfort from anything around you. People can't comfort you. None of the familiar comforts work anymore. There's nowhere to turn. No letup. You're just undone. Like an egg without a shell, as I have written.

When you're undone, it is as if you've been thrown out of the boat. You can't touch the bottom, see the shore, or even get ahold of the boat itself. You feel alone and desperate. You can't see what's ahead, nor can you reach back for what's behind you. You are at a complete loss. You're exhausted physically, emotionally, and spiritually. And yet the waves keep hitting you, one after another. You're tired. You can't battle it anymore. You have none of your own resources left. The problem has taken over, and you can't focus on the Lord. He's out of focus; everything's out of focus. All you know is the problem. And it is overwhelming.

Undone is not a place God wants us to stay. As we will see, His goal is to comfort us in our brokenness and then to lead us out of it. But you do have an enemy committed to keeping you undone. He will use whatever means necessary to shut you down and convince you that you'll never function, never be whole, again. The enemy wants you to believe that undone is the new normal.

Jesus enlightens Peter about the enemy's plan against him as they are sitting at the Passover meal. To his headstrong, passionate, willful disciple, Jesus says, "Simon, Simon, behold, Satan has demanded permission to sift you like wheat" (Luke 22:31). That's what the enemy wants to do—sift us, fragment us, take us apart. When Peter is older, long after Jesus has been crucified and resurrected, the seasoned disciple-turned-leader advises the early church with a similar warning: "Be of sober spirit, be on the alert. Your adversary, the devil, prowls around like a roaring lion, seeking someone to devour" (1 Peter 5:8).

Satan knows our failures and our weaknesses. He knows our fears and the areas in which we find ourselves insufficient. The Bible calls him "the accuser" (Revelation 12:10). Some of his words will sound very familiar to you:

"Nothing will ever change."
"No one will ever love you."
"You can't possibly do that."
"You're inadequate for this—you'll never pull it off."
"You've blown it again."
"You'll always be a failure."
"You're destined for mediocrity."
"Your hopes and dreams will never come to pass."
"God can't use you anymore. You've made too many mistakes."

These are the kinds of words the enemy will sow into our minds and hearts, but Jesus calls Satan "a liar and the father of lies" (John 8:44). We don't have to believe what the enemy says about us. We have the Word of God, which tells us what *God* says about us. Someone far greater than the enemy is living in our hearts and fighting on our side (1 John 4:4). Again, Jesus is praying for us. He is on our side. And the Bible assures us: "If God is for us, who can be against us?" (Romans 8:31 NJKV).

I have felt undone many times in my life. I was undone after I learned of betrayal in my first marriage. I was undone by my own sins and mistakes when one bad personal decision began to lead to another. Loss can undo us. Failure can undo us. Death—of a loved one, a dream, a relationship. Abandonment. Fear. But when we are undone, when we can't find any comfort, when it feels as if our adversary is prowling through our lives like that roaring lion, in these moments, we have an opportunity to know the deep comfort of God. Scripture calls Him "Comforter" (John 14:16 KJV). He uses the dark chapters of our lives to show us the power of His comfort and to draw us closer in intimacy with Him.

God does not create our ruins. The Bible says, "The Lord will surely comfort Zion and will *look with compassion* on all her ruins" (Isaiah 51:3 NIV, emphasis added). God sees us undone like that egg without a shell. He sees us floundering in that water. And He is looking at us with compassion. The verse from Isaiah goes on to say, "He will make her deserts like Eden, her wastelands like the garden of the Lord. Joy and gladness will be found in her, thanksgiving and the sound of singing." Undone is never the final chapter with God. He promises comfort. He promises restoration. He promises joy and gladness. Thanksgiving. The sound of singing. No matter what the enemy says or does, we can know God's comfort in our ruins. God will make of our ruins opportunities to woo us with His love.

Letting the Walls Down

I confess I fear becoming undone. I resist it. I build walls against it. I have been there more than once, and quite frankly, I hate the feeling. When I sense trouble on the horizon, I want to do whatever I can to shield myself from pain. But look at what God says: "When you pass through the waters, I will be with you" (Isaiah 43:2 NKJV). *I will be with you.* In the deep waters of hurt—the deep waters we fear having to experience in our tomorrow—God promises to be with us. If we can learn to let go in our pain, to let the walls down and let God in, then we will know a comfort that heals, that restores.

In the spring of 2007, my loved ones and I all noticed my mother's health had begun declining rapidly. She found communication difficult. It was hard for her to get comfortable. She was no longer able to sit in her recliner propped up by pillows. She was no longer able to enjoy the lovely saltwater aquarium Daddy had given to her for Christmas. She began to withdraw, and we knew the end of our time with her on earth was near.

For years I dreaded losing her. I feared the experience of that loss. My mother had suffered for many years due to degenerative arthritis and macular degeneration. I knew she would be much happier in heaven with Jesus and with all her loved ones who had gone before her. But she was my mother. I did not want to let her go.

When my oldest sister, Gigi, called me on a Monday morning to say that Mother was fading and that I needed to come home, I shifted into autopilot, packed, notified my children, and left for Montreat, almost a six-hour drive away. In some ways I felt numb. Mother's death was not unexpected, but I was not sure I was prepared. Questions surfaced as I drove. How would I cope in a world without Mother? Most of the way, I listened to worshipful music that comforted me and brought me into God's presence.

When I arrived, Mother was aware that I had come, and she greeted me. Each day she got worse. Family members came to see her, to tell her they loved her and would see her in heaven. We sat vigil, taking turns holding her hand, smoothing her brow, reading Scripture to her, praying, and playing the music she had compiled for her own mother's homegoing. She had always loved "The King Is Coming" as sung by our beloved "uncle" Beverly Shea. We also played Fernando Ortega's version of "Give Me Jesus." It was painful to keep watch. Mother struggled for each breath. She was very tired and growing weaker.

Those of us surrounding her bed prayed that the Lord would sweetly come and carry her to be with Him. As the hours lengthened, I found I was becoming angry with God for tarrying. This was His beloved child. She was tired, struggling. Why wouldn't He let her enter His rest? She had often quoted the verse, "Precious in the sight of the Lord is the death of his saints" (Psalm 116:15 KJV). Surely this was one of His saints whose death was precious to Him. I so wanted her to be free of the struggle, free from the horrible restrictions her worn-out body had placed on her.

While we waited, I kept in touch with my children and friends. I read an email to Mother that my daughter Noelle had sent. It was difficult for me to read, but in so many ways, it expressed the feelings of her adoring grandchildren. The days seemed to grow shorter, and soon Mother's kind doctor prepared us that it would not be long. On the final day, we gathered with our pastor, Richard White, as he read the Twenty-third Psalm and prayed for Mother. She turned her head toward him, and I took it as an indication that she was aware. We released Mother, telling her it was okay to leave us. We loved her and we were going to be fine. We would miss her, but there were many waiting for her on the other side. Then, with my father holding her hand, she slipped quietly into heaven.

With tears filling our eyes, we stood around her bed and sang the doxology:

> *Praise God from Whom all blessings flow;*
> *Praise Him, all creatures here below;*
> *Praise Him above, ye heavenly host;*
> *Praise Father, Son, and Holy Ghost. Amen.*[2]

It was a sweet family time. The familiar words and the act of worship at that moment brought comfort. The presence of death does not mean the absence of God. He was with us in our loss and pain.

We were all given thirty minutes to call our children before the press release went out. After I had called mine and let them know, I went back to my mother's body and stayed with her until the funeral home arrived. I held her hand, smoothed her brow, and brushed her hair. My sisters and I assisted in tenderly caring for the body we had loved so dearly. The body that had given us life. The body that had knelt so often at the throne of grace on our behalf. I didn't know beforehand how I would respond to my mother's death, but in those moments, it was a comfort to be able to tend to her body. It was my way of honoring her. And another opportunity for me to say good-bye. These were precious moments that reinforced how much I loved her.

When the funeral home removed her body from the house, I finally gave in to the grief. I could hardly bear watching my mother being carried out of her beloved home and driven down the winding driveway, leaving the mountain that had nurtured her for so many years. Mother had designed our home. She had cared for it and loved it with such creativity and joy. She had adored our mountain and these woods with which she was so intimately acquainted. I thought, "My mother is leaving the mountain for the very last time." And I broke. I stood there sobbing, letting myself come undone. Someone tenderly put their arms around me, trying to comfort me, weeping with me. But I wanted to say, "Please, please don't—I need to feel this grief. I need to weep."

It is important that we deal with hurts and heartache in a healthy way—that we learn to let God into the pain. The older I get, the more I return to those words Aunt Peggy said after she lost my uncle suddenly—she said she was going to "lean into the pain." Letting ourselves feel pain is difficult. It is messy. I don't like grieving or feeling undone. Opening up to the pain as I watched Mother's body being taken away from our home cut me deeply. But feeling undone is human. Grief is human. It is part of life. The pain of loss is human. God can use all these emotions to draw us in closer to Him. As He comforts us, He strengthens us. Jesus said, "Blessed are those who mourn, for they shall be comforted" (Matthew 5:4).

When we are undone, God can meet us in a unique, transformative way. Often, the more we work at holding ourselves together without turning to God, the higher we build up our walls. In the process we not only wall ourselves in, but we wall God out. And yet it is when we are undone, messy, and vulnerable that God does his deep, comforting work in us. God was there with me in those days leading up to Mother's passing, comforting me in stages, one moment at a time, and I now have those memories to help me as I continue to miss her and walk out the process of grief. As I let my walls down and experienced grief, I began to feel a release from the enormous pain. I could sense the calming tenderness of God. I still resist being undone. I don't like it. But I do know that He will be there and that comfort will come. For I have known His comfort. I have known His "I am with you."

I Am the Resurrection

Mary and Martha knew what it was like to come undone. They had watched as their brother Lazarus grew sicker. They had done all they knew to do, but his condition only worsened. Frantic, the two sisters finally sent word to Jesus. "Lord, the one You love is sick." Jesus had a special relationship with this family of siblings, and He would know who they meant in their message. Surely, He would come right away. But as the days passed, Lazarus faded and finally died. Their brother was gone, and there had been no word from Jesus.

Imagine Mary and Martha's grief. They were close to Jesus. They knew of His healing miracles. Of course, they had assumed He would want to heal their brother, His dear friend. They had put all their hope in what Jesus could do, and yet He hadn't come. Instead, they had watched their brother die, believing themselves abandoned by the One they relied on most. What could've been so important to keep Jesus away? Didn't He love them? Didn't He care?

Realistically, it would have taken some time for Jesus to get the word from Mary and Martha and then to travel to Bethany. But why didn't He drop everything and rush to get to His friends? Scripture says that once He got the word, it took Jesus two days to begin traveling. In fact, we read, "Now Jesus loved Martha and her sister and Lazarus. So when He heard that he was sick, He then stayed two days longer in the place where He was" (John 11:5–6). Consider the logic in these verses. Jesus loved His friends, so he stayed where He was. To our ears, that doesn't sound logical at all, does it? If He loved them, wouldn't He have gone to them right away?

Jesus knew what He was doing. "This sickness is not to end in death," He told his disciples, "but for the glory of God, so that the Son of God may be glorified by it." God is never in a hurry. His goal is not to meet our expectations but to point us to the larger, eternal purpose in what He chooses to do—to shift our focus. Mary and Martha, of course, were not privy to Jesus' thoughts. All they knew was that He had not arrived in time to save their brother. Then, four days after the burial, the sisters heard a commotion outside. "Jesus is coming!" someone said.

Martha was the one to respond. She was a woman of action—practical, straightforward, a take-charge kind of woman. I can just see her marching out of the village to meet Jesus in the road, her mourning clothes raising a cloud of dust as she approached him. She was at her wits' end with grief, and she was going to speak her mind. Meanwhile, Mary—pensive Mary. Scripture tells us that she stayed at home, perhaps too heartbroken, too disappointed to face Jesus. "It's too late," Mary must have thought. With her sensitive heart, perhaps she couldn't bear to look at Him, knowing that He could've saved their brother. She didn't want to blame Jesus, but she was confused. Hurt. Grieved on so many levels.

Martha, though, pushed through her sorrow to get to Jesus in the road. Standing in front of Him now, she doesn't mince words. "Lord," she says, "if You had been here, my brother would not have died."

You let us down, Lord. This is often our first response when life doesn't happen on our terms. We rise up in confusion and anger at God for not doing what we wanted or expected Him to do. I probably would've been so upset at Jesus I would have been reluctant to face Him. I tend to react this way. When things go badly, I first try to figure out some solution on my own. Then I get frustrated and upset. My thoughts go round and round. When I finally recognize the futility of it all, I settle down to pray, asking God to calm my heart and change my attitude.

Martha continues, "Even now I know that whatever You ask of God, God will give You." She knows that nothing is impossible for Jesus. She doesn't dictate to him, but still, like me, she may have been thinking, "Make it up to us, Jesus. Do something to take our pain away."

Jesus speaks right to the heart of her grief. "Your brother will rise again." A simple, disarming declaration. Martha seems to catch only an eternal meaning in the words. "I know . . ." she tells Him, "in the resurrection on the last day." She believes in the resurrection of the dead.

But Jesus is preparing to point Martha beyond her limited understanding. Not with condescension, but with tender love. He longs for her to understand. He addresses the pain; he doesn't sidestep it. But then He challenges Martha to shift her focus, to take her mind off her loss and to consider who He is—to affirm who He is. Jesus makes a statement and then asks a question. "I am the resurrection and the life," He says, declaring to her the truth that has echoed down through the ages. "He who believes in Me will live even if he dies, and everyone who lives and believes in Me will never die. Do you believe this?"

Do you believe this? Jesus seeks to lift our perspective to the larger picture—from the temporal to the eternal. Here He wants Martha to affirm her faith. Martha answers yes and affirms for both herself and anyone close enough to hear her that she believes Jesus is the Son of God. But she still doesn't grasp what this truth means for her. She doesn't realize that Jesus is not just speaking about eternity but also the present moment—right here, right now. Jesus is the resurrection and the life wherever He is. And He is with us. That is the ultimate comfort. Jesus, the resurrection and the life, is with us in our suffering. He is comforting Martha with this truth, and yet she doesn't quite see it. She goes to the house to get Mary.

"The Teacher is asking for you." Now we see Mary, undone in a different way than her sister and with different needs. Imagine what this must have meant to her, being so devastated and reluctant—to be summoned by the One who alone could make a difference. Jesus was asking for her. He understood her desolation. He knew her better than anyone. Yes, He had to have known how she felt. He could make sense out of what seemed so senseless. She gets up quickly, we are told, while the mourners, thinking she is headed for her brother's grave, follow her out. They had come to comfort the sisters, but they could not do it the way Jesus could. He knew them so well and loved them so tenderly.

I can imagine the tearstained face with which Mary meets Jesus as she comes to Him in the road. Her face is swollen and blotchy from crying. How she must have looked to Him. Vulnerable. Desperate. Undone. His heart is pierced as He looks into her eyes, into her pain. When she sees Him, she falls at His feet, grief stricken. "Lord," she says weeping, as the mourners weep behind her, "if You had been here, my brother would not have died."

I'm undone. I'm confused. I'm at a loss. Why, Lord? Mary isn't accusing, just honestly expressing her weariness and anguish. She is letting go of her grief. To stand vigil by a loved one's deathbed wrings so much out of you. Mary opens herself up so that Jesus can come closer. He looks at her with eyes that see it all. The pain, loss, confusion, exhaustion, heartache. We are told that He is "deeply moved" and "troubled." The meaning here for troubled is *angered*. Perhaps He is angered that death brings such misery. Angered at the curse of sin, at the despair crushing the hearts of those He loves.

"Where have you laid him?" He asks. The mourners motion for Him to follow, and we read those beautiful, simple words: "Jesus wept."

Jesus wept. He knew what He was going to do, but He loved His friends and was not immune to their pain. He entered their grief. He was with them in it—not just physically, but emotionally. *When you pass through the waters, I will be with you.* Jesus wasn't distant or removed. He legitimized the pain of those He loved. He felt the weight of their sorrow. "Surely," the Bible says, "He has borne our griefs and carried our sorrows" (Isaiah 53:4 NKJV). Jesus' presence in that pain—His empathy, His sharing of the load—brought comfort. "See how He loved him!" the attentive crowd exclaims, touched by Jesus' grief. And as Jesus comes to the tomb, we read again that He is "deeply moved within."

But here is where Jesus turns. He gets down into Mary and Martha's grief, into the mourners' grief, and then he gets ready to lead them out. He knows that death will soon be defeated for all time, and He moves the people toward that understanding. They already believed Lazarus would be raised on the last day in the resurrection of the dead, but Jesus has so much more for them. He is going to reveal a greater glory. He points to the eternal perspective.

Looking at the tomb, a cave blocked by a stone, Jesus gives a directive: "Remove the stone." No explanation. No niceties. Just take it away. He has allowed the people to grieve; He has honored their grief, grieving with them. But now He gives them something to do—an action that doesn't make sense. Will they trust him?

Martha had no way of knowing what God was going to do. It was a very odd request to have the stone removed. Always practical, Martha comes back with the obvious. "Lord, by this time there will be a stench." Her brother's body has been closed up for four days. Jesus reminds her of their conversation on the road. "Did I not say to you that if you believe, you will see the glory of God?"

No response. They have no idea what Jesus is preparing. Perhaps Martha doesn't dare to hope. Hadn't Jesus said, "Your brother will rise again . . . I am the resurrection"? But surely not . . . there is a hush. Quietly, the people do what He says. They remove the stone.

Standing before the crowd in front of the open cave, Jesus now prays, praising God for what He will do. "Father, I thank You that You have heard Me . . . that they may believe that You sent Me." *Let this be a sign of who I am.* Then He takes on the whole underworld of death. He puts death on notice, confronting it head-on. The intensity of evil must have been incredible. But death is not going to be the victor. Jesus calls out in a loud voice, breaking death's hold: "Lazarus, come forth!"

The echo of His voice booming against the rock. The silence of the people, as if the whole crowd has drawn its breath. The life force moves. Staring at the mouth of the cave, they see him come into view: Lazarus bound up in his grave clothes. "Unbind him," Jesus says, "and let him go."

A Bigger Picture

How did Jesus comfort Mary, Martha, and those mourners? He showed up on the scene—His presence was a comfort. He called them to take on God's perspective and to affirm his identity. "Do you believe this?" He entered their pain, feeling it with them, deepening their intimacy with Him. He called them out of their sorrow into a place of trust, asking them to act on that trust and be part of the miracle. "Remove the stone." And He demonstrated His supernatural power, breaking death's power over life, showing them who He is: Resurrection.

Look at the detailed involvement of Jesus in the lives of these people at their lowest moment. Yes, He could have gone to Bethany before Lazarus died and healed him. But look at what Mary, Martha, and the others would have missed. Sometimes God will allow circumstances in our lives to become extreme so that He can step in and give us an experience of His love, His comfort, and His power that changes us forever. He wants to show us who He is. He longs to reveal himself. Our desperation—like that of Mary and Martha—becomes His opportunity to meet with us, to identify with us, and then to walk us to another level of intimacy and trust.

What's more, what Jesus did that day was not just for Mary, Martha, and those who cared about Lazarus. We read in the Bible that word spread of Lazarus's resurrection and caused many people to believe in Jesus. So dramatic was the impact of the miracle that the chief priests and the Pharisees began plotting to kill Jesus. Indeed, so many people were putting their faith in Jesus the chief priests put a death warrant out for Lazarus too. Jesus knew ahead of time that letting Lazarus die and then raising him from the dead would result in this groundswell of faith. Unbeknownst to them, Mary and Martha got to play a part in the purpose of God. The price they paid was their suffering, their grief, their experience of being undone.

If Mary and Martha had not suffered, would we have missed all the truth Jesus shared with them? Think what Jesus told Martha: "I am the resurrection and the life." That is a truth read at the funerals of many today. It was what Jesus said to bring comfort to His friends, and it has been passed on through the millennia as a comfort for us. Because of Mary and Martha's suffering, we can be comforted in ours.

God always has a bigger picture in mind when He confronts our ruins. The resurrection of Lazarus was the last major miracle Jesus worked before His own death and resurrection. Perhaps the Lazarus miracle was also Jesus' way of preparing the people for what he would undergo, a way of building their faith against the despair of the cross. Our willingness to come undone, to trust God with our pain, to let Him in, to receive His comfort, and to allow Him to walk us out of our brokenness will always make a difference in the lives of other people, whether it be those watching our lives or those whom we will encourage later. As Scripture says, "Blessed be the God and Father of our Lord Jesus Christ, the Father of mercies and God of all comfort, who comforts us in all our affliction so that we will be able to comfort those who are in any affliction with the comfort with which we ourselves are comforted by God. For just as the sufferings of Christ are ours in abundance, so also our comfort is abundant through Christ" (2 Corinthians 1:3–5).

Knowing God's Comfort in Our Undone

Jesus shifted the focus of Martha, Mary, and the mourners—He called their attention to Himself. In our undone moments, God calls us too to put our focus on Him. I remember the day I realized that a marriage I had entered later in life was over. I sat down in a chair in my den and wept. I had done all I knew to do. Now the marriage was ending. I was exasperated, exhausted, broken. Years of pain and grief came pouring out.

Weeping there in my chair, I suddenly had the impression in my heart that God wanted me to praise Him. I couldn't and told Him no. I didn't feel like praising Him. The thought persisted, and finally, in obedience, I began haltingly to praise Him. I dragged my focus from my deep heartache and put it on God's character. Praying aloud, I praised Him for who He is. For how He had sustained me through all the stress. For having a purpose even in those ruins of my life.

I moved to my ABC list of God's attributes. "God, you are almighty, an anchor. You are beautiful and bountiful. I praise you because you are compassionate, a composer, a covenant keeper, my creator . . ."

Slowly, as I moved through the alphabet, focusing on God's character, I began to feel the burden lifting. It was as if someone were letting water out of a tub or air out of a balloon. The pain seemed to dissipate. The grief, the undoneness, began to pass. By the time I had run through my list, I could sense my perspective had changed. I felt calmed. Comforted. Quieted. "Like a weaned child with its mother," as David wrote (Psalm 131:12 NIV).

Even when you don't have the strength to pray as I did that day, you can still turn toward God in your heart. I mentioned my father's favorite prayer, "Lord, help me." When we're undone, we may not even be able to pray that. This is when we count on what the Bible says—that Jesus is praying for us, that the Holy Spirit intercedes for us. Paul wrote, "The Spirit also helps our weakness; for we do not know how to pray as we should, but the Spirit Himself intercedes for us with groanings too deep for words" (Romans 8:26). That verse is a great comfort to me. When I can't articulate my deepest hurts, then I can rest knowing Jesus is talking to God about me. The Holy Spirit is talking to God about me. And God is listening.

At other moments, you may be able to put your mind on a portion of Scripture, or even on a phrase like: "God loves me." "God is able." "I trust you, Lord." Or it may be just a word: "Father." "Helper." At times we can't hold on to more than that. Perhaps at other times you may find you are able to picture Jesus giving comfort, as he did to Mary and the mourners. "Jesus wept." Try putting your mind on that verse. Imagine Jesus "deeply moved" over your situation, your heartache. As you do these things, you are renewing your mind. You are adding God's truth to your thoughts. You may not feel at first as if this makes any difference, but over time the truths will begin to influence you. Remember the promise of Scripture: "You will keep him in perfect peace, whose mind is stayed on You" (Isaiah 26:3 NKJV).

Comfort doesn't mean the absence of grief. Grief is something we have to work through; it is a normal, healthy human expression. God doesn't necessarily take it away. Sometimes grief dissipates for a while, as it did for me that day as I praised. Or it may come in waves, recede, and surge again. But at other times, as with the loss of my mother, God comforts us by making the grief bearable. He helps us to function in spite of it. Whether or not the grief lifts, we can choose to believe God is present. That's what I learned after that walk on the beach in South Carolina. I could not put my trust in my feelings. I had to trust in the fact of God's presence, in His promise to be with me. Whatever you might be going through, God sees you. He knows your situation. And He hears your prayers. Take comfort in these facts.

POINT OF FOCUS

Blessed be the God and Father of our Lord Jesus Christ, the Father of mercies and God of all comfort, who comforts us in all our affliction so that we will be able to comfort those who are in any affliction with the comfort with which we ourselves are comforted by God. For just as the sufferings of Christ are ours in abundance, so also our comfort is abundant through Christ.

2 Corinthians 1:3–5

Encounter His Power

chapter five

ONE LATE FALL after having major surgery, I traveled to the Caribbean to spend time with my parents. It had been two weeks since the operation, and my doctor had given me permission to go. I wasn't fully recovered. I had developed an abdominal blood clot. But my doctor prescribed me some medicine and said he believed I would be fine. I needed to get away and catch up on some rest. I was trying to sell my farm and make decisions about where to relocate. My older daughter had entered college that fall and was having difficulty adjusting. The surgery had further drained me, and I was looking forward to the sun and the sand.

We were staying in a home right on the beach. The house belonged to a friend of my parents. Each year my oldest sister and her husband would accompany my parents on vacation there, and in recent years, I had joined them. It was a lovely spot. The pool was at the beachfront, and the bedrooms were all lined up behind the pool. I was delighted to finally arrive.

The time with my family was relaxing. We would have a leisurely breakfast in the mornings with discussion about current events and brief devotions led by my father or my brother-in-law. There would be rest and reading around the pool and afternoon walks on the beach with my father. In the evenings, we usually went out to dinner at a local restaurant and then came back to the house for a time of Bible reading and prayer.

All seemed to go well with my health until about five or six days into the trip, when I began to feel ill. I was having some abdominal pain and told my family I would have to stay behind while they went to dinner. I called my doctor in Virginia, and he instructed me to continue taking my meds, to monitor the pain throughout the night, and to call him in the morning. The next morning I was feeling a little worse. By the following nightfall, the pain had become so severe we realized I would have to be evacuated back to the States.

But despite my need, we were unable to make the evacuation happen. We learned that the airport was already closed for the evening, and officials told us the medevac plane would not be allowed to come in. I would have to wait it out till morning. Mother and Daddy prayed for me, and after that, the only thing Mother knew to do was to rub my back with some lotion. All she had on hand was antiwrinkle cream! This did not deter her—Mother was never easily deterred. She was so cute, coming into the room with that cream, trying to soothe me, comforting me in the stress of our dilemma.

On one level, I had resigned myself to the circumstances and felt peaceful. We had done all we could. We had used the resources at our disposal. The officials had made their decision. I couldn't change anything. My parents couldn't change anything. What options did we have? We finally had to say, "Okay, Lord, this is in your hands." My parents committed me to the Lord, praying that I would sleep well and that my condition would not grow worse during the night.

But once you decide to trust God, worry can creep in and threaten your decision. One moment you say, "Lord, I trust you. This is in your hands." A few minutes later, your mind starts turning, and you begin to sift through a range of hypothetical outcomes. "What could be wrong with me?" I wondered. Surely the pain I was experiencing had some connection to my surgery, but what if it didn't? In fact, I later learned my abdominal blood clot had become infected. I had misread the directions on my prescription and had taken too little of the medication. If that infection had spread, my condition could have become very serious, but at least I didn't know enough to worry about that scenario.

I worried about my children. Christmas was coming up, and I realized I wouldn't have the strength to do Christmas for them as I wanted. My husband and I were divorced, and my children needed the traditions that might make things seem less unstable, more normal. Now their Christmas would be interrupted because I wasn't going to be able to travel home. I would have to stay in Florida, and they would have to travel to me. I knew they wouldn't be happy without our family traditions for celebrating, but I was unable to do anything about it. Lying in bed on that island, I was powerless to change things.

We Need God's Power

Coming up against our own powerlessness can make us acutely aware of God's power. Waiting out the night on the island, I recognized just how dependent on God I truly was—totally dependent. I was experiencing pain that no one could alleviate. I had an infection that no doctor knew about, let alone one that anyone could contain. I needed to be in another country but had no way to get there. I needed doctors who could pinpoint and solve the problem quickly. I needed my body's immune system to fight. I needed God to prepare my children emotionally for a change in plans. I needed Him to keep me peaceful and trusting through it all. Everything I faced at that moment, both internally and externally, depended on God's power.

But the truth is even if my physical condition had been different, even if I had been able to work it out to spend Christmas with my children at home, I would have been just as dependent on God's power. We feel secure when we believe we are in control of our lives, but ultimately, God is in control. We do have choices. God has given us a free will. We can choose how to interpret our circumstances. We can choose our attitude about what is happening around us. We can choose to see our circumstances as hindrances, failures, catastrophes, fiascoes, and interruptions. Or we can look around and see them as opportunities. Yet even in our capacity to choose, we are not in control. We need God's power.

What is God's power? How do we encounter it? Do I want to encounter it? What difference does God's power make for me today? After all, if God is so powerful, if He is in control, then why do bad things happen? To good people? To our loved ones? To me? Why is life unfair? Why do devastating acts of nature occur? Why are terrorists allowed to hit their mark? Why do schoolchildren turn guns on their classmates and on themselves? Why do we struggle so? If God is so powerful, then couldn't He prevent all this? Couldn't He intervene?

One thing I have learned is that to live fully is to live in a double reality—to know our pain and loss but also to know God's love. We live in a fallen world with fallen people. This was not God's plan. He created an ideal world in which everything was at peace and in harmony. God gave our first parents a free will; they could choose whether to obey Him. They chose not to obey, and as a result, chaos entered the world, and bad things, terrible things, happen here. But God did not abandon us or the world. When humanity rebelled, God had a plan to redeem both us and the world, a plan that culminated in the death and resurrection of Jesus Christ.

Perhaps if we were God, we would have done things differently. But we are not God. When we truly recognize this fact, we can relax and let God be God. He is the one true hope we have in this life. Without God, without the promises of His unfailing love and unchanging character, we have no hope. We have no security or stability. We have no tomorrow. I am not saying trusting God is easy. It isn't. Relaxing and letting God be God is a daily battle. I am a worrier by nature, so this is always difficult for me. When I am struggling and desperate for God, I find it hard to cope. But desperate for God is what we are and what we always will be. God's power is what we need.

God's Power, Our Weakness

God is both sovereign and omnipotent—He has absolute authority, and He is all-powerful. These aspects of God's nature can be difficult to grasp with our finite minds. Sovereignty and omnipotence are concepts that seem distant and illusive. They make God seem distant and illusive. They sound like big theological words that have little to do with real life. In fact, the truths behind these words reveal important facets of God's character, and if we are going to trust in God's character, we need to seek to understand them.

Sovereignty may seem like an outdated concept to us, because in today's world there really isn't a ruler who is a true sovereign. We call the Queen of England sovereign, but she is not. She has influence, but she doesn't rule with absolute authority. God rules over all. He is the supreme ruler. He holds the highest status, commands the greatest respect, and has the final say. He is totally independent and self-governing.

When we talk about God's omnipotence, we are talking about His power. God is all-powerful. He is the most powerful. He does exactly as He wishes. He can make things happen. He can get it done. In His power, He is all-knowing and absolutely free. He cannot be stopped, hindered, or compelled. If God were not also love, goodness, and mercy, He would be terrifying.

In contrast, the Bible says that we humans are only dust. "As for man," we read in the Psalms, "his days are like grass" (Psalm 103:15 NKJV). In God's eyes, "the nations are like a drop from a bucket, and are regarded as a speck of dust on the scales" (Isaiah 40:15). What are we when compared with an all-powerful, sovereign God? What kind of power do we have if the nations are like specks of dust in God's sight? Who are we to think we actually control our destinies? As the Bible says, "Will the clay say to the potter, 'What are you doing?'" (Isaiah 45:9).

Let's bring this discussion down to where we live. We persist in believing that if we just try hard enough, we can gain complete control over our tomorrows, but as many of us have lived long enough to discover, we can do everything "right" in life and still have things go wrong. When my younger daughter was four, she was trampled by a horse. An adult horseman was with her. She was out in our pasture. She knew the horse. The horse just spooked. No one did anything wrong. I blamed myself for the accident, as if I could've stopped it, but I could not have controlled that animal. No one could've predicted what the horse would do in that moment. We all thought we knew the horse. But things still went wrong, and I had to look to God to heal my child's body and emotions. Thankfully, after a trip to the emergency room and stitches, she recovered from her injuries.

Coming up against our own powerlessness can scare us. The idea that we can dot every *i* and cross every *t* and still end up in a mess; that no matter what we do, pain can still overwhelm us; that even if we love and serve God with all our hearts, we can still suffer terrible loss—these realities make us insecure. They make us preoccupied with the "what ifs." Oh, that we could embrace God's perspective—we need His help to do it. God told the apostle Paul, "My grace is sufficient for you, *for my power is made perfect in weakness*" (2 Corinthians 12:9 NIV, emphasis added). Do you see that? God is saying it is okay to be human. We don't need to fear our insufficiency. Our weakness is the very environment in which God's power thrives. Encountering our own weakness is what sets the stage for us to encounter God's power!

God's Power in Our Weakness

When I am willing to be myself, when I am willing to let God work through my insufficiency, incredible things can happen. Through my weaknesses God can work and show His greatness. Paul caught this truth. Having understood what God said to him about weakness, he wrote, "Therefore I will boast all the more gladly about my weaknesses, so that Christ's power may rest on me. That is why, for Christ's sake, I delight in weaknesses, in insults, in hardships, in persecutions, in difficulties. For when I am weak, then I am strong" (2 Corinthians 12:10 NIV).

To Paul, the prospect of hardships, persecutions, and difficulties was not cause for fear but for confidence in God. And Paul was one to know. He was beaten, thrown in prison, stoned, flogged, and shipwrecked; he experienced hunger, thirst, and dangers of all kinds (2 Corinthians 11:23–27). He also struggled with some kind of troublesome hindrance throughout life (2 Corinthians 12:7–8). Three times he asked God to remove it. God did not, and Paul did not complain. Rather, he embraced the perspective that these sufferings gave God the opportunity to demonstrate His power and sufficiency. Paul boasted of weaknesses the way someone else might boast of accomplishments. He knew that through those weaknesses, God would be glorified.

Think about Lazarus. His death is what gave God the opportunity to demonstrate power *over* death. Our dead places, our devastations— the places we are helpless to restore—are the environments into which God enters with resurrection power. "O death, where is thy sting?" we read in Scripture. "O grave, where is thy victory?" (1 Corinthians 15:55 KJV). When we encounter God's power, we encounter Him overcoming the deaths in our lives. Whatever our circumstances, God can stand at the mouth of the grave and cry, "Lazarus, come forth!" And Lazarus must come forth. For death has to give way in the presence of Jesus.

Through adversities God's power shines. Paul's testimony of this fact carries down through the ages. His perspective, molded by his knowledge of God's character, enabled him to trust God in the uncertain, stormy circumstances of life. This man, who was intimately acquainted with hardship, was able to declare, "I have learned to be content whatever the circumstances" (Philippians 4:11 NIV).

I was not as steady as Paul while waiting for morning to come during my ordeal on the island. Trust and fear. Rest and worry. I seemed to oscillate between them. But that is okay. Our part is to make the choice to trust God. We don't have to work up a lot of faith and purge all our doubt. We just make the choice to believe. In the Gospels, a father who wanted Jesus to heal his son said, "I do believe; help my unbelief" (Mark 9:24). This father was struggling with doubt, but he made a choice to trust. That is what we do. Even in fear, we can make the choice. God then inhabits our choice and helps us to apply it in our lives. In fact, He even helps us to make the choice. The Bible says, "For it is God who works in you both to will and to do for His good pleasure" (Philippians 2:13 NKJV).

I don't want to make it sound like choosing to trust God is easy—as if it is easy to say, "Oh, God will handle this financial mess. I don't have to worry." Or, "God can take care of my out-of-control teenager. It's out of my hands." Trusting God can be a struggle. It can be a minute-by-minute renewal of our decision. Still, we must learn to surrender—to believe that God in His power and authority can handle our situation. God's perspective is eternal. His purpose in our lives is not limited by time, space, or circumstances. While we see just our little corner of life, God sees the whole.

When we surrender to God in our weakness, when we choose to trust Him, we experience freedom. We realize that we don't have to be the all-powerful ones. We don't have to be strong. We don't have to be supersufficient. We don't even have to be sufficient. This doesn't mean we settle for mediocrity or cease to do our part, but it does mean we learn to embrace the fact that we are not in charge. We use so much energy both trying to stay in control and worrying that we might lose it. But we don't have to be everything to everyone. We don't have to do it all. God is sovereign and omnipotent, and He already knows what will happen. Instead of fretting and asking, "What can I do to control this?" we can surrender and ask, "What does God want to do in the midst of this?"

The medevac plane was the first to land that next morning on the island, and we were there to meet it. I was in a lot of pain while flying, but when we landed in Fort Lauderdale, an ambulance was there to take me to the hospital. I was able to get the medical attention I needed, and I recovered. The children fared pretty well. We did spend Christmas in Florida, not at home, but we had a good family time; and I had enough strength before New Year's Eve to travel back to Virginia. I would've preferred not to have gone through the experience and to have been able to do Christmas differently for the children, but God took care of us, turning the challenge into an opportunity to show us the power of His love and care. In our powerlessness, we encountered God's power. He showed us more of Himself, and that is His promise, His desire, in every circumstance we face. He longs to reveal more of Himself.

In the Storm

I love the picture of God that is painted in Psalm 18. The psalmist starts out by praising God and telling of his horrible predicament. The psalmist was overwhelmed. He was about to die. Then in his distress, he cried out for God, and God heard him. I picture a small, helpless child whimpering in fear and panic, and then the sound of that whimper echoing down the great corridors of heaven to the very ear of God. Hearing His child, God moves into action, roaring, "How dare anyone tamper with my child?" The Lord gathers Himself up with all His terrifying power to rescue His own. He reaches down into the tumult and tenderly takes hold of His child, drawing him from the grip of his adversaries and setting him down in a place of peace.

Why does God do all this? Why respond to His child's cry with such power and force? The psalmist says, "He rescued me, because He delighted in me" (Psalm 18:19). What a beautiful picture and truth! When the psalmist called out to God, did he know what his prayer would set into motion? Did he know all that would happen in the heavenly realms to bring about his rescue? Probably not. The psalmist was in the dark. He was not in control. All he knew in his anguish was the sureness of God's character, and that was what he was counting on.

This passage of Scripture reminds me of a favorite print I own, a watercolor by artist and dear friend Carolyn Blish that hangs over the fireplace in my den. The painting depicts Jesus standing in the midst of a turbulent sea with arms outstretched, hair and robes tossed, and a profile revealing a look of great intensity. The waves are heaving spray. The sky is dark and menacing. This is a scene from the gospel account of Jesus calming the storm. Mark's narrative describes it: "He got up, rebuked the wind and said to the waves, 'Quiet! Be still!'" (Mark 4:39 NIV).

Leading up to this storm, Jesus had been busy traveling around Galilee, healing the sick, casting out demons, rebuking the scribes and Pharisees, and teaching the multitudes. As word about Jesus spread, people were coming with their needs from all over the region. This particular day, they had gathered at the shore of the Sea of Galilee and were pressing in on Jesus with such intensity He got into a boat and began to teach the people from there.

That evening, after Jesus had finished teaching, He and His disciples rowed out across the sea. They had made no preparations. They just up and left as they were. But as the boat was making its way, an intense storm arose without warning. The Sea of Galilee is famous for its sudden, fierce storms. Due to the lake's location, it often becomes the colliding point for cool and warm air masses. Storms can arise unexpectedly, drop to the center of the lake, and stir up waves that are extremely high, putting vessels in danger.

Dark clouds rolled in, and the waves were not lapping—they were crashing into the sides of the disciples' boat. Lightning was flashing, the thunder was deafening, and the wind threatened to spill the men into the water. In all the confusion, these seasoned fishermen no doubt did everything they knew to save themselves. They tried to scoop the water out, but it came in faster than they could keep up, and the boat began to fill. I can imagine them trying to dump overboard everything that wasn't necessary. Still they began to sink. Scrambling to keep the vessel righted, they couldn't hear one another over the great roar of the wind. These disciples—these seasoned, highly experienced fishermen who had fished their entire lives on these waters—were terrified.

Think about this. For more than a year and a half, the disciples had talked and walked with Jesus. He had taught them about God. They had worshipped together in the synagogues. They had played and laughed and shared life together. These men knew what Jesus could do. They had seen Him heal the sick, turn water into wine, and yet they looked at this raging storm with terror in their hearts. All they could see was the storm. In panic and desperation, they finally turned to Jesus, who was asleep in the back of the boat.

The men looked at Jesus and couldn't believe it. The very idea that He was asleep while they were trying desperately to save Him, themselves, and the boat! The storm raged, the sea churned, tossing them up one way and down the other, and Jesus was not paying attention.

Above the roar of the wind and waves, they yelled to Him. "Teacher, don't you care if we drown?" This is so human. So often we look at our situation, see the worst-case scenario as inevitable, and then read it to mean we have been abandoned or forgotten by God. We see the storm. We are overcome by fear. We see our demise. We feel alone in it. We want safety and security immediately, and we think that Jesus is asleep on the job! We ask God if He cares. There at the end is when we finally put our focus on God—once we've decided we're finished. The circumstance is the all-consuming thing. God is an afterthought.

Notice it was after they had exhausted their own efforts that these men even decided to turn to the Miracle Worker. As a last recourse. So often we do the same in our storms. The last thing we do is look to God. We try to fix things ourselves, and in the process, we produce pitiful results, the evidence of our own weakness. These strong, experienced, and normally steady fishermen were powerless in the face of the storm. They were in way over their heads and totally inadequate to save themselves. If only we could see our weakness right off—even "boast" about our weakness like Paul—and invite God to demonstrate His power, as Jesus was about to do.

I can imagine the storm swirling around them as Jesus is aroused from sleep. I see Him rubbing the sleep from His eyes, stretching a bit, looking at the waves and the wind as if they are no threat at all. Jesus was in charge in that storm. He knew who He was and what was going to happen. I can see Him with that intensity Carolyn Blish portrayed in her watercolor. Rising up and taking control over the nature He created, Jesus says those words that I hear Him speaking over the storms in my life and in my heart—storms of fear, anxiety, and worry. "Quiet! Be still!"

Immediately, nature recognized Jesus' authority and obeyed. The storm simply stopped. No slow abatement. All was instantly calm. The boat was still. The waves and wind hushed. It was as if there had never been a storm. Jesus had demonstrated His power, and the disciples in their helplessness and terror had encountered it.

Then Jesus turned to focus on the disciples, and I don't sense a rebuke here—more that Jesus was expressing His own sadness. In their fear, they had accused Him of not caring, when nothing could have been further from the truth. He observed what was happening in their hearts and called it like He saw it. He asked, "Why are you so afraid? Do you still have no faith?" *Didn't you know you were safe with Me? Haven't you seen me take care of you before? Guys, remember what I've been doing, the things you have seen. Don't you trust me?*

Aren't we all like the disciples? When things are fine, we think we've got it together, but then a storm arises. We try to manage it on our own, doing all we know to do. Even good and appropriate things. But the storm is way too much for us. Fear and panic set in, causing us to lose our perspective. *Don't you remember what you've already seen me do?* I can hear God asking that of me. The Lord does such powerful works in our lives, but we are so weak. When a new trial comes, our hearts melt. Instead of seeing the storm through the eyes of confident faith, we see it as overwhelming. We fail to remember all the ways God has helped us before. *You're still afraid? You still don't trust? Don't you remember?*

God's people, the Israelites, were notorious for forgetting. One of God's big complaints against the Israelites was that they failed to remember how He had provided for them time and again. With every new challenge, their default response was fear and grumbling. Are we any different? Our storm may be the bills we can't pay, a difficult diagnosis, or a broken relationship. From storm to storm, we struggle to remember what we have already seen of God's power. As the waves are about to cover our heads, we cry out, "Don't you care that I'm drowning?"

God knows we have this tendency. He knows our weakness. He knows how hard it is for us to trust. But Jesus didn't silence the storm in response to the disciples' faith crisis. He drew attention to their lack of faith for their sakes, but He quieted the wind to demonstrate His power, to show His friends—and us—that He is in control. He stilled the waves to show us who He is: Omnipotent Creator. Sovereign Lord. God wants to reveal Himself in our storms so that we will see who He is and dare to trust Him with our tomorrow. That's what Jesus did for the disciples. He showed them His power, and by doing so, He shifted their focus to Himself. In the eerie stillness after the storm, we hear them saying, "Who can this be, that even the wind and the sea obey Him!"

Retraining Our Minds to Trust

One of my favorite choruses says, "Turn your eyes upon Jesus, Look full in His wonderful face, And the things of earth will grow strangely dim In the light of His glory and grace."[1] In trouble, Jesus should be the first place we look. When we look at Jesus, our storms seem less powerful and our hearts take strength. But often we do the reverse: like the disciples, we look at the storm and we fold in fear. God wants to help us learn to look at Him from the outset.

One of the ways we can retrain our minds is by remembering what God has done in the past. We've talked about keeping a journal and reflecting on our experiences of God. Even as I keep that ABC praise list in my mind for easy recall, you might want to keep in your mind a short list of significant life experiences with God or memories of times when God demonstrated His power to you. Make a habit of meditating on the ways God worked in those situations. Ask Him to keep showing you new things about Himself as you remember. In building up your mind this way, you will have an easier time drawing on your memories—your track record with God—when life takes unexpected turns.

Scripture memory is another way to train our minds for future storms. In memorizing Scripture, we feed our minds with God's truth, and that truth will rise to the surface when it is needed. Jesus said, "But the Helper, the Holy Spirit, whom the Father will send in My name, He will teach you all things, and bring to your remembrance all things that I said to you" (John 14:26 NKJV). If we put God's Word in our minds, then He will bring it to our "remembrance." I can't count the number of times I have found myself in a tough situation only to have phrases or passages from Scripture come to memory, seemingly out of nowhere, as encouragements to me. On the other hand, if we don't know what God's Word says, how can He bring it to our minds? Try memorizing the verses highlighted in the Point of Focus feature at the end of each chapter in this book. Or memorize some of the other verses that strike you as you read. Maybe there are specific verses that keep coming up in your devotional time with God. If they keep coming up, then perhaps God wants you to see something you are not yet getting. Why not try memorizing those truths?

Praise music—music that lifts up God and His truth—is another tool I use to build up my mind and spirit. I listen to it as I take walks, as I drive. I even use it as background music in my office. I usually keep it playing softly. That way, if there is a lull in my work, even for a moment or two, those lyrics are allowed to filter in and remind me of some truth about God. I surround myself with praise music. I turn up the volume of praise in my house. I want my home to be filled with the praises of God. The music lifts my heart and builds up my spirit in the truth of who God is. When I need comfort, certain songs touch my heart. When I need strength, other songs remind me of the One who is on my side. As with Bible verses, God will bring certain songs to mind just when I need them. Lyrics or melodies will find their way into my consciousness, reminding me that God is with me.

Learning to trust God is a process, as we are discovering, and we have a part to play in developing ourselves so that we can more readily do it. Trusting God isn't natural for us. Author Brennan Manning wrote a book titled *Ruthless Trust.* In it he writes, "Unwavering trust is a rare and precious thing because it often demands a degree of courage that borders on the heroic."[2] How does it feel to trust God in a storm more forceful than any we've ever known? It feels crazy. It feels out of control. That's why the disciples couldn't do it. Trusting God is not for wimps. Waiting in faith to encounter God's power is tough. If we hope to fare better than the disciples, then we will have to keep returning with determination to the character of God. We must drill down to the bedrock of who God is and make it our priority to know Him. Jesus was intimate with the Father. He was one with the Father (John 10:30). Trust wasn't an issue for Jesus. He could sleep through a storm, and He wants the same for us. God longs for us to know His character so we can live resting in our storms, expecting His power, and trusting Him for tomorrow.

POINT OF FOCUS

But he said to me, "My grace is sufficient for you, for my power is made perfect in weakness." Therefore I will boast all the more gladly about my weaknesses, so that Christ's power may rest on me.
2 Corinthians 12:9 NIV

Receive His Help

chapter six

I REMEMBER WATCHING WITH horror the television accounts of the 2004 Asian Tsunami that devastated Indonesia, Sri Lanka, Thailand, and other countries. The news played and replayed the sights and sounds of the mighty wave as it surged forward, taking everything in its path, only to inhale and surge again. Nothing was safe. What was left in the tsunami's wake was unrecognizable, damaged beyond rescue, or dead.

Another disaster scenario played out in 2005, of course, when Hurricane Katrina slammed the Gulf Coast of the United States. Mighty waters rushed in, carrying off people, animals, cars, and everything else in the force of the current, before eventually receding, leaving behind a devastated, stinking, contaminated wasteland. The interviews with survivors were sobering. I listened to one woman give her account from the living room of a home owned by my parents in Montreat. I remember her telling of the water rushing toward her, of trying to outrun it, of grabbing hold of a tree as the water rose, and of debris rushing by, banging against her body. I could only imagine the sheer terror of the experience.

Floods, fires, earthquakes, storms. Those who have faced these terrifying events have experienced the reality of our human frailty and helplessness. What can you do against a 150-mile-per-hour wind? What can you do against a ten-foot wall of water? What can you do when the earth beneath your feet literally begins to move, to open, and to pull the structure of your home down on top of you? As a survivor, how do you pick up your life and move forward after losing perhaps everything, even family and friends?

If you have not experienced the trauma of a natural disaster, then perhaps you have lived through personal disasters that have created lasting damage in your life. The psalmist wrote, "The floods have lifted up, O Lord, the floods have lifted up their voice, the floods lift up their pounding waves" (Psalm 93:3). The psalmist was no stranger to the "floods" life can bring. Disaster had often made its way into the psalmist's life. Many times the noise of it had gotten to him. The floodwaters had gotten high and their sound deafening, and the waves had pounded away at him. He had been battered and bruised, in danger of losing his grip.

Does it seem as if the floods of hardship have lifted up their pounding waves and sent them crashing down on you? Have you known what it is like to be battered and bruised by the debris of life issues? Have you known the feeling of trying to hold on in tragedy, loss, or trial, realizing you are close to losing your grip?

I have known such moments in my life—moments when I struggled to hold on to something, anything, that would prevent me from being swept away. How I longed to get to solid ground, to some secure place where I could stand, if even for a moment. The year I lost my mother was such a time. Mother was very ill, and each time I went home, I feared it would be the last time I would see her. I would leave the house with a profound sadness, choking back the painful emotions. She was slipping away, and I dreaded the day when I would have to face life without her. In addition, the ministry I founded and loved was in a major transition, and I was in the midst of some difficult personal challenges. Change seemed to be happening on so many significant levels, and I just didn't think I could handle one more thing. I was hanging on for dear life and growing weary in the effort.

During one of my devotional times, I read, "A bruised reed He will not break and a dimly burning wick He will not extinguish; He will faithfully bring forth justice" (Isaiah 42:3). In those images I saw myself: A bruised reed—vulnerable, weak, fragile, bruised by life, bruised by my own choices. A dimly burning wick—having once burned brightly, now nearly burned out, almost down to the nub, barely flickering. Then I saw what God promised. The verse said he would not break me in my bruised condition. He would not let me burn out. I might feel like He was cutting it close, but He saw me. He would help me. He would not let those waters carry me into oblivion.

A Bruised Reed

One of the myths we can find ourselves believing is that when we know God, especially when we are trying to serve Him, life should run smoothly. If it does not, then we may condemn ourselves for having failed somewhere along the line, or we may feel unloved and abandoned by God. We wonder why God isn't keeping His end of the bargain. Doesn't He see us floundering? We reach what we believe is the end of our capacity to survive, and we expect things to get better. Surely, we think, they must get better. But sometimes they don't. We ask, "How much more can I take?" We feel battered by life. We feel bruised.

Let's take a closer look at the reed. Some are growing by a pond near my home. They look tall and proud, standing straight and appearing very strong. They are encircled with lovely foliage and have heads like little cigars, swaying gently in the breeze. They look serene, as if they belong in the pond's environment. And yet, they are terribly weak and vulnerable. They cannot endure any kind of strain. A strong gust of wind or a small animal running by can knock them over. Any slight amount of force can bruise or bend them, leaving them doubled over and even more vulnerable.

What are some of the things that bruise us? Prolonged illness. Financial stress. Troubled relationships. Loneliness. Rejection. Unkind words. Betrayal. Unconfessed sins. People's opinions. Failure. I am sure you can add to this list. These are the kinds of experiences and traumas that weigh heavily on our hearts, preoccupying our thoughts. They leave us hurting, weakened, doubled over like the reed.

But God, in our bruisings, has not left us alone. Life may seem just about as great a strain as we can handle, but God's Word promises that He is with us. He sees us in our condition, so close to the edge. He isn't condemning us for our helplessness. He doesn't condemn the reed for being bruised or the wick for being nearly extinguished. God looks on us with compassion. He strengthens the reed; He relights the wick. The verse from Isaiah says He will "faithfully bring forth justice." Often when we are at the end of our rope, we want justice to be done. We feel abused or wounded, and we want God to set things right. He promises He will: "He will judge the world in righteousness and the peoples with equity" (Psalm 98:9 NIV).

Focusing on the Helper

In our pain, we often get stuck at, "How much more can I take?" This is when we need to shift our focus from the pain to God's character. What does Scripture say about who God is in our distress? The psalmist calls Him "a very present help in trouble" (Psalm 46:1). That means He is standing by ready to help at all times, even at this moment. "The Lord is your keeper," we read again in the Psalms, "the Lord is your shade on your right hand. . . . He will keep your soul" (Psalm 121:5, 7). We are told we can "draw near with confidence to the throne of grace, so that we may . . . find grace to help in time of need" (Hebrews 4:16). And again: "We may boldly say: 'The Lord is my helper; I will not fear. What can man do to me?'" (Hebrews 13:6 NKJV).

The Lord is my helper; I will not fear. All through Scripture we come across God's promise to help. His help is always available to us, and it is free. There is never a moment when God is not poised to help us. At times we may judge that God is not acting like our Helper. We may feel disillusioned or betrayed by God, asking, "But why has He allowed this bruising? Why the debris banging against me, wounding me, as I try to hold on? He could have stopped it, but He didn't. How could He love me? Where is compassion? Where is His help?"

There are no easy answers to these questions about suffering. They are difficult. Through the ages, we have suffered and asked why. I don't want to paint the picture that when you are a Christian, life is always rosy. It is not. In fact, many times, you struggle all the more. What I do know is that when we have God in our lives, we are connected to the only source of help and goodness in this world. He may not help us in the ways we expect or desire. Or at the time when we believe that He should. He doesn't promise to infuse us instantly with new energy. He doesn't promise to make things better on our terms. Things may actually get worse before they get better. But God does promise help. He promises His presence, the forgiveness of our sins, the hope of eternal life, and the peace that passes all understanding.

What did Jesus do when he was in distress? He kept his focus on God. In bruisings and in sorrow, He focused on the Father. Often we think Jesus had it easier because He was God. But Jesus knew ahead of time what He was facing. His life was a constant advance toward deeper gloom, for He lived always in the shadow of the cross. He knew what lay ahead. He knew the heart of His countrymen. He knew that many were not with Him, that they were not His friends, that they were going to one day crucify Him. The process of crucifixion is one of the cruelest deaths humanity has yet to devise, as was so vividly illustrated in the movie *The Passion of the Christ*. But Scripture tells us that Jesus was determined to go to Jerusalem. He did not back away. He went purposefully because He loves you and me.

How did Jesus do it? Many times in Scripture we are told that before a major event in Jesus' life, He took time to pray and to be alone. In my hectic life, this is a hard discipline. I am a doer. I have a hard time being still. I want to start tackling the day or the project immediately. I am one of those people who doesn't read directions—I just want to start. If ever there was a busy man, it was Jesus. So many pressing needs surrounded Him. But He took time to pray and to commune with God—to focus on the Helper. He knew where His strength came from.

Jesus also kept his eyes on God's purpose for Him. He said, "My food . . . is to do the will of him who sent me and to finish his work" (John 4:34 NIV). That march toward the cross was Jesus' purpose, and He kept His eye on the goal out of love for both the Father and us. He endured it "for the joy set before him" (Hebrews 12:2 NIV). He saw ahead to the joy of our salvation. He looked beyond the brutal death, the mocking, and the beatings. He looked beyond it, and He saw you and me. He saw us washed in that blood and clothed in His righteousness. That was His joy. Jesus loved us that much. And His love is unchanging.

Trusting in God's Love

When we are bruised and bent down by life, we can take comfort in God's unconditional love. He deals with our sin, but He is merciful. He deals with us tenderly and in ways that reach our innermost being. He does the preparatory work in our hearts so that permanent change will take place. There may be no outward signs of this work at first, but we can trust in God's promise. He says, "I will seek the lost, bring back the scattered, bind up the broken and strengthen the sick" (Ezekiel 34:16).

All of Scripture tells of God's love. We read, "I have loved you with an everlasting love; I have drawn you with loving-kindness" (Jeremiah 31:3 NIV). And: "But because of his great love for us, God, who is rich in mercy, made us alive with Christ even when we were dead in transgressions" (Ephesians 2:4–5 NIV). Paul writes of his prayer that we "know the love of Christ which passes knowledge" (Ephesians 3:19 NKJV).

These are powerful verses—and they are difficult to grasp. A love that passes knowledge? We cannot conceive of such a love. We are used to conditions. If I want a house, I have to meet the condition of paying the mortgage. If I want to be in shape, I have to exercise. If I want someone to do something nice for me, I assume that I'll need to do something nice for him or her in the future. "You scratch my back, I'll scratch yours" is an accepted way of doing things in our society. We live with conditional love and hidden agendas every day. Love can be conditioned upon our behavior, our looks, the size of our bank account, our sphere of influence. It can be dependent on reciprocity. We even have conditional love for ourselves. How often do we spend days beating ourselves up about opportunities we've missed? Or reacting to other people's opinions, regretting past mistakes, and recalling hurtful memories and feelings? We don't love ourselves without conditions, so how can we expect God to love us that way?

Yet the Word of God promises an "everlasting love." A love that never runs out and cannot be threatened. I am a proud grandmother. My oldest grandson is a joy to my heart. When he was a small boy, he would come to visit me, and during the course of his visit something would inevitably get spilled or broken. When it happened, he would look for my reaction. Was I going to get angry? Punish him? He learned that my love for him is not based on his actions. I love him just because he is. Yes, there are appropriate times for instruction and discipline—but always with love, because he is mine, and I want what is best for him. My love for him is not perfect, because I am not perfect. But God is perfect, and His love for me is perfectly unconditional. He is my Helper. I will not fear. What can man do to me?

Admitting Our Need for Help

Hanging on the cross, Jesus chose to be helpless. He chose to be beaten beyond recognition, gasping for each breath. The Bible says, "He was wounded for our transgressions, He was bruised for our iniquities; the chastisement for our peace was upon Him, and by His stripes we are healed" (Isaiah 53:5 NKJV). Jesus could have called legions of angels to His rescue. He could have stepped down from that cross and wiped His tormenters off the face of the earth. But He did not. He chose for our sakes to hang there helpless and to rely on the help of the Father.

If Jesus made Himself helpless, then helplessness must be a valid, necessary experience. We don't like feeling helpless. We resist our vulnerability. We want to believe we can change things—that we are in control. We try to figure out what to do or how to manage people and situations. We connive. We exert a great deal of energy doing this. It makes us feel productive and strong—for a time—until we finally realize we are going in circles. Still frustrated. Anxious. Angry.

Let's go back to what Paul said about weakness. He said that he would boast about his weaknesses. That when he was weak, then he was strong. Paul knew his weakness was the environment in which God's power was perfected. The same principle operates here. In our helplessness, God's help in our lives is enlarged. Rather than hide our frailty and our vulnerability, we need to admit our helplessness to God. It is okay to be the bruised reed. We don't have to fix our bruisings or try to cover them up. We can come to God bruised and bent over like the reed, and He will meet us where we are.

God is rich and generous with His help, and He wants us to count on Him. The Bible says, "He has filled the hungry with good things" (Luke 1:53). There may be times when we are convinced that God wants us to have a difficult life. That if we leave the choice to Him, He will pick the toughest road for us. This is not true. Satan would have us believe this of God, because it makes God less than who He is—a loving parent who wants the best for us. While God is out to make us holy, not necessarily happy, God's plans for us are good. If we can just make ourselves vulnerable to God's Spirit and admit we need His help, then we will create an environment for that help to be manifested.

Perhaps the biggest hindrance to admitting our need for God's help is pride. Even when we are figuratively gasping our last breath, we still hold on to our way, not wanting to make ourselves vulnerable. Steeling ourselves. Protecting ourselves. Maybe this is because God's help isn't always the help we want or expect. Maybe we don't think we deserve His help—we're unable to accept God's unconditional love. Or maybe we are still holding on to the belief that we can handle things on our own, controlled by pride and our ingrained sense of independence.

Pride hinders blessing; it gets in the way. God wants to help us, but in our refusal to acknowledge our need, we can keep Him out. By wearing a mask and pretending we have things under control, we keep God and others away from our need. God wants us to be transparent. The Bible says that "we all, with unveiled face, beholding as in a mirror the glory of the Lord, are being transformed into the same image from glory to glory" (2 Corinthians 3:18). The unveiled face speaks of transparency before God. We are transformed as we remove our masks—as we let go of our own efforts—and look to God in our need, in our battered condition, in our helplessness. If we cover or "veil" our need, we can delay or hinder our own transformation.

Asking God for Help

The narrow street was crowded that day. Maybe she wouldn't be noticed. After all, she wasn't a leper, required to declare her presence in public. She would just slip through the crowd and avoid drawing attention to herself. People were pressed in around the Rabbi, following Him as He made his way to Jairus's house. Jairus was an important man in the synagogue and had pleaded with Jesus to save his dying twelve-year-old daughter. Now Jesus was walking in the direction of his home.

The woman had found her way into the procession. She didn't want to bother the Rabbi or even touch Him. If she could just touch something on Him, the edge of His garment, then maybe . . . maybe. Did she dare to hope? Could the bleeding really be stopped? It had been twelve years—such a long time. A long time to be marginalized. A long time to seek help from doctors who had no answers. She had spent all her money, but instead of getting better, her condition had grown worse. For twelve years. Grown worse.

Had the bleeding kept her from marrying, from finding love? Had it prevented her from having children? Or perhaps it had ruined her marriage. She certainly wasn't allowed any social life, because a woman with an issue of blood was considered unclean according to the Law. How much rejection had she suffered? How much isolation? Leprosy would've been a better fate. At least she would've had a community— somewhere to belong, people with whom she could talk and share life, however limited. With the bleeding, though, no one could have anything to do with her. All of her tomorrows were like her yesterdays. Disappointment was a constant. And yet, somewhere in her heart, hope must've been alive, for she had decided to seek out Jesus. She would have heard the reports of His healings. Maybe, she thought, just maybe, He would heal her too.

Oblivious to the people around her, the woman pressed her way through the crowd, keeping her eyes on Jesus, focusing on Him. She could see Him just ahead, His prayer shawl draped over His shoulders, hanging down over His back. If only she could touch that shawl. That's all she wanted. Was that too much to ask? She knew He was busy. He wouldn't want to be interrupted. She would just edge her way in, touch His garment, and slip away before anyone noticed.

She was close enough now. She could try. Straining over someone in front of her, reaching out toward Jesus, in one difficult motion, she touched the very edge of His shawl. She had done it! The crowd kept carrying her forward, but in that instant, she felt something happen inside of her. Yes, some kind of sensation. A warmth? A shifting inside? Whatever it was, she knew her body had changed. The Bible says, "Immediately her bleeding stopped and she felt in her body that she was freed from her suffering" (Mark 5:29 NIV). *Freed from her suffering.*

But before she could slip away, Jesus asked, "Who touched me?" He didn't ask because He didn't know who touched Him. Jesus knew exactly who had touched Him. He knew the woman well. He knew her life story, her need, and her desperation. He asked the question because He wanted this woman to acknowledge her need and to publicly embrace her healing. He gave her the opportunity to experience acceptance among those who would have rejected or avoided her. He wanted God to get the glory for the work.

Did the woman try to shrink back in fear into the crowd? Everyone around her denied touching Jesus. No doubt she overheard the disciples say to Him, "What do You mean who touched You? It's crowded here. Lots of people are touching You." But Jesus had felt the power go out of Him. He recognized that the woman had acted on her faith. This wasn't an ordinary touch. Jesus never heals or helps by accident. His miracles are always deliberate and meant to draw us closer.

Realizing she couldn't slip away, the woman stepped forward. Would He humiliate her? Condemn her for being out in the crowd against the Law? I wonder if her heart almost quit beating as she realized He had noticed. I wonder if she thought she was now in trouble, fearing she had taken something she didn't deserve. Shaking with fear, we are told, she fell at His feet and told Him the "whole truth." She poured out her need, confessing why she had reached out to touch Him, telling Him she had been healed.

Then, bowed to the ground like a bruised reed, she waited. So open. So transparent. Her heart in His hands. Such humility there at

His feet. Such sweetness. She had taken the risk of being out in public, doing what she ought not do—touching a rabbi. And now she would take the penalty if that was what Jesus would give her. Waiting in that moment, perhaps she resigned herself to it, expecting His words to come down on her like stones. But when He spoke, it was not like that. Not like that at all.

"Daughter," He said.

He called her daughter. This is the only time in the Bible that Jesus addresses a woman by this title. It is a term of endearing relationship. With that word Jesus said, "Mine." He said, "My offspring." "One who has rights and privileges." "One for whom I am responsible." That word said no more rejection. No more isolation. No more loneliness. In a word, she who had been excluded was now included. She who had been an outcast now belonged. In a word, Jesus had affirmed her desperation and her effort to reach for His help. In a word, He healed not only her body but also her spirit.

Then Jesus told her that her faith had healed her. He said, "Go in peace and be freed from your suffering."

What more wonderful message could Jesus have given her? Think of the message in those words. To the tormented heart, "Go in peace." No more turmoil or confusion. To one who for years had known only bondage, "Be freed from your suffering." The woman had touched Jesus' garment and been healed in her body, but He called her forward to affirm and free her heart. She had sought her healing secretly, hiding herself in her shame. Jesus wanted her to step out in the open so He could *remove* the shame. He called her out so she could acknowledge her helplessness and be set free. He wasn't going to heal her body and leave her with a broken heart. He wanted her to leave from that place healed completely. "Daughter," he said. "Go in peace."

The Freedom of Desperation

As He did with so many others, Jesus met this woman in her need, her desperation, and then He moved her forward. He gave her a new life, a new beginning. She came to Him wanting physical healing, but she received so much more. That is God's nature—to give us more than we can think to ask (1 Corinthians 2:9; Ephesians 3:20). I had a friend in England who used to say, "God doesn't know how to fill a cup. It always overflows." God is generous. Often we come to Him with our own agenda, but He has something far greater in mind for us. He has an eternal perspective. We are like children asking for what we think we need when we think we need it. But God gives us what we really need in the perfect time and in the way that will bring us closer to Him.

God also gives in ways that will draw the attention of others. Jesus could've ignored this woman and kept on walking. Not only would she have missed out, but no one else would have known what happened that day. Jesus wanted God to be glorified in this woman's healing. He wanted God's help to be seen. People in the crowd might have known her—known about her struggle and the twelve years. Perhaps they had condemned her, telling her she was being punished by God for some sin. Perhaps they had written her off and called her crazy for spending all that money looking for cures. Think what it communicated when Jesus called the woman out and honored her "crazy" desperation by healing her.

Think what it said to them when He called her "Daughter." He used such intimate language addressing an "unclean" woman for her benefit but also for the crowd's—and for ours. So many of us believe God is exclusive. We believe we must be a certain kind of person before He will include us. We tend to think He is looking for ways to exclude us. I have certainly felt this way. But in reality, God is always looking for ways to include us. Jesus met this woman in her desperate, bruised, vulnerable condition and told her while she was in that helpless state, "You belong."

We can learn a great deal from this woman of faith. She truly was desperate to be well. She was doing as much as a person could to find the help and healing she needed, but she had come to the end of herself. Can you relate? Sometimes you do all you can to help yourself, and it's still not enough. The doctors couldn't heal her. Her resources were gone. Her illness had gone from bad to worse. But still she wanted to get well. And that desire caused her to act—to make the effort to seek out Jesus. Are you that desperate? Her need was so big and she so desperate that it would've taken much more than a crowd to stop her from trying to reach Jesus. When we get to the place where, as was true for this woman, nothing can prevent us from reaching out to touch Him, He is there. He is always there. Whatever our condition or state of mind, He is always waiting for us.

Once she got to Him, the woman reached out and touched Jesus' shawl. She did her part. In that simple action, she acknowledged her own helplessness and reached out to the only One who could help her. She "asked" for His help. That was all she could do. And she found it. When I am faced with crisis and struggle, there are some things that are beyond my control, but I can do my part. I can do what I know to do and leave the rest to God. My mother used to say, "Let God take care of the impossible, and I'll do the possible." We are not to be passive. We understand there is only so much we can do in certain situations, but we do it. We do the possible. In this way, God allows us—invites us—to participate in the process of His work.

Participating in God's activity is one of the greatest privileges and joys He affords us. He chooses to make us His partners. In doing so, He stretches our faith and expands our capacity for ministry in the lives of others. This woman got to participate in her own healing. Jesus didn't just pass by and make her a passive recipient of the miracle. He allowed her to be a part. And look at what her participation hinged on—her desperation. God had let this woman become so desperate in her condition that she actively sought out healing at great risk to herself. Her desperation is what drove her to participate in the miracle. So often we expect things to come to us. That way we never have to get messy enough to ask for God's help. But our fear of becoming desperate—of being exposed as that vulnerable, bruised reed—is what hinders us from playing a part in what God wants to do.

When He called her out, Jesus told the woman that her faith had healed her. There are many theological takes on these verses and on the role of our faith in God's work in our lives. Even as we seek to understand what Jesus meant, I do think it wise to be careful about putting so much weight on our faith that we make healing about our own effort to believe. Healing is not meant to spotlight us—it isn't about the quality or quantity of our faith. Healing is meant to call attention to God. I don't know why He chooses to heal some and not others. Why did my mother suffer so many years with crippling degenerative osteoarthritis? She had stayed home to raise the family, and when we were finally grown and she was free to travel with my father, she was unable to do so. Surely she was a woman of great faith. Many people prayed in faith for her healing. But God did not heal her on this side of heaven. I do not understand, and I do not think I am meant to understand. Living with unanswered questions is part of our faith journey. With or without the answers, we can continue to press through the crowd to get to Jesus.

Taking Off Our Masks Before God

Taking off our masks before God simply means learning to be honest and to share our feelings openly with Him. If we are the bruised reed, we share that with Him. If we feel He has betrayed us in our struggle, we tell Him that. Taking off our masks means learning to do what David and the other psalmists did. They got vulnerable and weak in front of God. They let God into their desperation, weakness, frustration, and need. It wasn't always pretty or neat. It could be messy.

When I'm struggling, I love to read the Psalms. They help me express my own emotions to God. The psalmists don't hold back. They bare their hearts to God, and we get to eavesdrop. David is a great example of an imperfect person who longed for God. He got into trouble. He was a murderer, an adulterer, a sinner. He often felt overwhelmed by his circumstances. He suffered betrayal and heartache. He faced unbelievable odds. And he knew to whom he needed to turn in his times of distress. When David was frustrated or feeling helpless about something, he told God how he felt. He didn't sanitize his feelings, making them more presentable. He took off his mask. He let his feelings out. The other psalmists are equally transparent—let's look at Psalm 77:

> *Will the Lord reject forever?*
>   *And will He never be favorable again?*
> *Has His lovingkindness ceased forever?*
>   *Has His promise come to an end forever?*
> *Has God forgotten to be gracious,*
>   *Or has He in anger withdrawn His compassion? Selah.*
> *Then I said, "It is my grief,*
>   *That the right hand of the Most High has changed."*

(verses 7–10)

Take a look at the same passage in The Message. The drama comes through differently in our vernacular!

> *Will the Lord walk off and leave us for good?*
>   *Will he never smile again?*
> *Is his love worn threadbare?*
>   *Has his salvation promise burned out?*
> *Has God forgotten his manners?*
>   *Has he angrily stalked off and left us?*
> *"Just my luck," I said. "The High God goes out of business*
>   *just the moment I need him."*

This psalmist is trying to understand where God could be in his circumstances. He feels abandoned, forgotten, grieved. He wonders if God has failed in His promise. The psalmist expresses these emotions and questions without reservation. No mask anywhere in sight. But then look at what happens. After expressing his grief, he shifts his focus! He remembers what God has done before. The psalmist is walking the same path we are learning to walk.

> *I shall remember the deeds of the Lord;*
>> *Surely I will remember Your wonders of old.*
> *I will meditate on all Your work*
>> *And muse on Your deeds.*
> *Your way, O God, is holy;*
>> *What god is great like our God?*
> *You are the God who works wonders;*
>> *You have made known Your strength among the peoples.*
> *You have by Your power redeemed Your people,*
>> *The sons of Jacob and Joseph. Selah.*
>
> (verses 11–15)

Do you see what is happening? As the psalmist's focus changes, so does his perspective. When he takes his eyes off his problems and his hurts, when he *remembers* what God has done for him and for his people in the past, he reinforces his faith in who God is and in God's power to take care of his tomorrow. The psalmist receives God's emotional help right here in the course of the psalm, and the process begins when he takes off his mask.

Even Jesus went back to the Word of God. During the time He spent in the wilderness, what did He do? He went back to the Scriptures. We can do the same. Why don't you try exploring the Psalms, looking for passages with which you can identify or those that express your emotional ebbs and flows? Or try reading Job. Now there was a man who experienced desperation! His life got worse and worse, with loss upon loss, and even his wife told him to curse God and die. What a comfort she was! Make sure you are using a version of the Bible you enjoy reading, one that you can understand, and ask God to lead you to passages that will help you articulate your own emotions most fully to Him. God can use His Word to meet you where you are and to lead you out.

Taking Off Our Masks Before Others

Taking off our masks is also something we do with others. God wants us to be real with Him and with one another. Other people are God's instruments in our lives. If we never admit our need to others, we can hinder the help God wants to bring. When my first marriage ended, a friend of mine was also going through a divorce. One of the first things she did was start attending a divorce recovery group. I couldn't do that. I didn't want to sit in a group as people talked about their failed marriages and reminded me of my own. I also didn't want to expose myself as "Billy Graham's daughter" to a group of struggling people whom I didn't know. And yet, my struggle was every bit as common as anyone else's. I allowed my pride to keep me away. It would have been humbling to admit I needed help. I convinced myself that I could handle things on my own, and I have to say I didn't do it very well. Now I regret staying away from that kind of support. I might have discovered more about the divorce process and the emotional pitfalls. I would have realized that I wasn't alone, that others had traveled the same path. I might have been strengthened and have saved myself a lot of heartache.

Either we can be victimized and become victims, or we can be victimized and rise above it. Often it is easier to play the victim than to take off our masks and ask for help. We get comfortable with our victim status. It becomes our identity and is hard to give up. The Israelites often played the victim card, and I love what God finally tells them: "You have circled this mountain long enough. Now turn north" (Deuteronomy 2:3). Turn north! It's time to move on! Self-pity, fear, pride, and negativity paralyze us. Taking off our masks takes courage, but if we don't do it, we will retain our victim status and end up stunted.

Early on in my first marriage, my husband and I needed some help, so I decided to go see a counselor. I was very nervous and anxious. It had been implied that Jesus was enough—that He was all I needed. I didn't yet realize all the ways that Jesus uses other people in our lives, and I feared that my needing a counselor made me spiritually deficient. Still, I made up my mind to try. I needed help. And that meant taking off my mask.

When I phoned for the appointment, I made sure it was the last slot of the day. Trying to be inconspicuous, I entered the building through the back door—and stepped into a room where someone else was waiting! I was mortified then, but today I don't worry about what others think about my choice to seek help. If I need help, then I want to be sure to do my part to find help. I do see a counselor now periodically just to make sure I'm on the right track. He has been a great help as a sounding board. His office is on the main street of a nearby town. I drive a car with personalized license plates, but I don't slip in the back way. I park in front and walk right in the front door.

I am still amazed at the number of people who come up to me after I have spoken at a conference or an event and, having heard me say that I have experienced depression and go to a counselor, tell me, "Thank you, I thought I was alone." So many people are afraid to admit their need. They feel isolated with it, embarrassed, shamed. Or they have been marginalized for it. But it is okay to need and to ask for help. Needing help is not a weakness. Nor does it mean Jesus is not enough. Seeking help is courageous, and it is empowering. In doing it, we are saying that our need has value and that we have value.

Perhaps you are not ready to go to a counselor's office, or perhaps that is not even the kind of help you need. God may be challenging you to reach out and talk to a trusted friend or a pastor. Or to share more of your feelings with your spouse. Maybe God is prompting you to seek out some other kind of help. Whatever the case, be open to God's leading. Of course, be judicious about what you share and with whom. Before you open up to someone, make sure you know that person. Is the person trustworthy? Does the person have a depth of relationship with God? Does he or she seek to live according to God's Word? Is the person discreet? Can he or she keep a confidence? Spend time watching that person's life, and ask God for wisdom. But do not be afraid. God will direct you as you seek Him. He created us not to be islands but to need one another. It can be injurious to us if we remain isolated in our suffering. We can get ill, suffer a breakdown, pretend to be what we are not—it takes a toll when we keep things bottled up inside. We must be able to take off our masks and talk to someone.

God sends His help into our lives through so many channels, and it is available to you whatever your condition, whatever your issues. Receiving that help will involve choosing to move out of victimhood and take off your mask. I want to encourage you to do that—to reach out to God and ask for His help. It's not too late. Even if you feel unworthy, even if you are in a mess of your own making, even if you feel beyond help, you can receive God's help. God wants to help you, even this moment. His Word says He is a "very present help," and He is nearer than your breath. He cares about every detail of your life. He is eager for you to call on Him. Don't be afraid. He is with you. Ask!

POINT OF FOCUS

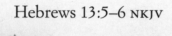

For He Himself has said, "I will never leave you
nor forsake you." So we may boldly say:
"The Lord is my helper;
I will not fear.
What can man do to me?"

Hebrews 13:5–6 NKJV

Rest in His Peace

chapter seven

I REMEMBER A STORY I heard someone use years ago to illustrate what peace was like. Once there was a man who decided to hold an art contest to find the painting that would best depict peace. Artists from all over the land submitted their work, and on judging day, before a curious and attentive audience, officials unveiled numerous paintings until only two were left.

The first depicted a placid lake, perfectly still, reflecting the varied red tones of sunset as sheep grazed nearby. The audience became quiet with awe. No doubt this painting would take the prize.

Then the remaining work was unveiled. You could hear the crowd draw breath.

A huge waterfall roared down a cliff face. Storm clouds overhead hung low, dark, and threatening. Suddenly, something startling came into view. Right at the edge of the massive falls was a small, skinny tree. In one of its branches, a tiny bird had built a nest. She was resting there on her eggs. This was the winning scene.

My Peace I Give to You

How do we experience that kind of peace? How do we rest like that bird in the midst of danger, chaos, or storm? We are a stressed-out people. I certainly feel the burden of life's stressors. I can become consumed in worries—those "little foxes that spoil the vines" (Song of Solomon

2:15 NKJV). A loved one is having financial problems, and I cannot do anything to help. I have several deadlines looming. Bills have to be paid. I have to pack for a speaking engagement, and like most women, "I have nothing to wear." The blouse I was planning to wear came back from the cleaners with the same spots! What I intend to share at the event may not suit what my inviting committee has in mind, which always causes me to question myself. My shredder has overflowed and spilled onto the floor beneath my desk. My flowers outside are wilting. The phone is ringing, and correspondence is accumulating. I am tired.

As I was writing the above, I was distracted by some noise on the flat roof above my office. I went outside to investigate and discovered that a flock of crows had found a puddle of water up there to bathe in. When I disturbed their swimming party, they took off and in the process sprinkled some water on me. I had to smile. It is just like God to remind me of His care. If not an image of a bird, as in the illustration above, then He will use actual birds. Those crows may not have been resting serenely, but they didn't seem to be worried about anything. They were just enjoying God's provision. They didn't sit around discussing where they would find water, fretting over whether there would be enough for all of them. I am reminded of what Jesus said: "Therefore I tell you, do not worry about your life. . . . Look at the birds of the air [noisy crows]; they do not sow or reap or store away in barns, and yet your heavenly Father feeds them [provides them with a pool of water on the roof]. Are you not much more valuable than they? Who of you by worrying can add a single hour to his life?" (Matthew 6:25–27 NIV).

And yet your heavenly Father feeds them. Why can't I get ahold of that truth and learn to rest in it? My Father knows my schedule. He knows the pressures. He knows about the spots on my blouse and my drive to please others. He knows my fears and my stresses, my concerns for my loved ones. He understands. He doesn't condemn me for my worries. He invites me. He says, "Come." "Come to Me, all who are weary and heavy-laden, and I will give you rest" (Matthew 11:28).

Those are the words of Jesus. Jesus had a full schedule. He had people pressing Him at every waking moment. He didn't have a nice mattress and pillow to rest on like I do. At that point in His life, He didn't even have a home. He was constantly interrupted. He had to answer hostile questioners and bickering disciples. His cousin John the Baptist was in prison and would soon be beheaded. His hometown had rejected Him, and one of His closest friends would betray Him. Nothing about Jesus' life externally was conducive to peace.

And yet, Jesus knew peace. He went to sleep in a boat during a violent storm. He kept His cool. He remained calm, revealing the tensions he must have felt perhaps only in the garden of Gethsemane when he agonized in prayer about his coming death or at the temple when he disrupted the money changers. And He did get quite harsh with the scribes and Pharisees. But even in conflict or in displays of emotion, Jesus was anchored. He knew who He was. He understood His purpose. He knew He was in the Father's will. He maintained peace on the inside, and He offered that same peace to others: "Come unto me." Just before going to the cross, He told his disciples, "My peace I give to you" (John 14:27 NKJV). Whatever was raging around Him, Jesus had a peace that was His own.

If Jesus said, "My peace I give to you," then we must be able to know that peace—a peace, Paul wrote, "which surpasses all understanding" (Philippians 4:7 NKJV). Some of us may have the wrong idea about peace. Often we think peace is something we come by through external action or accomplishment. "If I get my to-do list completely checked off this week, then I can at least feel a little more at peace over the weekend." "If I can just get my husband to watch the kids for a few hours, then I can finally get a little peace and quiet." Even with our affluence, luxuries, time-saving appliances, ease of transportation, and creature comforts, we are stressed—to the max. Clearly, we are not finding the solution in our relationships, our "stuff," our jobs, our status, or our achievements. My daughter and I chuckle over a greeting card she sent me some years ago. A haggard young mother is walking around and around her block, talking to herself. Inside the card, her children say something like, "We don't know why Mom is walking around the block but all we can make out is 'Peace and quiet. Peace and quiet. All I want is a little peace and quiet.'" Young mothers can relate!

While the externals of life can certainly impact our state of mind, peace is not necessarily related to our circumstances. Peace does not depend on what is happening around us. The peace that "surpasses all understanding" does not have to do with the conflicts we may or may not be experiencing. Someone once said, "Peace is not the absence of conflict; it is the absence of inner conflict." I can be sitting under a canopy on a beautiful tropical island, feeling the wind in my hair and the sun on my toes, but if my heart does not know peace at that moment, I won't feel peaceful. When dictionaries define peace, they use words like tranquility, security, harmony, and silence. Those words speak to me of inner qualities. Peace is something we carry on the inside, as Jesus did when He walked on the earth.

Real peace comes from God. The Bible calls peace one of the "fruit of the Spirit" (Galatians 5:22–23). I love what Isaiah says: "Lord, You will establish peace for us, since You have also performed for us all our works" (Isaiah 26:12). Peace is not something we have to—or can—manufacture. God establishes our peace. He gives it to us, as Jesus promised. The verse also says that God has already taken care of our works. He has already gone ahead of us into tomorrow and prepared a way to sustain us in the conflicts we will face. We seem to constantly wear ourselves out trying to do, trying to fix—or else we worry. But God has already taken care of our works. All of our works. And as we put our faith in that truth, we tap into His peace.

Trusting in a Sure Thing

Peace comes when we can place our trust in something sure. Jesus was sure about God, His Father. He walked with His Father. He was one with His Father. He knew His Father's character was certain, unchanging, completely reliable. We can have that same certainty. Scripture says, "You, Lord, in the beginning laid the foundation of the earth, and the heavens are the works of Your hands; they will perish, but You remain; . . . they will also be changed. But you are the same" (Hebrews 1:10–12).

God's character is sure. One of the qualities that makes God sure is His justice. "God is a just judge," David wrote (Psalm 7:11 NKJV). As we have read, God promises to "faithfully bring forth justice" (Isaiah 42:3). On receiving the Nobel Peace Prize in 1993 along with Nelson Mandela, former South African president F. W. de Klerk remarked that justice was necessary to peace.[1] Without justice, he said, there can be no real peace. We have a God who is always just. Life may be unfair, but God promises that in the end, it will be just. We expend a great deal of energy defending ourselves, rationalizing our actions, and being angry over wrongs, but as my former father-in-law used to say, "God keeps the books." The injustices we suffer in this life will one day be righted. That is a truth in which we can rest.

In his Nobel acceptance speech, President de Klerk also said, "The greatest peace, I believe, is the peace which we derive from our faith in God Almighty; from certainty about our relationship with our Creator. Crises might beset us, battles might rage about us—but if we have faith and the certainty it brings, we will enjoy peace—the peace that surpasses all understanding."[2]

Peace depends on our certainty about God. The Lord establishes and gives us peace, but peace is something we have to protect with vigilance. With uncertainties and crises all around us, we have to be on guard concerning our certainty about God. I have also heard this definition of peace: "Peace is not the absence of conflict but the presence of creative alternatives for responding to conflict." One of our "creative alternatives" for responding to the inner conflict produced by fear and anxiety is turning our eyes from the turmoil we face to the character of God. This practice of shifting our focus, as we are discovering, requires diligence and discipline, but we have the tools. God has given us all that we need to meet the day as it comes. He has given us His Spirit to live within us. We have the Bible—His Word, His promises. And we have His everlasting love.

Our part is to feed our spirits with God's truth and to nurture our faith in His character. President de Klerk talked in his speech about developing a framework for peace. He said, "Peace does not fare well where poverty and deprivation reign."[3] Personal peace does not thrive in poverty of spirit. We cannot neglect nurturing our souls and spirits and then expect peace to reign in our hearts. We trust God for the impossible, but we must do what is possible. There are too many things in this life that will rob us of our peace if we do not keep our eyes on God. The framework for our peace is His character.

What to Do when Peace Goes Missing

It is important that we tune in and recognize when peace is missing from our lives. When peace goes missing, we feel discontent, anxious, restless, and unsatisfied. We are uneasy, often spinning our wheels, preoccupied with what is troubling us or perhaps trying to cover our anxiety with some activity or behavior.

If we lack peace in our hearts, then we need to stop and pray. It is important that we be open to God's leading and direction. If you are experiencing a lack of peace, it may mean you are headed in the wrong direction. Peace is an inner compass. When we don't have peace about something—a decision, a relationship, anything at all—we should turn to God and ask more questions. God is not rushing us. He will make His direction known.

When a lack of peace causes us to stop and refocus, search our souls, and evaluate ourselves spiritually, then it can be a change agent for good. If our lack of peace produces an honest motivation to discover God's purpose and plan for the situation in our lives, then that lack of peace becomes an opportunity for spiritual growth. But soul searching must be accompanied by a willingness to obey. Sometimes it is only in hindsight that we see God's direction most clearly. In the meantime, I have found that I just need to keep obeying the little bit I do know. I keep walking through the doors that I believe God is opening, and I trust He will reveal the next step. Sometimes I feel like I am stumbling around in the dark, but I know that He holds me and has promised to guide me and to show me the right way.

It is important to be aware that a lack of peace in our lives can also be the work of Satan. This is why it is so critical we stay close to God. He will help us discern the enemy's work. The Bible says, "We are not ignorant of his [Satan's] devices" (2 Corinthians 2:11 NKJV). Jesus explained the aim of those devices. He said the enemy comes to "steal and kill and destroy" (John 10:10). Satan is after our relationships, our purpose in God, our very lives. He knows where we live and he hates us. When a lack of peace paralyzes us in our purpose or causes us to get sidetracked or to start taking things into our own hands, then I believe our distress is being used by Satan to take us off course. It is to his advantage to disrupt our peace, to get us off-kilter, to throw us into confusion, and to provoke us to fear. If we are operating out of fear and instability in our hearts, then what kind of decisions will we make? We become mired in anxiety. We exhaust ourselves trying to devise our own solutions. We are right where the enemy wants us—in a vulnerable position with our focus on ourselves.

There are also times when we can become the agents of our own lack of peace. Tragedy and difficult circumstances can certainly disturb our peace, but in the midst of challenges, we often do not make it easier on ourselves. We can create our own turmoil by constantly analyzing, questioning, and imagining possible outcomes. We keep going around the same mountain. We get ourselves into a swivet. I am very guilty of this. As I have said, I am a worrier. Beyond worrying about actual problems, I tend to see problems behind every bush. For me, everything has a downside. If I do well at something, then I worry people will expect even more of me next time. If I can pay my bills this month, then I worry that I won't be able to pay them next month. Often, I just plunge ahead, carrying this heavy load until I can't go anymore. I am working in my own strength, my own reasoning, and I am trusting only myself. How unreliable is that?

Anxiety and worry do not honor God, and they destroy the possibility for peace and rest. This is where the discipline of shifting my focus to God and His character comes in. God knows my weakness. He does not condemn me for it, and He is on hand to help me. There is a reason I have posted this Bible verse above my kitchen sink: "Trust in the Lord with all your heart and lean not on your own understanding; in all your ways acknowledge him, and he will make your paths straight" (Proverbs 3:5–6 NIV).

Someone who practiced this verse, trusting God under tremendous pressure, was King Hezekiah of Judah. In 2 Kings, we read that Hezekiah was under threat from his powerful enemy, the king of Assyria, who had sent an army to take Jerusalem. The leader of that army had gotten up before the people of the city and started undermining Hezekiah's credibility. Hezekiah had told his people to trust God to fight for them, but the messenger from Assyria said that Hezekiah was deceiving them. Jerusalem would be taken, he taunted, for no one could escape out of the hand of Assyria, as that nation's track record had shown.

Hezekiah was stressed, to put it mildly! He had cause to be worried and frightened. His enemies surrounded him, breathing out threats. They were maligning God, saying that Hezekiah's God was no match for the king of Assyria. Not exactly a situation in which one might find inner peace. Hearing of the messenger's words, the Bible says, the king "tore his clothes, covered himself with sackcloth and entered the house of the Lord" (2 Kings 19:1). But Hezekiah knew what to do. He sent word to the prophet Isaiah and asked him to pray. What was the king's first response in a crisis? To seek God. And look at God's response through Isaiah: "Do not be afraid" (verse 6).

The Assyrians held off the attack for the moment, but then Hezekiah received a threatening letter. Again, he did not waste time wondering what to do. He didn't chew his fingernails. He didn't strategize. He didn't build up his defenses and munitions. He didn't run. He didn't hide. He didn't deny the facts. He certainly acknowledged the threat, and it frightened him; but instead of focusing on the threat, Hezekiah turned to God. The Bible says he took the letter and "went up to the house of the Lord and spread it out before the Lord" (verse 14).

We are told that Hezekiah prayed, and I find it instructive to look at where he started. He didn't spell out the problem for God. He didn't tell God what to do. He didn't even start with the letter. Hezekiah began his prayer by focusing on God's character and person. He prayed, "O Lord, the God of Israel, who are enthroned above the cherubim, You are the God, You alone, of all the kingdoms of the earth. You have made heaven and earth" (verse 15).

Hezekiah goes on to pour his heart out before God about the Assyrians' warnings and the danger Judah faced. The king is transparent about his fear and his indignation at the way the Assyrians have mocked God; he wants God to be glorified. But he started his prayer by declaring who God is. He went directly to the Lord, taking his mind off that threatening letter for a few minutes to remind himself of God's power and sovereignty. In doing so, Hezekiah made God's character the basis for his prayer and for his ultimate request: "Deliver us." This wasn't a selfish prayer. Hezekiah wanted deliverance for the nation so "that all the kingdoms of the earth may know that You alone, O Lord, are God" (verse 19). Hezekiah affirmed God's ability to deliver them from the enemy. And God answered in a mighty way—in one night. God did a much better job than Hezekiah ever could have done if he had taken matters into his own hands.

Hezekiah's example is such a good one for us. He shows us how to respond when crisis hits, when our peace is taken from us, when fear takes root and we can't seem to break free of it. In these moments, we start focusing on who God is. We remind ourselves of what He can do. We praise Him for what He has done in our lives before. We get caught up in the character and nature of God. Don't waste precious time in a crisis worrying yourself sick or building a defense. Go right to reminding yourself of who God is. As you do this, and as you begin to pour out your concerns and requests before God, the Bible promises that "the peace of God, which surpasses all understanding, will guard your hearts and minds through Christ Jesus" (Philippians 4:7 NKJV).

Learning to Be Still

Our lives can be so busy, so frenetic. I have already told you that I am guilty of letting the tail wag the dog. It is typical for me to head into one room to do something, do ten other things on my way, and then wonder what my original purpose was! I stay wound up, and when I do have a break, I often need days just to quit vibrating. How can I experience the peace that surpasses all understanding when I can't seem to ever settle down?

Peace can become a practice, not something we seek from God only in a time of crisis. Scripture says, "Be still, and know that I am God (Psalm 46:10 NKJV). I have found that resting in God's peace often means finding ways throughout the day to quiet myself and be still. When we are still, we can tune in to what God is speaking to our hearts and minds, and centering on God brings peace. When Jesus would visit Mary and Martha at their home in Bethany, Martha's habit was to serve, while Mary's was to sit at Jesus' feet and listen to Him. During one visit, Martha got aggravated and complained to Jesus that Mary wasn't helping. Jesus replied, "Martha, Martha . . . you are worried and upset about many things, but only one thing is needed. Mary has chosen what is better, and it will not be taken away from her" (Luke 10:41–42 NIV). Mary could have been helping her sister. It would have been a good thing. But she chose not to be sidetracked. She chose to be still and listen to Jesus. She chose to set aside the immediate for the eternal. And Jesus said she chose well.

Even in busyness, we too can choose "what is better" by pulling away from the fray to focus on God. I have discovered that one of the best ways to become still and quiet before the Lord is to spend purposeful time meditating on Him. This is one way we can "practice" God's presence. I do not mean meditating in some New Age sense but rather quieting our minds and turning our thoughts to the Scriptures and to God's character. Frederick Buechner wrote, "To *meditate* is to open the mind to a single thought until it fills the mind so completely that there is no room left for anything else."[4] For us, that "single thought" is God.

If you desire, I encourage you to try any of the practices I describe here. Richard Foster's book *Celebration of Discipline* is also an excellent resource. J. Boyd Nicholson once wrote, "Meditation, the lost art, is like a balm to the weary mind. It is to hear the Lord speak peace to the storm within, or to raise the believer above the storm and see it from God's point of view. This is what sustains the mind in times of stress, refreshes it in times of weariness, comforts it in times of sorrow. For thinking with God is a veritable balm to the mind."[5]

Ideally, we would set aside ten or fifteen minutes for practicing stillness before God, but we can meditate on God anywhere. I can do it while working in the yard or sitting at a traffic light. I turn my thoughts inward, breathe deeply, relax my neck muscles, and let my mind become absorbed in a favorite verse, a phrase about God, a promise, or one of God's attributes. I keep several verses written on index cards in my car so I can remind myself of those truths at any time. I may take an attribute from my ABC list and ponder it for a while. Coca-Cola used to have a slogan, "Relax with the pause that refreshes." These moments of meditation can refresh us. God gave us an imagination to use, and when we give ourselves to mulling over His truth and listening to Him with our hearts, we choose, as Mary did, what is better.

When I do have the time to focus on God without distraction, I tend to practice stillness in the following way. First, before I begin to meditate on Him, I ask God to help me in the meditation. I ask the Holy Spirit to guide me. He knows my desire to slow down. He knows my desire to hear from Him. When we set aside time to draw near to God, Scripture promises He will draw near to us (James 4:8). God delights in revealing more of Himself, and we can ask Him to do that.

When I begin my meditation practice, I usually lie down on the floor and take a moment to breathe deeply and steadily, calming my body and my nerves. If I am out of practice with this, then calming myself down through breathing may take some time. When I am ready, I let my mind turn to a passage of Scripture. For this example, let's use Matthew 11:28–29: "Come to Me, all who are weary and heavy-laden, and I will give you rest. Take My yoke upon you and learn from Me, for I am gentle and humble in heart, and you will find rest for your souls."

As I use this passage for meditation, I first imagine myself feeling very heavy, very weighed down. I am worried and anxious. I am fretting about everything. This is not difficult to imagine, because I usually come into this discipline this way. Then I think about the word "Come." It is a word of invitation. It is inclusive and warm. No one invites someone to come unless he wants or needs them nearby. God is inviting me to come. The invitation isn't general but specific: "Come to Me." There is a direction, a destination. God wants me to come close to Him. In my mind's eye, I may imagine responding, "Who, me?" I often feel so inadequate and unworthy. But here is the God of the universe, the Creator—*my* Creator—seeking me out to come close.

What has qualified me for this invitation? God specifies those whom He wants to come near: "all who are weary and heavy-laden." Those who are exhausted from trying. Those who feel they keep missing the mark or can never get ahead. The overworked and overburdened. God is inviting us. Society says we should be able to handle whatever life dishes out, but God sees us near the breaking point. He is saying, "It's okay. Admit your need to Me. Allow yourself to be weak and inadequate. Confess your limitations. Be where you are and let Me heal you." If we can't allow ourselves to admit that we are weary and heavy-laden, how will we be able to respond to God's invitation?

Then God says what I have been longing to hear: "I will give you rest." He will give us rest. Not the Serta mattress. Not the bottle. Not the sleeping pill. Nothing and no one but God Himself gives us the rest that we need. I pause with this thought. God gives me rest in my body and in my mind. He gives me His perspective on my circumstances. He does this personally. Rest is His gift to me. I cannot buy it or bargain for it. When I accept His invitation, rest is a free gift. He provided it through the cross. He died so I wouldn't have to carry burdens. He bore my griefs and carried my sorrows (Isaiah 53:4). He looks at me now and says, "Daughter, you do not need to drag that burden around."

I focus on the word "rest." Dictionaries talk of rest as freedom from activity, peace of mind, relief from anxiety or disturbance. To rest can also mean to lean on something for support. When we are resting at home, we are being supported—by a bed, perhaps, or a chair. But when we rest in God, He is the one holding us. He is the support. Who better to hold us than the One who made us? He is more than capable. Scripture says, "The eternal God is a dwelling place, and underneath are the everlasting arms" (Deuteronomy 33:27). What security! His arms are our everlasting supports. He will not drop us—ever.

Stretched out on the floor, I imagine being held by God. He cradles me. The Bible says, "He gathers the lambs in his arms and carries them close to his heart" (Isaiah 40:11 NIV). I picture the face of Jesus. He isn't looking at me with disapproval or disappointment. His face is strong and tender. His smile is calm, loving, and inviting. He will give me rest. I trust in that fact.

Now I visualize Jesus asking me to release my burdens to Him. All of my anxieties, worries, doubts, and fears—whatever is weighing me down. We all have our pet anxieties, our favorite burdens, issues we like to mull over and carry around with us. Jesus sees even those burdens we try to hide. "Bring those to Me," He tells me. He is not reprimanding me for my lack of trust. He wants me to be free. He says "Come—what are you waiting for?" I picture myself giving Him each fear, each worry, one by one, as I unload my burden onto Him.

I imagine Him saying to me, "Now take my yoke upon you." *Take Myself. Take Me. Exchange all that anxiety and fretting for My presence. Focus on Me. I am gentle and peaceful. I will give you rest, the thing you're longing for the most. Only come and learn from me. I Myself will be your teacher. Let Me teach you those things you want to know. Let Me give you the certainty you need. Learn from Me. I am gentle and humble in heart. Here with Me you will find rest for your soul.*

Hearing God's Voice

Learning to rest in God's peace is connected to learning to hear God's voice. Not many people have heard God speak in an audible voice. I certainly haven't. I sense impressions in my heart and my mind that I believe are from God, and I measure those against the principles set forth in the Scriptures. But because God is Spirit, it can be challenging to know at times whether we are hearing from God about something or projecting Him onto our own thoughts, feelings, wants, and tendencies. We do the best that we can, trusting God will help us know the difference. God wants us to hear His voice. He is not playing hide-and-seek. He is not out to trick us. How could we trust a being who leads us to believe one thing when the opposite is true? I wouldn't do that to my grandchildren. God won't do that to us. He wants to reveal Himself to us and draw us into intimacy.

God speaks in a variety of ways. There are no formulas like, "Do A and B, and C will result." God doesn't fit in a box. He can show up to surprise us in as many ways as He is diverse. Certainly, reading the Bible is the best way to hear from Him. We can hear from Him when we listen to His Word being taught or preached. How many of us have sat in a worship service and felt as if the preacher were talking directly to us? Often on Sunday morning, my pastor will say something that speaks directly to my heart about an issue that I have been discussing with God throughout the week.

Practicing stillness as I just described in the previous section helps me to tune in to what God may be saying in my heart. At the same time, I can be very busy or preoccupied and experience God breaking in through the static and chatter. For instance, I might be running errands in town, see someone, and have an unkind thought. Right there God's Spirit may speak a word of conviction to my heart and remind me that He loves that person I was just judging.

A couple of years ago, I was wrestling with a decision. I had framed it as "either-or." As I was waiting at a traffic light, thinking the decision over, I heard what I believe was God's voice speaking to my mind. He was questioning me: "Have you thought that it might be 'and-with'?" That was an aha moment for me. I wasn't straining to hear from God. I was just thinking. Suddenly, a simple question came through and shifted my perspective.

At about that same time, I had been asking God for direct confirmation about a decision. I was walking the beach, asking God for something specific. I was very anxious about this decision I had made. Was it the right one? What should I do? On my iPod came a chorus about giving God thanks. I realized it was already settled. God had shown me. Now I was to give thanks, and I did. Interestingly, in the ensuing months when I would second-guess myself on the decision, that chorus would play on the radio, the choir at church would sing it, or it would have cycled around again on my iPod. I understood through this song that God was assuring me.

How do we know when we are hearing God's voice? We are back to that question, "How do you know when you are in love?" When you hear God's voice, there is a spiritual recognition. One way you can cultivate your ability to recognize His voice is by spending time regularly in the Scriptures, learning God's truth. When we consistently focus on the principles He has set forth in the Bible, we will be more apt to sense whether our thoughts or seeming moments of clarity are on track. If what we believe we are hearing doesn't line up with the Bible, then it cannot be God's voice. God doesn't contradict Himself.

Hearing God's voice can be very subjective. Some people declare with certainty that God has told them certain things. They are dogmatic. Unless I know the integrity of a person's walk with God, I tend to be a little skeptical. When we intone God's name in this way, we must be careful. Our words can become manipulative. If God is speaking, He will confirm it—in Scripture, through godly counsel, through circumstances, and in other ways. There have been times when I thought for certain I was hearing from God on something, only to come back later and realize I might have been wrong. We do the best we can to hear God, in faith, but we still only "know in part" as long as we are on earth (1 Corinthians 13:12). We are to maintain humility and transparency before God. We must be careful that in saying we have heard from God we are not being presumptuous. My attitude is to be one of "I believe I am hearing from God" and then to trust Him to redirect me if I have heard wrong.

What we do know is that God does speak, and that He wants to speak, to His people. In Scripture we read, "He will surely be gracious to you at the sound of your cry; when He hears it, He will answer you. . . . Your ears will hear a word behind you, 'This is the way, walk in it,' whenever you turn to the right or to the left" (Isaiah 30:19, 21). God will answer us in His own way and time. And that answer will bring peace. Let's look at the way Jesus stepped into a chaotic situation, spoke clarity, and brought peace.

Jesus Brings Peace

It was the evening of Resurrection Sunday. The God of eternity was fresh from victory over death. The history of the human race had changed profoundly and forever. Cosmic changes had occurred. The crucified Jesus was alive! Soon God was going to seat Him at His right hand in heaven. Can you imagine what must have been going on in heaven? The saints clapping and high-fiving. God grinning from ear to ear. The angels on tiptoe to see what was going to happen next. Momentous things were taking place! And what did Jesus want to do? He wanted to talk with two discouraged men.

These men had just heard from the women who had gone to Jesus' tomb and found it empty. The women claimed to have seen two angels there who explained that Jesus had been crucified to fulfill the scriptural prophecies but that now He had risen from the dead. The band of Jesus' followers struggled with the women's claims—they seemed so outrageous. And yet the disciples wondered. Could it be? Excitement and hope surged through the band of Jesus' followers as word spread. Peter and John had run to the tomb to find out for themselves. But nothing had come of it. Like everyone else, these two men, now traveling on a dusty road out of the city back to their town of Emmaus, were confused. Things had not turned out as they had hoped and expected. Their shattered dreams had been replaced by hurt, pain, and heartache. They felt disillusioned, uncertain, and anxious. They had a lot more questions than answers.

As the men walked the seven miles to Emmaus, they tried to sort through the events of the preceding days. They had thought they had it all figured out. They had believed Jesus was the Messiah. Jesus was going to be the conqueror and ruler and establish His kingdom on earth. But nothing of the sort had happened. A far cry from it. Jesus had been brutally tortured and murdered instead. He didn't live up to their expectations. Now their world was upside down, and their hearts were broken with grief. They had witnessed so much cruelty and pain, and along with Jesus, all their hopes had died. What had they left to believe in?

While discussing things with each other, trying to make sense of what went wrong, trying to answer the whys, the men are approached by a stranger. We are told it is Jesus, but the Bible says they "were kept from recognizing him" (Luke 24:16 NIV). We are just like these men. How often do we become so absorbed in our pain that we fail to recognize God working in our lives? In our despair, God may send us encouragement through others or through circumstances, only to see it go right over our heads. We miss His assurances, His messages of peace. While God seems to have prevented these two men from knowing Jesus here, no doubt their vision was also blurred by disillusionment. They were so focused on the problem that when Jesus walked up and joined them, they didn't recognize Him. We are just like them. We have our eyes on the ground.

So here we have Jesus coming alongside His weary, overwhelmed disciples and asking them a question: "What are you discussing together as you walk along?"

They stop in their tracks, and still stuck in their pain, they look at Him with shock. One of them asks his own question: "Are you only a visitor to Jerusalem and do not know the things that have happened here in these days?" *Are you the only one who doesn't know this?* They are incredulous, flabbergasted by His lack of knowledge of current events in Jerusalem. The whole city and surrounding towns had been fixated on the crucifixion of a man whom no one could deny was a prophet. Even the sun had stopped shining for several hours in the afternoon while this prophet had hung on the cross. An earthquake had opened graves! How could the stranger not know?

But Jesus' sympathetic and courteous manner invites the two men to speak frankly. Express their doubts and questions. Tell their story. "What things?" He asks.

I think this is one of the most ironic portions of scripture in the Bible. Here we have two men telling Jesus all about Himself! They talk about His powerful deeds and miracles. They talk about His teaching. They tell *Jesus* about His own betrayal, the trial, and the crucifixion. Then they say three very sad words, common to those with broken hearts: "We had hoped." We had hoped He was going to be our Savior. We had hoped He was our Messiah. We had hoped He would redeem Israel. We had hoped for another outcome. *We had hoped.*

This is classic disappointment. "We had hoped" says that hope is now gone. It's over. Might as well resign ourselves to it. Three days have already passed. And now, the men tell the stranger, there is this puzzling development of the missing body. They explain what the women said after their visit to the tomb—how they had come to the disciples talking about seeing two angels who claimed Jesus was alive. Other disciples had also gone to the tomb but hadn't seen anything or anyone. So now these men were settling for disappointment and going back home. They didn't bother sticking around to investigate the women's claims. It was easier to go back home to their comfort zone. Back to the familiar to pick up where they'd left off. Did they really think they could do that? How close they came to missing the blessing.

I love the fact that Jesus listens to these men and lets them pour out their hearts. He lets them explain things to the very One who knows more than they will ever know about what happened and about the vast implications! He doesn't interrupt or rebuke. He lets these two disciples grapple with the events, the confusion, and the pain. He asks a question to which He already knows the answer ("What things?") so they can express themselves, and so He can meet them where they are.

When Jesus does speak, He turns the men's focus to the real issue, to what is hindering them: their unbelief. "How foolish you are and slow to believe all that the prophets have spoken!" Jesus isn't condemning or ridiculing the two disciples. He is letting them know they are not looking at the whole picture. They were slow to trust in the words of the prophets. They had failed to understand and to grasp the significance of the prophecies. They had expected a triumphant Messiah and had missed the part about the suffering Savior.

True to form, having met the men where they are, Jesus proceeds to take them further. On that dusty road from Jerusalem to Emmaus, Jesus patiently explains it all to them. He tells them what the prophets had written and foretold about the Messiah—about Himself. He teaches them step by step, line by line, taking them back to the beginning—back to basics. We read, "And beginning with Moses and all the Prophets, he explained to them what was said in all the Scriptures concerning himself."

As Jesus opens up the Scriptures for these men, He is sensitive and available, not aloof and arrogant. There is something very winsome about Jesus. Talking with the two disciples, shedding light on the events they had witnessed, patiently explaining things to them, Jesus is drawing these men closer to Himself. This is what peace is about—hearing God's voice, understanding His perspective, moving closer to Him. Jesus' voice calms, brings clarity, draws us into deeper relationship. The men become so excited and intrigued by Jesus they want to hear more. As they approach the village, they invite Him to stay. The Bible says they "urged him strongly." I love that Jesus isn't pushy or aggressive, that he waits on an invitation.

Once the three sit down at the table to eat, Jesus takes over the role of host. He takes bread, gives thanks, and then breaks the bread and gives it out. As He is doing this, the two disciples suddenly realize who it is sitting before them. Perhaps they see the scars in His hands—and seeing them, realize who He is. We read, "Then their eyes were opened and they recognized him."

That instant, just as He is recognized, Jesus disappears. He is gone. The men are left stunned at the table. But they are not hallucinating. They know they have seen Jesus, and they connect the dots with their experience on the road: "Were not our hearts burning within us while he talked with us on the road and opened the Scriptures to us?"

Despite the fact that they have just traveled seven miles on foot from Jerusalem, despite that it now is night and bandits might be out on the road, the men return immediately to the city. They have to go back. They need to tell the others. They have discovered new energy, new excitement, and new insight. No longer are they weighed down by a heavy load of confusion or anxious with stress and uncertainty. No longer are they focused on their own disappointment and heartache. They have encountered Jesus, and their perspective has changed radically. They know they can't keep all this to themselves.

What a return trip! I can see the men talking over each other as they realize how their hearts had burned within them when Jesus was talking. I would have loved to have overheard their conversation: "Yes, I can see now." "No, I didn't recognize Him." "I'm embarrassed I was so doubtful, but He was so kind." "How could we not have seen?"

When they get to Jerusalem, they find the other disciples gathered together and begin excitedly to tell them about their encounter with Jesus—how He talked with them, how when He broke bread they recognized Him. "It is true!" they say. "The Lord has risen . . ."

But as they are still talking, Jesus appears again. We read, "Jesus himself stood among them and said to them, 'Peace be with you'" (Luke 24:36 NIV). *Peace be with you.* There was no more important or relevant message for His weary, confused disciples. They had known only chaos, pain, desperation, and despair since that Thursday night in the garden of Gethsemane when Judas betrayed Jesus. All of them had fled—running in fear. Now Jesus has come to them personally to calm their hearts. To speak into that confusion. To settle it all with a word: Peace.

Do Less, Be More

It is important to remember that it is not up to us to figure out how to "achieve" peace. Peace is not something that we *do*. It is something that He *is*. We tap into who Jesus is and keep our focus on Him. He enables us to rest in His peace.

As we saw in our meditation practice, Jesus says that we are to take His yoke and learn from Him (Matthew 11:29). The Message Bible translates "learn from me" as "learn the unforced rhythms of grace." I love that idea. When we learn the ways of Jesus, we find rest. Jesus describes Himself as "meek and lowly in heart" (KJV). Meekness speaks of kindness, patience. Lowliness speaks of humility. He describes His yoke as easy and His burden as light (Matthew 11:30 KJV). When we are walking closely with Jesus, situations, conversations, and relationships do not have to be forced. There is an ease in our relationship with Jesus. We don't have to strive to gain His peace. That is self-defeating. With Jesus, we get to trade in our "stuff" for His peace, tranquility, and harmony. We accept His invitation to come, and He gives us what we long for—peace. All we have to do is come.

Jesus describes our relationship with Him using the image of a vine. He is the vine and we are the branches (John 15:1–11). Branches on a vine don't wrestle to get on the vine or to stay in place. They don't wake up saying, "Oh, I have to hang on to the vine today. I've got to work hard to stay in place." They are already part of the vine. They don't struggle and strive to get connected. They don't worry if they are doing it right. They relax, allow the vine to hold them, and grow with the vine, getting their substance from it.

This does not mean we do nothing in our relationship with God. Certainly, throughout this book we have been looking at ways we can know and trust God more fully. In this chapter, we've talked about putting our trust in Him, keeping our focus on God, turning to God in crisis, stilling ourselves before Him, and other of those "possible" things that we can do to enhance our experience of what we already have in Christ. But remember what Jesus said: "My peace I give to you" (John 14:27 NKJV). And what Isaiah said: "You will establish peace for us" (Isaiah 26:12). God is our source. He is our vine.

Perhaps our restlessness in life comes in part from feeling like we always have to be doing something to keep God happy. I don't believe the Christian life needs to be so difficult and effort centered. Oftentimes we make it too complicated. Like the Pharisees, we've added layers and layers of shoulds, oughts, dos, and don'ts—things God perhaps didn't ever intend for us to get absorbed in. It is our human nature to think we can somehow earn a place with God. As we've discussed, that way we feel like we are in control. And yet, this approach only leads to more burdens and more agitation. It is counterproductive. We do not have to worry or strive. God doesn't want us to strive. It is God's great delight to give of Himself—to give of His rest, His peace, His joy. Jesus said, "Fear not, little flock; for it is your Father's good pleasure to give you the kingdom" (Luke 12:32 KJV). Even in the midst of turmoil, even when we are dealing with unpleasant and difficult circumstances, God wants us to rest in Him and to know His peace. His request is so simple: "Come."

POINT OF FOCUS

Come to Me, all who are weary and heavy-laden, and I will give you rest. Take My yoke upon you and learn from Me, for I am gentle and humble in heart, and you will find rest for your souls.

Matthew 11:28–29

Hear His Invitation

chapter eight

ILOVE TO GET an invitation. Invitations make me feel special and sought out. An invitation for dinner at a friend's house, a wedding ceremony, a picnic, some fund-raising event, an opening of some kind—whatever the occasion, I enjoy being included. My church holds small dinner groups every six months. Though I am rarely able to attend due to my travel schedule, my church family never fails to ensure that I am invited, and they always seem delighted when I show up.

We need to feel as if we matter to others. No one likes to be left out. When we are excluded, we feel rejected, sidelined, unappreciated, and overlooked. Rejection is very painful. It says we're not valuable. We're not respected. We're not wanted. All of us have experienced rejection of some kind. The kid picked last to play on the team or not picked at all. The teenager left sitting at home while all her friends go out. The adult passed over for the promotion he or she really wanted. We experience cliques in school, at church, in our communities. If you're not part of the "right" clique, then the message is you don't fit in. You don't belong. That hurts, doesn't it? We all need to feel like we belong.

The most painful kind of rejection is what we experience at the hands of loved ones, those who are supposed to nurture and protect us. Maybe the person to whom you've committed your life chooses someone else over you—or some*thing* else over you, like work, activities, or possessions. A loved one changes his or her priorities, cutting you out of the picture. A circle is drawn by people you believed were your friends, and you're left on the outside. These are painful experiences. I have known deep, life-altering rejection over the years, and it has left scars.

But God is not like those who have cast us aside or excluded us or failed to see us as valuable. God loves us with an "everlasting love"—a love that never quits—and He always wants to be with us (Jeremiah 31:3). God invites us. There is never a moment when He is not calling to us, if we could only hear His invitation. He says, "Come." Come if you are weary (Matthew 11:28–29). Come if you are thirsty (John 7:37). Come closer to Me. Come belong in Me. Come find sustenance in Me. Come be healed in Me. Come into relationship with Me and live in My love. God's invitation isn't just for a few of us, either. God invites *all* of us to come. Scripture says, "Everyone who thirsts, come to the waters" (Isaiah 55:1). *Everyone who thirsts.* That's me. That's you.

Trying to Measure Up

We have such a hard time believing God would accept us, let alone invite us to come closer. Could He actually want us? So often we transfer the attitudes and behaviors of people onto God. We tend to think that God is exclusive like those who have rejected us. That He is looking for ways to exclude us. That if we blow it or make a mistake, He will wash His hands of us. We strive so hard to measure up. We make our lists of things we believe are acceptable to God, and we exhaust ourselves trying to do them. My uncle Clayton Bell used this illustration in one of his sermons: A farmer was dissatisfied with the size of his chickens' eggs; they weren't big enough for him. So he went out and looked for the largest ostrich egg he could find. He carried it into his henhouse one morning and said, "Try harder!" Isn't that how we feel sometimes? We are trying our best, but we just don't see ourselves measuring up to the standard we think God has set.

Author John Eldredge writes in his book *Wild at Heart* that "every man is haunted by the question, 'Am I really a man? Have I got what it takes . . . when it counts?' "[1] *Have I got what it takes?* I think we all struggle with that question in one form or another. Do I have what it takes to please God? To cope with life? The rejection we've faced has a way of underscoring our feelings of inadequacy, causing us to answer the question in the negative. No, we don't have what it takes—we don't measure up. We believe God is disappointed in us. We're disappointed in ourselves. So what do we do? We do our best to cover up our sense of failure, perhaps with busyness, anger, or even addiction. Or maybe we try to prove ourselves. We try to show God and others that we are okay. But the truth is we are not okay. We need God's help.

Sometimes we ourselves can generate the sense of rejection we feel. We do this by comparing ourselves with other people. It seems that every week another catalogue arrives in my mailbox. The models in the catalogue are thin—no muffin tops in these pages. They have perfect skin, their hair is long and silky, and their teeth are straight and gleaming white. Then I catch a glimpse of myself in the mirror! My aging image doesn't fare well by comparison. I get discouraged and feel defeated. Again, I don't measure up.

We don't even need catalogues or magazines to know this experience. How many of us have looked at others and silently wished we could trade lives with them? They can pay their bills; they have good jobs; their families are stable; they have new cars and nice homes; their kids are well behaved. By comparison, my life looks ragged, lackluster, or a failure. What's worse, I feel powerless to make it any better. I am just too tired.

The Bible calls comparing ourselves with others a foolish waste of time. We read, "When they measure themselves by themselves and compare themselves with themselves, they are not wise" (2 Corinthians 10:12 NIV). I like this verse from Galatians: "That means we will not compare ourselves with each other as if one of us were better and another worse. We have far more interesting things to do with our lives. Each of us is an original" (Galatians 5:26 The Message).

Everyone has issues. Everyone is dealing with hurts and weaknesses. We all struggle in some area, so what use is it to compare ourselves with one another? We only end up feeling the sting of low self-esteem. We begin to see ourselves as unworthy of love or acceptance. We cement in our minds the false belief that God too will reject us. Can you see how comparing yourself to others can hurt you? My older daughter is a marathon runner. She tells me that when she is running a race, if she glances back to see what the other runners are doing, she can lose a whole step and possibly the race.

For us the equivalent of losing the race is becoming deaf to God's invitation. All our efforts to measure up to others, to our own standards, to what we believe are God's standards—all of it keeps us broken, distracted, weary, and unable to hear His call. God isn't standing over us measuring us to see if we're good enough. As I've shared, we think He is looking for ways to exclude us, when, in fact, God is longing to *include* us. He loves us as we are. He is not surprised by our issues, nor is He shaking His head in disapproval. God accepts us right now, just as we are, and He invites us to come.

God Pauses for Us

But why would God waste His time with me? Why would He be so bent on inviting and caring for me when I'm not important? Why would God care about my small, pitiful situation when people in this world face such grave circumstances and issues? God has the rest of the universe to take care of—why invite me?

Let me ask you something. Which do you think is more important to God: Your getting to work on time or the HIV-AIDS crisis in Africa? Your need for money to pay your bills this month or the plight of street children in South America? Your battle with the flu keeping you home in bed or the young mother's battle with stage-four lymphoma? In every case the answer is both are important. God cares about everything we humans suffer, great and small. No one's need is insignificant. God cares about it all.

My friend Lysa TerKeurst tells the story of an encounter she had on an airplane after a speaking engagement. She describes it in her book *What Happens When Women Say Yes to God*.[2] I have also heard her share it at events. Taking her seat on the airplane, Lysa felt exhausted and longed for some rest, but the two empty seats on either side of her filled up, so she decided instead to take out a book manuscript and do some work. Soon the man beside her expressed interest in what she was doing. "What are you working on?" he asked her.

She told him the title of her book—*Leading Women to the Heart of God*—and they began to have a conversation about God. Lysa, a woman who is passionate about God, proceeded to take out her Bible and share some verses that related to what the man was saying. As she was doing this, she distinctly sensed God telling her to give the man her Bible. Now this, as I have heard Lysa tell it, was her "Bible Bible." Important notes, thoughts, and insights could be found in the margins. It was her "tearstained" Bible. Her children had drawn in this Bible! Give it away? She began having a mental discussion with God.

"I'll go home and buy him a Bible, God," I've heard Lysa say. "Really, I'll get his address and mail it to him." But she kept sensing God say, "No, I want you to give him yours."

When she and the man had finished talking, Lysa removed some loose papers and put the Bible in his hands, saying, "I'd like for you to have my Bible."

The man looked at the book, the well-worn pages, the aging cover. He told her he couldn't possibly take it.

But Lysa insisted. She said, "Sometimes the God of the universe pauses in the midst of all His creation to touch the heart of one person. Today, He paused for you."

What a powerful moment and an awesome truth! Sometimes God pauses the universe to touch our lives! We really are that significant to Him. God sent that man to Lysa because He loved him. God asked Lysa to sacrifice something, her Bible, because He wanted to make sure the man could hear His invitation. God had his eye on that man, right down to the seat assigned him by the airline.

We buy into the myth that God is too big to worry with our details. How many of us have said, "I don't want to bother God with that"? Our perception of God is that He is distant. God is somewhere up there, out there, and maybe every now and then He glances our way. He's not really interested in the small things that concern us. If someone I know is diagnosed with cancer, then, yes, I'll call on God. But if I lose my watch, that's no reason to bother Him.

Oh, if we could only hear God's invitation! He is neither distant nor disinterested. Far from it. God became what we are—human—and went to the cross in order to draw us into an intimate, personal relationship. That was God's greatest "pause." He stopped the universe and died so we could be invited.

God never tires of our needs. When my children were small, I could tell by looking in their eyes if they were not feeling well. I could tell by the way they walked if they had had a good day or a bad day. I could tell by their tone of voice whether they were disappointed or angry. I focused on my children, not that I got it right every time, but the details of their lives were important to me because *my children* were important to me. God is a much better parent than any of us. He is detail oriented. He is watching over us at all times. He wants us to come to Him with everything that concerns us. That kind of dependence honors God and moves His heart. It expresses the truth of our human condition: We cannot meet our own needs.

I addressed this earlier in the book, but while I often find it helpful to think of God in parenting terms, I realize some of us were raised by a parent who was critical, neglectful, absent, or abusive. Unknowingly, we can transfer these qualities to God. As I have written before, and I do so here with great kindness and respect, my father was gone much of the time. Though my father did his best, often it seemed that when I needed him most, he was farthest away, busy with other people. I viewed God as similarly distant. It took work to adjust my view of God, and even today I work at it. I have also told you how my father showed me God's grace at a critical point in my life. My father's "welcome home" in our driveway in Montreat and the grace he showed me at that time illustrated as nothing else could the outrageous nature of God's grace and the depth of His love. Still, my father is human, and he couldn't do it perfectly. God is not my father, and my father is not God. God is the only perfect parent.

I encourage you to prayerfully work through past hurts that may be hindering your relationship with God. He is asking you to "Come." The relationship He offers isn't just for the "superspiritual" people who seem to have it all together. It is for you right where you are. God is personally inviting you. What is preventing you from hearing His invitation? What is keeping you from trusting Him? Ask Him to help you work through those issues. He loves you. He wants to be close to you. And He will do whatever it takes to help you respond to Him.

Renewing Your Mind

Part of staying open to God's invitation involves what the Bible calls renewing our minds. We read, "And do not be conformed to this world, but be transformed by the renewing of your mind, so that you may prove what the will of God is, that which is good and acceptable and perfect" (Romans 12:2). Renewing our minds means just what it says. When we renew our minds, we are reprogramming our thoughts. We are taking out old, false ideas and replacing them with God's truth so that we can think in a new way. This is so important. Our thoughts influence so much more of our lives than we can imagine.

In order to trust God, in order to believe that He loves us and is inviting us into a closer relationship, we must renew our minds about Him. We can begin by confronting our notions of what God is like. How do you look at God? Do you see Him as a brooding taskmaster who is hard to please? As someone just waiting for you to mess up? As one who is never satisfied? Unpredictable? Capricious? Do see Him as indifferent? Uninvolved?

Once we acknowledge these thoughts, we can go to the Bible and choose instead to believe what God's Word says about God. We've spent time in this book seeking to know more about God by looking at Jesus. Jesus came to show us God's nature. Through Jesus, we see God's tenderness and gentleness. We see His humility and kindness. We see His consistency and love. We see His eagerness to touch wounded lives. We also see His power and His ability to bring peace. As we let go of our old ideas and embrace these truths about God, our faith in Him will begin to grow.

Renewing our minds takes time and discipline. A lifetime of incorrect thinking doesn't necessarily change overnight. Even having examined God's character in Scripture, you may still be unsure of Him. Let me say here that uncertainty about God is okay. Discovering God's character and learning to trust Him is a process. How I wish my flowers grew and blossomed instantly. They don't. They need sunshine. They need watering and fertilizing. They need time. So it is with us as we seek to grow spiritually, especially as we try to change our view of God. It comes down to consistently renewing our minds.

We are touched by a variety of influences in this world. Often we dwell on things that are not true. We chew on ideas that we read or on thoughts we hear others express. The ideas seem reasonable to us at the time, and they may contain some truth. But they are not wholly true, and often they settle into our thinking until they become a part of us. Many people of influence speculate about God and His nature. For centuries artists have depicted their images of God. Writers, including this one, try to describe Him. Popular movies portray God in new ways. Television hosts may say things about God that include enough truth to sound good and draw applause. But the nature of God is not created by or subject to television hosts, Hollywood, world events, art, books, or even preachers. God's nature is unchanging, and it is proclaimed by the Word of God. In the Bible, God describes Himself. The best way we can learn about God is to absorb the Scriptures, to fill our minds with it. Everything comes back to that.

Paul describes our efforts to correct our thinking as a battle: "We are destroying speculations and every lofty thing raised up against the knowledge of God, and we are taking every thought captive to the obedience of Christ" (2 Corinthians 10:5). What does this verse mean? Destroying is a very strong word. We are ruining, demolishing, and annihilating. God is saying something important here. He will not tolerate false notions about Himself. He is a jealous God. He has told us not to make false images of Him—that is one of the Ten Commandments (Deuteronomy 5:6–22).

In the process of renewing our minds, we must be determined like Paul to destroy any false thinking that we have about God no matter how eloquent, reasonable, or popular. Again, everything we believe must be measured against God's Word. This is not to say I don't consult other sources. I read or listen to a number of people whom I trust to interpret the Bible faithfully and whose work has stood the test of time—people like A. W. Tozer and C. S. Lewis, to name just two. But we must know the Bible for ourselves and let it be our ultimate standard. While certain works of the imagination can challenge us to enlarge our thinking, it is always wise when we hear, see, or read something about God to check it out with what He has revealed about Himself in the Bible. I am blessed to have a heritage of people who have held a high view of Scripture; they helped me to affirm the centrality of God's Word as I developed my worldview. Like Paul, they taught me that the ideas we choose to embrace must be held up to the knowledge of God in Scripture. We cannot rely on ourselves, our own opinions, or the opinions of others to determine for us who God is and what He is like.

Once we have destroyed our false thinking and replaced it with truth, that truth will be challenged in our lives. This is when we have to practice what Paul called "taking every thought captive to the obedience of Christ" (2 Corinthians 10:5). What does that mean? It means becoming aware of what we think, measuring it by the truth of God's Word, and ridding ourselves of those thoughts that are not honoring to God. This takes work and diligence, but we have the Holy Spirit within us to help us. He prompts us, and as we respond, He enables us to align our thinking with God's. This is an ongoing process.

In *In Every Pew Sits a Broken Heart*, I write about how I worked at taking thoughts captive and renewing my mind as I walked through the process of forgiveness in my first marriage. As I write this book, I am struggling with the issue of negativity. I mentioned it earlier. I always seem to see the downside of everything. I can't seem to look at things in a positive light. This is hard on me and on those around me. I was not always like this. I don't like it, and I have decided to renew my mind.

Here is one exercise that is helping me. I have chosen a relevant Bible verse and memorized it. I have typed it in a large font and posted it on my bathroom mirror. I have also written it on an index card and put it on the dashboard in my car. The verse reads, "God is able to make all grace abound to you, so that in all things at all times, having all that you need, you will abound in every good work" (2 Corinthians 9:8 NIV). Notice that the word *all* is used four times and *abound* twice. Notice the words: "God is able."

When negative thoughts come, I take those thoughts captive by turning my mind to my verse. I acknowledge that "God is able" to overcome all the things causing me to be negative. He makes His grace "abound" to me. I can be thankful and joyful about His grace—He gives it to me personally to appropriate in my thought life. This is a grace for "all things" and "all times," not just for some things or some times. God gives me what I need when I need it so that I am able to move forward and abundantly do what is before me. No matter what the negative thoughts may be, God's grace has my situation covered. Sometimes it is enough just to remind myself that "God is able." I may not be able, but He is.

Is this process of renewing my mind magic? No. It is a discipline. A discipline that allows God, by the power of His Holy Spirit, to enter into my thought process through His truth in order to bring about change for His glory and my good. What are some of the issues you are dealing with right now? Why not go to the Bible and ask God to lead you to some passages that will encourage you? Try doing what I described above. Write out those verses and put them in places where you will see them regularly. Memorize them. Develop the habit of turning to them in your mind when you start to sink into old patterns of thinking. Practice meditating on the verses the way we did with Matthew 11:28–29 in the last chapter. Get serious about renewing your mind and taking unproductive or harmful thoughts captive. This is a battle!

Another exercise I practice is one my mother taught me years ago. It is what I call personalizing the Scriptures. I find this exercise so helpful. Often when we read the Bible, we forget that it is not just a book about those who lived long ago. The Bible was written for you and for me. When my mother, for whom I was named, was young and struggling with her faith, she personalized Isaiah 53:4–5: "Surely he hath borne *Ruth's* griefs, and carried *Ruth's* sorrows: yet *she* did esteem him stricken, smitten of God, and afflicted. But he was wounded for *Ruth's* transgressions, he was bruised for *Ruth's* iniquities: the chastisement of *Ruth's* peace was upon him; and with his stripes *she is* healed" (KJV). Taking these verses as her own marked a critical juncture in my mother's walk with God. He loved *her*. He carried *her* burdens. He went to the cross for *her*. As she absorbed that truth, the effect in her life was powerful.

Why don't you try this yourself? Read the following verses and insert your name. Go to the verses right in your Bible and write your name in there. I do this often in my Bible. Here are a few verses to start with:

> You [*Your name*] did not choose Me but I chose you, and appointed you that you would go and bear fruit, and that your fruit would remain, so that whatever you ask of the Father in My name He may give to you.
>
> *John 15:16*

> I have loved you [*Your name*] with an everlasting love; therefore I have drawn you with lovingkindness.
>
> *Jeremiah 31:3*

Fear not, [*Your name*,] for I am with you; be not dismayed, for
I am your God. I will strengthen you, yes, I will help you, I will
uphold you with My righteous right hand.

Isaiah 41:10 NKJV

Isn't that a comforting exercise? You can do that with the whole of
Scripture. The more you take in the truth, meditate on it, and make it
your own, the better you will be able to hear God's voice and recognize
His invitation.

Come and Have Breakfast

It had been many days since the resurrection. Many days since Mary
had first reported the tomb was empty. Many days since Peter and John
had raced to the tomb, also finding it empty. Since then everything had
shifted. Jesus had begun appearing to people, and the disciples didn't
know what to expect. They didn't know where Jesus was going to show
up next. They would be eating in a room behind locked doors, and suddenly He would be there, standing in their midst. They weren't used to
encountering Jesus this way. They had been used to living with Him.
Traveling with Him. Eating with Him. Now that He had risen, I can
imagine they weren't sure how to adjust. Jesus talked about needing to
ascend to His Father. What did that mean? He had breathed on them
and said, "Receive the Holy Spirit." It all seemed so strange. There was a
new normal, and the disciples couldn't get their minds around it. Scripture tells us, "They still did not understand from Scripture that Jesus
had to rise from the dead" (John 20:9 NIV).

Now seven of the disciples had gone back to what they knew best—
fishing. So much was uncertain for them. They had experienced a
rollercoaster of emotions as they had watched the trial and execution
of their best friend. They had witnessed Him die such a brutal death.
After suffering profound grief, they had learned the tomb was empty

and He was alive. There was great joy. But what were the implications for them? What did the future hold? They had no idea. So they went back to the one thing they did know. The one thing that made them feel secure. Fishing. Their old way of life. Their comfort zone.

Isn't what these disciples did true of us? When life has been turned upside down, when we are confused and uncertain, we reach for what we know, what we find to be familiar and comfortable. Limbo is a very hard place to be. For me, it is the place I begin to make mistakes. I don't like the feeling when my toes don't touch the bottom and I can't see the shoreline. In limbo I struggle to trust God. This must have been where the disciples were. They wanted something certain, and they knew fishing. They had spent the better part of their lives doing it until Jesus had called them to be fishers of men. So they went back.

Did that mean they were settling for less than the call of Jesus? Was the return to fishing a sign of resignation or defeat? Had they given up on being fishers of men? Who knows? Maybe they were just trying to figure out what to do. I can hear them saying, "Jesus interrupted our lives, and we gave Him everything as we followed Him. Now how do we take care of our families? Do we form a fishing company?" They knew Jesus had talked about God's kingdom, but what were they supposed to do with that information? They didn't understand what kind of kingdom. They thought the kingdom meant power and conquering, victory and governing. But that had proven not to be the case. So they went back to fishing. Were they going backward? At the very least, they were not moving forward.

The Bible tells us the men were at it all night—lowering their nets, hauling them in—and that still they caught nothing. I am not sure how serious they were about fishing that night. Maybe they were just a bunch of fishing buddies out for relaxation. Maybe they were trying to cope. Maybe they wanted a night together to talk over what they'd been through. Whatever the case, here they were, experienced fishermen who had caught nothing. They must have been a bit embarrassed, and I'm sure they felt tired, defeated, and frustrated. Their efforts were futile.

We might say that in going back to fishing, they had leaned on their own understanding. And when we lean on our own understanding, trying to figure things out for ourselves, we come up with nothing. We fall into futility at best and sin at worst.

As dawn breaks, these expert fishermen who haven't caught a single fish see a figure on the beach. The man calls out, "Children" (John 21:5). I love that. He calls these big burly, rugged, weather-worn men "children." Children are dependant, innocent, impatient. Perhaps there is a slight hint of rebuke from Jesus. Not a harshness, but something like, "Oh, how foolish you are to go backward instead of forward with Me. You are being impatient. Learn to depend on Me."

Then He asks them, "You do not have any fish, do you?"

When God asks us a question, it is not because He doesn't know the answer. He wants us to acknowledge and face where we are. So what is He trying to get these men to do? He is asking them to admit their own failure, their own lack, so that He can step into their dilemma and guide them to fulfillment. These men have been at it all night. They should've had a boatload of fish, but they don't have anything. Jesus' question forces them to acknowledge that their efforts have failed, that going back to the familiar has not helped them. The question spotlights their inadequacy.

The disciples confess. "No," they call back. Now watch what Jesus does.

"Cast the net on the right-hand side of the boat and you will find a catch." *Your efforts aren't working. Try it My way.*

Can you see them wrestling this great big wet net over to the other side of the boat? It must have been quite a sight to see—a boat crowded with seven big fishermen trying to move this large net over, a struggle no doubt made harder by the fact they had been up all night. But they do it. They admit and accept their inadequacy in having tried it on their own.

I marvel at the fact that the disciples follow the direction of someone they still do not recognize. Why would they do that? They're complying with someone they think is a stranger. I probably would've said, "What does he know? I'm tired. I want to go home and take a nap." But they listen to this man, this stranger, and do what He says, which I think is amazing. Maybe they just figure, "Well, why not? We've tried everything else, why not try this?" It's already been called to their attention they have nothing. Maybe they were desperate. Maybe their families were at home waiting for food.

I don't know why they didn't yet recognize Jesus. Maybe there was mist over the lake. Maybe they were too far away. Maybe the early dawn light prevented them from making out His familiar features immediately. Maybe they were just too tired—or so focused on their task they couldn't see Jesus. I am like that. I let other things blur my vision of Jesus. I get so tired that I don't recognize Him when He shows up in my life, whether through people, circumstances, or in other ways. I get so focused and busy doing good things that I miss seeing Him. That doesn't stop Him from wooing me, from calling and inviting me. Wherever I am, He still confronts me with Himself.

So the disciples were obedient. They did what the stranger said. They moved the net over to the other side. I recall my pastor having said, "Christian intelligence is obedience." Obedience is the key to a fruitful Christian life. We don't like the word *obey*. It insults our independence. But we are not independent. We do not belong to ourselves. As the Bible says, we have been bought with a price—the blood of Jesus (1 Corinthians 6:20).

The disciples obey, and look what happens! We are told they can't even haul the net in because it's so full of fish. At this moment, working there in the boat, John has a moment of recognition. Hasn't he lived through this experience before? Yes. When Jesus first called him to be a disciple—to become a fisher of men—he, Peter, and James were dealing with the same scenario. An all-night fishing trip. No catch at all. Then a man, Jesus, showing up and borrowing their boat as a platform so He could teach the people on shore. And after that, His instruction: "Put out into the deep water and let down your nets for a catch" (Luke 5:4). They caught so many fish that day, their nets started breaking. And then Jesus said it, "Do not fear, from now on you will be catching men" (verse 10).

Now, in the early morning light, John has an aha moment. He remembers, and he realizes it is Jesus on the shore. Our past experiences with the Lord help us to recognize His presence in our lives. That is why it is so important to remember what He has done for us. As I've shared, that is why I journal—my journals are records of what God has done in my life. They help me to recall the ways He has answered prayer, how He has worked in situations I thought were impossible, and the promises He has made to me.

"It is the Lord!" John tells Peter. Can you imagine the joy? The excitement?

Peter hesitates only long enough to put on his clothes before jumping in the water and swimming or wading the hundred yards to shore. But why put on his clothes? If you were going to jump in the water, why would you bother? By religious standards, it would not have been appropriate for Peter to meet his teacher or rabbi while undressed. But perhaps Peter also still felt some shame for denying Jesus before the crucifixion. Perhaps he felt unworthy to meet Jesus and wanted to cover up. Was he still feeling vulnerable? Maybe he wanted to make himself more respectable. Don't we do that? We're back to that desire we have to prove ourselves to God. We think we can make ourselves more respectable by covering ourselves—by doing good things and keeping the rules. But God just wants us to hear His invitation and say yes. And Peter did that. He said yes before there was even an invitation! He wades to shore as the other disciples tow in their boat and the load of fish.

Why was Peter so eager to get to Jesus before the others? The passion of his personality aside, Peter would have already seen Jesus since the resurrection. No doubt he had experienced Jesus' unconditional love and forgiveness. Maybe Peter needed more of that love and acceptance. Who doesn't want to be around someone who loves you totally even with your failings? I have a little sign in my kitchen window that reads, "A friend is someone who understands your past, believes in your future, and accepts you today just the way you are." Perhaps Peter's eagerness stemmed from his overwhelming gratitude for the forgiveness he had received and his deep love for Jesus.

When Peter and the others get to the shore, Jesus is there waiting for them with a warm, glowing fire; fish and bread are already cooking over the flame. He asks, "Bring some of the fish which you have now caught."

God always looks for a way to include us in His plan. Whether He gives us a chance to use our gifts and talents or positions us in a place to help someone else, He invites us to participate. Life with God is not a spectator sport. We do not simply sit by and observe. He asks for what we have, and what we bring to Him in obedience He uses.

Peter drags the net, loaded down with fish, to shore. The Bible gives us the detail that the disciples caught 153 fish. I imagine they were so completely overwhelmed by the fact that while their own efforts had been fruitless, their act of obedience had resulted in a net full of fish that they sat down to count just how many fish they had in hand. When we act in obedience, there is an abundance of supply.

Then Jesus says, "Come and have breakfast." What a beautiful, simple invitation. *Come and be nourished. Come and be fed. Come and be taken care of. Come and be included.* He invites them just as they are— wet, tired, disheveled, and most likely very smelly!

Jesus invites them to eat what He has prepared. This is what God does. He prepares. Way back in Genesis, God prepared the sacrifice of Jesus so that we could share in an intimate relationship with Him. God prepared the way of salvation. What Jesus does on the beach is an illustration of what God has done for us all along. God has prepared the way for us. He has prepared nourishment and sustenance for us, and He invites us to partake.

Now, we read, the disciples know that this is the Lord. Could they now see Him in the full light of the sun? Was it in the way He prepared the breakfast? The way He invited them? The Bible says Jesus took the bread and the fish and gave it to them. He served them. The last time the disciples sat down to a meal with Jesus was for the Passover meal before His arrest. There Jesus had given them the bread and the wine, explaining it represented His body and blood, the blood of a new covenant. At that meal, Jesus had pointed them to a bigger picture.

Here, too, Jesus is suggesting the bigger picture. This experience is not just about food, fish, and fishing. Jesus is teaching the disciples more about following Him. In serving them breakfast, He provides what they had tried so hard to prepare for themselves. They had struggled all night, while He had it ready for them all along. Jesus invites them into the flow of doing things His way. It is a better way. The men, it seemed, were trying to go backward, but Jesus is moving them forward into a new phase of their calling and into a new kind of relationship with Him. It won't be the old way. But it will be more fulfilling than they can dream.

His Invitation Is Lovely

All night long these disciples had been in the dark—literally and figuratively. Only as they saw Jesus and focused on Him could they hear His invitation. *Come. Come and be fed. Come into a deeper relationship.* The men were fed with physical sustenance as well as with spiritual food, and their eyes were opened with new understanding. They saw Jesus preparing and providing what they had been inadequate to provide. The difference called them into greater dependence on Him.

Just as Jesus invited His disciples into deeper intimacy and dependence, so He invites us. He invites us for love. For nurture. For comfort. For wisdom. He invites us to learn from Him and to step into the "unforced rhythms of grace." God wants to be in relationship with us. He wants us to draw near, and He will do anything to get our attention. The God of the universe will pause in the midst of it all to make sure we hear His invitation.

God's invitation can come through people, circumstances, experiences, and other things in life. Sometimes it is only in hindsight that we realize God is inviting us to something more, to something greater than what we have known. God has used much of what I have suffered to woo me. I know that now. Through my struggles, He was inviting me into a deeper, more meaningful relationship with Him. In those difficult years, I didn't always feel wooed. Hardly. I would not have thought God was using my experiences as His invitation. But today I can look back and see that through it all, I experienced the grace, love, and peace of God I never would have known otherwise, and I can hear His invitation. *Come closer.*

God's invitation is not a command. His invitation is gentle and winsome. If someone *orders* me to come, then there is something in me that wants to back up. But when we hear God's invitation through Jesus, it is lovely. "Come" is an invitation to be where He is. God wants our company, our presence. He wants to give to us, feed us, sustain us, care for us, nurture us, and grow us. His desire is to take us in our imperfection and fashion us in such a way that He can fill us with Himself. His is a gracious, inclusive invitation. May our response be a resounding yes!

POINT OF FOCUS

I have loved you with an everlasting love;
Therefore I have drawn you with lovingkindness.
Jeremiah 31:3

Embrace His Forgiveness

chapter nine

WHEN I THINK of forgiveness, I often think about the story of the prodigal son, told by Jesus in Luke 15. "A man had two sons," Jesus begins (verse 11). The younger son demanded his inheritance from his father and went off to live in a far country. Now in that culture, when a son insisted on taking his inheritance from his living father, he was cutting himself off from the family. By demanding his inheritance, he was telling his father, "I wish you were dead. I reject everything you stand for. I want my own life. I'm going my own way." There would have been a public ceremony severing this boy from the family and from the community. He was disowning his family, and they were disowning him. There was no way back, and the son would have left home knowing this.

So the son goes off to the far country. He lives irresponsibly. Eventually he runs out of both money and friends. Then there is a famine. Nobody wants to party with him now. The good times are over. He ends up out in the field feeding someone else's pigs. This was about as low as a young Jewish man could get. He is hungry—even the pig's food looks appetizing to him. He has hit bottom.

While in the pigsty, the Bible says, the son "came to his senses." He begins to think about his life with his dad—how much better it was. He thinks about how much better it was even for his father's servants. Finally, he decides, "I'm going to go to my father. I will tell him I've sinned against him and against God." The boy wants the security and protection that only his father can give. He has no right to those things

153

now, but there is something dawning on the son about his father. Something causing him to believe that he can go home again—that there is a way back. This boy knows his father's heart; he understands his father's heart is gracious and forgiving. Somehow he must believe that he will be forgiven and accepted. Not as a son—he doesn't go back asking to be accepted as a son. But as a servant. A field hand, a day servant. The lowest of the servants. This is the boy's intention.

We are told in the story that back at home the father is watching for his son. We don't know how long the father watched, whether for a week, a month, a year, or even years. But the father is watching that road, looking for, hoping for, his son's return. I'm sure the townspeople said things like, "You're a silly old fool. Let him go. He's no good. Don't bother with him. It's a waste of time. Be glad you have a 'good' son who stayed at home. You've got other things to do." But the father kept watching.

We are told that while the boy is still a long way off, the father spots him. Maybe the father saw just a wisp of dust in the distance. Could it be? At long last? No doubt the father could see the ragged clothes, the matted hair, the defeated posture, the bare feet. Maybe he even smelled his son before he saw him. It didn't matter. This was his son coming home. His father's heart leaps, and he says, "That's *my* boy!" The father's heart, we read, is full of compassion. That word *compassion* suggests a feeling felt in the gut, a feeling deep inside that moves you to action. You cannot have compassion and do nothing. This compassion compels the father to run toward his son. A man of his dignity and stature in those days would not have run. He would've walked and paced himself. To run, he had to pick up his robe and show his legs. That was a scandal. It just wasn't done.[1]

Imagine that the villagers have gathered out on the road. No doubt the word has spread that the son is on his way home. They know this boy has no right to come home. Maybe they are holding rocks in their hands. Maybe they're ready to spit on him. Or to jeer and tell him to go back—that he has no right, no place here. He has been told he could never come home, and yet here he comes anyway. The crowd is agitated. People are murmuring. Then, all of a sudden, they see this blur. And they realize it is the father running. Their attention is drawn away from the son and now is focused on the father. The father is *taking* the attention from his son. The father is taking on the son's shame. As he reaches his son, he embraces and kisses him again and again so that the bystanders know there is a way back, and that the father has provided it. Forgiveness is granted fully and freely.

But the father goes further. He calls his servants and says, "Kill the fatted calf. We are going to have a party." This is not just some cow out in the field but a calf reserved for special occasions. He says, "Get the robe reserved for distinguished guests. No more rags for my son. Get the family's crest ring and put it on this boy's finger. He's a restored member of the family. He has the authority of the family behind him. And bring sandals—no more dust for his feet. He's not a slave anymore. This son of mine was dead and now he's alive. He was lost and now he's found."

Embracing Forgiveness

What an incredible picture of forgiveness! Notice the father embraces his son before the son even says a word. There is no condemnation. No blaming. No judgment. Only unconditional love. The father gives his son a safe place to confess his sin. Our hearts long for that kind of mercy, acceptance, and safety. We don't deserve it. And this boy didn't deserve it. It was just grace that his father showed him. Amazing grace. Outrageous grace.

It is so powerful that the One telling this story is Jesus. Jesus, the "express image" of God (Hebrews 1:3 NKJV). Jesus, who came to demonstrate what the Father is like, is now *telling* us what the Father is like. Who better to know the significance of the father's forgiveness in the story than Jesus Himself, the One who makes our forgiveness possible?

I've told you about my own prodigal experience—the time I went home, drove up the mountain to my parents' house in Montreat, after making such a horrible mess of my life. It was a time of profound humiliation for me. I had made a decision that had caused damage. I had gone against everyone's advice, and I felt the shame of it. I had negatively impacted not only my own life, but also the lives of my children and my loved ones. I'd been told not to do it. But like the prodigal son, I thought I knew what was best for my life. I was willful, stubborn, and sinful. Now I was living with an overwhelming sense of self-condemnation. And yet, when I pulled my car to the front of my parents' home, my father was waiting for me in the driveway. As I got out of the car, he wrapped his arms around me and said, "Welcome home."

What was my father communicating with that welcome? Like the prodigal's father, he was demonstrating grace. His actions said, "I love you. I accept you. I forgive you." And through my father, I felt God saying those things too. My father's welcome illustrated God's invitation; it was God's "Come."

Later in my stay, our pastor in Montreat preached a Sunday-morning message that had to do with brokenness. At the end, he gave an opportunity for those who felt a need to deal with their own brokenness to come forward. I felt that this was my chance to be made whole, and yet my first thoughts were that I couldn't go forward. I was Ruth and Billy Graham's daughter. Everyone would see me. I would be embarrassed. There was the shame. But the pull to go forward and settle my heart with God was so much stronger than my shame. Somehow I found enough courage to get up and walk.

I was the only one who responded that morning—and everyone did see me—but it didn't matter. I desperately wanted to let go of the shame and the hurt. I wanted to be whole more than anything else. When I got to the front of the church, my pastor embraced me, took me to his office, and let me weep, pouring my heart out to God. My father's "Welcome home" had been God's invitation, and my going forward in the church that Sunday was my response. That is when I fully understood and embraced God's forgiveness.[2]

What is the difference between grace and forgiveness? Grace is a gift that we do not deserve. Forgiveness is a form of grace extended to us. It is a free gift from God. It is release from a debt that we owe for our sin and cannot possibly repay no matter how we may try. We can do nothing to earn forgiveness. It is simply the gift of a loving Father who sees us stumbling, dejected, broken by our sins and mistakes, trying to make our way back to Him. The Bible says, "For by grace you have been saved through faith; and that not of yourselves, it is the gift of God; not as a result of works, so that no one may boast" (Ephesians 2:8–9).

Embracing God's forgiveness is an act of faith. When I went forward in the church—and afterward, as I sat with my pastor in his office, letting go of all that pent-up emotion, pain, and regret—I was taking the first step in believing God had forgiven me. By then I had been at home with my parents for some time, and the truths illustrated by my father's welcome had filtered down into my heart. I could begin to embrace God's free gift.

God promises us forgiveness when we come to Him in repentance. His grace draws us, and when we embrace His love and forgiveness, believing that He has accepted us, we experience the completeness of His grace. We may not have the right words or be able to express ourselves in words at all; but God sees the intent of our heart, and He forgives freely. The words we say, the place we happen to be, the posture we assume—these are not what matter in God's eyes. The Bible says God looks at the heart (1 Samuel 16:7).

Like so much in our relationship with God, embracing God's forgiveness is a process of growth. It begins with God's conviction of our sin and our repentance. Then we take a baby steps. We acknowledge God's promise to forgive us and accept that forgiveness by faith. Moving into the fact of our forgiveness—choosing daily to live in the freedom of forgiveness—can take some time. We have to learn to renew our minds and reject the self-condemning thoughts, the opinions of others, and the enemy's voice telling us we've blown it. Embracing God's forgiveness can be an encounter like the one I had at the church, one in which we experience a depth of healing and find ourselves able to leave the past behind. It can also involve taking hold of our forgiveness day by day. God meets us as individuals. What I experience may not be what you experience. God and His principle of forgiveness are the same. He just may express Himself in your life differently than in mine. He is a God of variety and surprise.

The Issue of Feeling Forgiven

God's forgiveness is a fact. It is a central truth about who God is. The Bible says that when we come to God, admitting our sin, repenting of it, we are forgiven: "If we confess our sins, He is faithful and righteous to forgive us our sins and to cleanse us from all unrighteousness" (1 John 1:9). So often our problem is *feeling* forgiven. We may understand with our minds that God has forgiven us, but somewhere inside we feel we don't deserve it. We can't imagine being forgiven. Long after the sin has been acknowledged and carried to God, we still feel the burden of guilt and shame. We drag it around with us, unable to believe at the gut level that God really has set us free.

While I was at home during those months in Montreat, my father made a very simple statement to me: "We all live under grace and do the best we can." What a grace-filled statement from a man who had every right to condemn me! We all need to hear those gracious words. We need to hear and know that it is okay to be human. We are going to fail and make mistakes, and when we do, there is grace. God knows we're not perfect. The Bible says, "Just as a father has compassion on his children, so the Lord has compassion on those who fear Him. For He Himself knows our frame; He is mindful that we are but dust" (Psalm 103:13–14).

God's grace comforts, brings joy, relieves, rescues, sets free, and transforms. There is such sweetness in grace, but so often we feel that it isn't for us. We live life as if we are constrained, hindered, blocked, and held down. We feel uncomfortable, joyless, censured, and hopeless. That is not what God wants for us. Jesus said, "If you love Me, you will keep My commandments" (John 14:15). He did not say, "If you don't keep my commands, I won't love you anymore. I won't forgive you." He doesn't say His forgiveness is based on results. It is based purely on love. Unconditional love.

God is a forgiver. We struggle believing this because we don't feel worthy of forgiveness. We assume God must want something. That there must be a catch in it somewhere. We work very hard trying to prove ourselves. We go to church every time the doors open. We pray and have our devotions each morning. We memorize Bible verses. We take a casserole to a sick neighbor. We tithe, we volunteer. We do all the things we think we're supposed to do to make God happy. And these are good things. But we don't have to do them to earn God's love or His grace. God's grace and forgiveness have already been given. The work was finished on the cross. He has done it all.

I think about the two thieves who were crucified with Jesus. One cursed Him, demanding Jesus save Himself and them. This thief was defiant. The other thief recognized his own guilt. He turned to Jesus and said, "Remember me when you come into your kingdom" (Luke 23:42 NIV). He acknowledged his sin and received forgiveness. He didn't pray the sinner's prayer. He didn't go forward at a revival or affirm the "four spiritual laws." He didn't even use the words "forgive me." He simply recognized his wrongs and asked Jesus to remember Him. He got much more than that. He received forgiveness and the promise of eternal life. God always gives more.

In talking about grace, I do not want to minimize God's holiness. We have a holy God who has a standard of righteousness that we can never attain. We stand guilty before God. But through Jesus Christ, God met His own demands. Jesus took our guilt and shame to the cross. He nailed them there, and He offers us complete forgiveness and freedom. We stand in His righteousness—not our own, which can never satisfy God. When God looks at us, He sees Christ's righteousness. We need to acknowledge and repent of our sin, but then God wants us to leave it with Him! That's why Jesus died—so we *could* leave it with Him. We don't live disregarding God's standards of morality and the truth we find in His Word, somehow believing that He will forgive us anyway. That cheapens God's grace and makes the cross of little value (Romans 6:1–2). And yet grace is what it is—free. When we start trying to earn it or to prove that we deserve it, we are off track. We will never deserve God's forgiveness. We are all sinners saved by His grace.

The Fact of Forgiveness

Knowing that we are forgiven and accepted by God frees us to trust Him. If you know you are loved and accepted by someone unconditionally, if you are secure in your relationship with that person, then trust comes more easily. On the other hand, it is difficult to trust someone if you wonder whether that person is going to reject you, betray you, or hurt you. God is not like people who have let us down. He will never reject or betray us. He is like the prodigal's father, waiting for us, watching the road, poised to run out and meet us where we are so He can forgive, accept, and restore us. He sees us in our brokenness—and He loves us and has compassion for us.

One of the ways we can deal with doubts about our forgiveness is by turning our minds back to the fact of our forgiveness. When teaching about different aspects of forgiveness, I often use the analogy of a child's toy blow-up clown. The clown is weighted in the bottom, and when the child hits it, the clown may fall knocked over for a moment, but the weight in the bottom rights the clown again. The fact of our forgiveness is like that weight in the bottom. Our emotions, our doubts, the opinions of others, the enemy's voice—these things are what come to knock our faith down. But the weight in the bottom, the fact of our forgiveness, keeps righting us so we can live in the freedom of God's grace.

Scripture says we are forgiven, and we must embrace that truth. Here are a few verses you can use to renew your mind to the fact of your forgiveness. You may have some other favorite verses. Find the ones that speak assurance to you and try memorizing them. Write them out and put them in places where you will see them. When you start to feel the burden of guilt and shame—as if God will never forgive you, as if your life will never count for anything—or when you begin to notice the hum of fear under the surface of your thoughts, make a conscious choice to turn your mind away from the fear, away from the negative thoughts, and to put your mind on the truth. Ask the Holy Spirit to help you take that truth into your heart so that it becomes real to you.

Then I acknowledged my sin to you and did not cover up my iniquity. I said, "I will confess my transgressions to the Lord"— and you forgave the guilt of my sin.

Psalm 32:5 NIV

For as high as the heavens are above the earth, so great is his love for those who fear him; as far as the east is from the west, so far has he removed our transgressions from us.

Psalm 103:11–12 NIV

"Come now, let us reason together," says the Lord. "Though your sins are like scarlet, they shall be as white as snow."

Isaiah 1:18 NIV

Remember these things, O Jacob, for you are my servant, O Israel. I have made you, you are my servant; O Israel, I will not forget you. I have swept away your offenses like a cloud, your sins like the morning mist. Return to me, for I have redeemed you.

Isaiah 44:21–22 NIV

In him we have redemption through his blood, the forgiveness of sins, in accordance with the riches of God's grace that he lavished on us with all wisdom and understanding.

Ephesians 1:7–8 NIV

If we confess our sins, He is faithful and righteous to forgive us our sins and to cleanse us from all unrighteousness.

1 John 1:9

The cross, of course, is the central demonstration of God's forgiveness, and it reminds us of the cost of forgiveness. Our forgiveness isn't cheap. It was bought with a price—the blood of Jesus Christ. He paid the price for us totally and completely. I find it helpful to go to the Scriptures and meditate on the narrative of Christ's passion. Several years ago, I hung a crucifix in my room as a reminder of what Jesus did for me and of the costliness of His gift.

I encourage you to find some ways to remind yourself of the cross and of what it means. I have a copy of the film *The Passion of the Christ*. As difficult as it is to watch the brutality Jesus suffered on my behalf, I am deeply moved as I try to somehow comprehend the cost of my forgiveness. When I give time to thinking about what my forgiveness cost God and to imagining what Jesus suffered, when I dwell on the details of what He endured, I come to a place of profound gratitude and trust in God. How could I doubt God's forgiveness when He gave everything He had for me?

Condemnation versus Conviction

When we continue to carry around guilt and shame, we open ourselves up to condemnation. Condemnation tells us that we have blown it and there is no way back. Our sin has stained us forever. We are worthless. We might as well resign ourselves to it. We have no hope for a future. Those are condemning words, and they run contrary to the Word of God, which promises us a future and a hope (Jeremiah 29:11). The Bible says, "Therefore there is now no condemnation for those who are in Christ Jesus" (Romans 8:1).

Through the eyes of condemnation, we see ourselves as never measuring up. Not only do we have our own feelings of guilt and shame working against us, but as I have shared, we also have an enemy constantly accusing us. He is called "the accuser" (Revelation 12:10). He accuses us because he knows how effective it is. He uses our own self-talk against us. He constantly points out our failures and flaws, how badly we've failed, how we'll never be good enough. We begin to think that God must look at us in the same way. We project onto God the condemnation, criticisms, accusations, and negative views, as if they are all coming from Him. We ask ourselves, how can God love us, much less forgive us, when we are such failures? The concept of God's all-encompassing grace is beyond us.

Unfortunately, many of us have become used to thinking and living this way—as if we are outside of God's acceptance. We spend our energy desperately trying to earn our way in, or we decide to give up and quit trying. We adapt to the false belief that we will forever be on the outside looking in. We adapt and we live with it. Why is this? Perhaps it is partly a function of personality or the result of life experience. Perhaps it is also because the voice of condemnation is so familiar.

Condemnation is not the same thing as conviction. Someone has said that condemnation is from Satan, but conviction is from the Holy Spirit. Condemnation reminds us of where we have been; it keeps us chained to the sin. Conviction reminds us of where we should go—to God for His free gift of forgiveness.

If we will let it, conviction can move us forward. It signals to us where we've gone wrong so we can do something about it. God uses conviction to guide us back to Himself and to His ways. I find it easy to be critical of people and to judge them on a whole range of issues. Usually I do this in my thought life. God has said, "Do not judge, or you too will be judged. For in the same way you judge others, you will be judged, and with the measure you use, it will be measured to you" (Matthew 7:1–2 NIV). That is serious stuff. I don't want God to judge me in the way I judge others. Yet I still fall into the sin of judging, and when I do, God convicts me. I feel discomfort, uneasiness, in my heart and mind. I recognize I am wrong. God gently reminds me of His love for those on whom I am being hard—He died for them too. This conviction then moves me toward God, and I ask Him to forgive me and to give me a more charitable view. You would think I would've learned by now. I don't like having to go back to God, saying, "Lord, I've blown it again. Please help me to change." But God's habit is forgiveness.

If we ignore the prodding of conviction, then we are robbing ourselves of the experience of God's forgiveness. We are hardening our hearts, and God says the one who is hardened "falls into trouble" (Proverbs 28:14 NIV). But a broken and contrite heart, we read in the Psalms, God will not despise (Psalm 51:17). If God is convicting you about sin, then it is because He wants to free you with His forgiveness and to renew you in some area of your life. Don't mistake conviction for condemnation. Remember, condemnation says there is no way back. With the heavenly Father, there is always a way back—forgiveness is always available. The conviction you feel is meant to compel you toward that forgiveness so you can embrace it.

Obeying God's Prompting

Sometimes responding to conviction means more than just asking for God's forgiveness. Our sins often involve other people, and God convicts us to seek their forgiveness too (Matthew 5:23–24). For years, I let a close relationship go from close to distant to nonexistent. There had been hurt feelings, misunderstandings, and harsh words that eventually led to silence and, when necessary, to superficial politeness. The change was painful. I missed the former relationship and its closeness. Once in a while, I would think about trying to bridge the chasm, but I would chicken out. I let distance remain the status quo.

Then God began to convict me. I ignored it. For years. I figured that if the other person wanted a relationship, she could come to me. As time went on, I assumed she wasn't worried about it. She didn't seem troubled. But God's conviction began to press on my heart. I became increasingly uncomfortable with the situation.

· Finally, I decided I would go to see my friend. This was a big step for me. Normally, I run from confrontation. I do not have a confrontational temperament. Usually my back has to be seriously up against the wall before I will confront anyone. I get tongue-tied and nervous. I'd much rather ignore the problem and hope it goes away. In this case, though, God was not going to let me off the hook, and I knew it.

I called my friend to ask if I could come for a visit. I had not been to her home in a long time, and I drove there with my stomach in knots. When I arrived, I was welcomed, and we spent a cordial evening with lots of catching up about children and life. I loved the family, and we laughed over shared memories. But I felt the underlying tension. We spent some time talking, and I told my friend how much I missed the intimate relationship. I said that one of the great sorrows of my life was that we were no longer close. I began to sob. The pent-up hurt and anxiety were released. I asked for her forgiveness for my part in the breach.

My friend listened sweetly and gave me a hug. She said she also had missed the close relationship. Soon afterward I left for home, relieved and content that I had paid attention to God's conviction in my heart. I did not know what God might do in the relationship from that point on, but that was not why I went to see my friend. I went out of conviction. I went because I believed God wanted me to go. I obeyed God's prompting. I sought my friend's forgiveness, and I left the results to Him.

The Freedom of Forgiveness

God gave us life to enjoy—life is His greatest gift. Imagine you gave someone you love a beautiful new convertible. Instead of enjoying it, he kept it in the garage, worried about putting miles on it, worried about getting it dirty, worried about getting a ding in the door, worried he wouldn't drive it correctly, and worried about getting a ticket. He never took the car out; he just worried about it all the time. How would you feel? You wanted your loved one to enjoy your gift, but to him it was a burden. We do the same thing with God's gift of life. Rather than enjoy it, so often we sit and worry about whether we are getting it right.

As I have shared, my mother had an amazing capacity to find and to make joy wherever she went. Some years ago, my two sisters and I were traveling with her. The circumstances were less than ideal. A dark, dirty hotel. No food service. Our passports had been taken. There was political tension in the area. It was late, and we were weary from traveling, so we collected what food we had between us—some crackers and apples—and we sat around a little table in Mother's hotel room.

Right away, the three of us girls began noting the grim circumstances. Not Mother. Instead, she started to sing: "If Jesus keeps you polished you will shine. 'Course you will shine. If Jesus keeps you polished you will shine." How can you keep complaining in the midst of that kind of mirth? We all joined in, and soon we were laughing—not to mention the happy memory we made!

My mother knew how to live. I want to be able to follow her lead, finding joy in the simple things: Hearing the birds singing in the morning. Seeing a beautiful sunset where I live in the Blue Ridge Mountains. Giggling with my grandchildren. God has given all of us a great capacity for joy. Life is full of opportunities for delight and pleasure, and God wants us to experience them—to listen to the birds, to watch the sunsets, to revel in life's unexpected gifts, to enjoy other people, to delight in the laughter of children. So often we miss out because we are burdened. Burdened by the cares of this world. Burdened by guilt, shame, and the weight of sins we've already taken to God probably many times over, seeking His forgiveness.

God's forgiveness sets us free. It gives us a fresh start to become who God created us to be. The things that encumber and hold us back are lifted, and we are liberated! That sin is gone. God erases it from His memory. He removes our sins from us "as far as the east is from the west" (Psalm 103:12). As Corrie ten Boom wrote in her book *Tramp for the Lord*, "When I confessed them to the Father, Jesus Christ washed them in His blood. They are now cast into the deepest sea and a sign is put up that says, NO FISHING ALLOWED."[3]

That is grace. If we can embrace it, we can come to know a freedom and a joy for which we were designed. God has freed us to live, freed us to enjoy life and love. But more often than not, we walk around joyless under a yoke of past sin and feelings of failure. Jesus invites us to trade our heavy load of guilt and our feelings of not measuring up for His yoke, which is pulsating with the joy of life (Matthew 11:28–30). That is what God offers us through Jesus.

At the Well

Though it was the hottest part of the day, the woman went to the well at this time perhaps because she was sure to avoid the other women of the town. She knew all too well the condemning glances and not-so-subtle comments the women would make when they saw her. She had experienced her share of rejection. Deep down she felt she deserved it, so she didn't blame them. If she were one of them, she would ostracize her too. Life had not turned out the way she had thought it would, the way she had dreamed of it as a young girl. But now she found it didn't really matter. She had gotten used to it. Her mask was in place. Her heart had callused over a long time ago. It was better that way. Better not to feel the rejection when it happened.

She had grown accustomed to going to the well by herself, but little did she know, today she would have a divine appointment. As she approached, she saw a man sitting there. He looked very dusty and tired from his travels. Was He alone? She didn't notice anyone else around. She could see that He was Jewish. She braced herself for whatever He might say to her, if He even acknowledged her presence at all. Jews did not like Samaritans—the animosity was age-old. Even though ethnically they were "cousins," Jews avoided contact with Samaritans at all costs. She was a Samaritan and a woman—and a notorious woman. Three strikes against her.

As she gets closer, she plans to just slip by, draw her water, and leave, trying to be as inconspicuous as possible. But then, He smiles. "Give Me a drink," He says (John 4:7). She is startled. The man has spoken to her, and without any disdain. Something about Him seems different; He doesn't seem to have the prickly personality of so many men she has known. His face doesn't reveal any disgust. He seems very pleasant, even kind. He seems . . . approachable.

And He asked her for a drink of water. A Jewish man asking something from *her*? She isn't sure how to interpret His words. There in the noonday sun, He is asking her to do Him a favor. To soothe His thirst.

She asks, "How is it that You, being a Jew, ask me for a drink since I am a Samaritan woman?" She points out their differences. Doesn't He realize He shouldn't be speaking with her?

But rather than answer, He begins telling her things she doesn't understand. "If you knew the gift of God, and who it is who says to you,

'Give Me a drink,' you would have asked Him, and He would have given you living water." What kind of talk is this? It confuses her. What does He mean?

Being practical, she points out the obvious—the well is deep, and He has no bucket with which to get water, so how can He get her any of this "living water"? Besides, is He presuming to be greater than their ancestor and father Jacob, who dug the well long ago?

Patiently He begins to explain. He tells her that everyone who drinks from this well will get thirsty again, but if they drink the water that He offers, they will never thirst. His water will become like a spring on the inside, welling up to eternal life.

She doesn't quite get His meaning. He is trying to point her to a bigger picture, but she isn't seeing it. What she does like is the idea of not having to keep coming back to the well in this heat, exposing herself to public humiliation. So she says, "Sir, give me this water."

"Go, call your husband and come here," He tells her. Now this is a dilemma. What should she do? Technically she isn't married. She will have to explain. She supposes she has nothing to lose. Everyone knows about her anyway. "I have no husband," she replies.

Then this man stuns her. He looks at her kindly and says, "You have correctly said, 'I have no husband'; for you have had five husbands, and the one whom you now have is not your husband; this you have said truly." He calls out her sin. He exposes her past. He states it all matter-of-factly. He doesn't condemn her. He doesn't demand that she change. He doesn't say, "Get your act together." He doesn't even call her what she is, a sinful woman. Rather, in kindness, He confronts her with herself. This is the first step in any relationship with God. We see ourselves for who we are, sinners. Seeing ourselves is what makes His acceptance so profound.

The woman is astonished and looks around. Who told Him this information? Those town gossips! But the two of them are the only ones there. She realizes she has been more honest than she intended. She surprised even herself in speaking the words out loud to this stranger:

"I have no husband." But there is something about Him—an honesty, a sensitivity. Something that makes her want to trust Him. "Sir," she says, "I perceive that You are a prophet."

Immediately, steering the conversation away from her own life, she begins a theological discussion. Of all things, she wants to talk about the proper place to worship! Samaritans worship here, Jews worship in Jerusalem . . . But the man is undeterred. He explains that the place of worship doesn't matter. His is not a neat theology. It has nothing to do with place or status or rules or regulations. It has everything to do with the Spirit. It has everything to do with truth. God looks for people who worship in honesty and transparency: "Those who worship Him must worship in spirit and truth."

She hears what He is saying, but she is not quite clear on His meaning. "I know that Messiah is coming," she says. "He will explain it all to us."

Suddenly, without warning, He tells her who He is. In a rare moment, He identifies Himself as Messiah and to an outcast, an outsider. He wants her to understand. He says, "I who speak to you am He."

Freed from Shame

This woman's life is changed! She is so excited about what Jesus has told her that she leaves her water jar and runs back to the city to tell the people—the same people who have rejected and ostracized her—to come and see the man who has lovingly exposed her for who she is and has shown her who she can be. She asks, "Could He be the Messiah?" The townspeople are curious. What could the man have said to this sinful woman? What could've made her so open, so free? A sinful woman whose life had been one of shame, darkness, and covering up? They go out to the well to see and hear for themselves.

The woman had come to the well with one need, and Jesus confronted her deepest need—her need for wholeness through forgiveness and acceptance. He offered her a new beginning—hope. He offered her truth. But how did this woman embrace Jesus' forgiveness? We do not read that Jesus tells her she is forgiven. He simply calls attention to her shameful past, to her sin. Sometimes that is all we need. His presence, His acceptance, His truthtelling are enough to bring conviction—to remind us that if we just turn to Him, we can be free.

What we do see in the story is evidence of an inward change in this woman's life. She puts aside the hurt and opens her heart to Jesus. She puts away her shame and marches back into town. She puts away the rejection of others and invites the townspeople to come experience Jesus. She becomes an evangelist! She who once slinked through the shadows is now calling to everyone, "Come with me!" Shame no longer has power over her. Her encounter with Jesus has released her from shame. She has let it go.

Shame is tied to the belief that we cannot be forgiven. We've been humiliated. We've blown it. We don't measure up. We're not adequate. We don't make the grade. In shame, we resign ourselves to the outsider's posture—the same posture this woman would have assumed in her life. But God's forgiveness takes us out of shame's prison and into freedom. This woman is telling other people what Jesus said to her. She's talking about the Messiah. Because of her testimony and the apparent change in her life, many people believe, and Jesus is given a greater ministry in that area. This woman—this sinful, rejected woman who supposedly had ruined her life with her choices—changes the course of history.

Take His Free Gift

Here was a woman who saw herself as unworthy and inadequate. Jesus didn't see her that way. I often tell people that Jesus was very hard on the self-righteous religious people of His day but very tender with those who committed sexual sin. This woman had attempted to satisfy her deepest felt need for acceptance and love in all the wrong ways. The more she tried to fix it, the worse she made it. She must've experienced rejection and abuse at the most profound levels. With each man she met, her hopes would rise—would this be the one to satisfy her longing?—only to be dashed as yet again she was mistreated or turned away. She went from one man to another until, finally, she gave up and settled for so little.

But Jesus knew it all. He knew her wounded, longing heart. He didn't see her at her end. He saw her the way she could be—as whole. He saw her the way He created her to be. He accepted her where she was and addressed her deepest need without reproach. He didn't make excuses for her. He didn't say, "Bless your heart, you've had a hard childhood. Your father ran off, and it's understandable you're at this place in life, looking for love." He didn't say that. But He also didn't condemn. Like the father in the prodigal story did for his son, Jesus met the woman where she was, loved her in that place, and then released her from shame with His grace so she could move forward.

Jesus' love and grace broke principles over people, not people over principles. We tend to do the opposite. People need the safety of grace-filled acceptance, but so often we feel as if we have to change them before they can enter the doors of the church. We want them to fulfill steps A, B, and C. We want them to say certain words or phrases before we acknowledge them as "good." I love and support God's church. I believe it is His instrument for expanding His kingdom on earth. But I am afraid some of our churches can create an atmosphere in which sinners do not feel welcome. It should be just the opposite! The very first premise for our coming to church is that we need help. We are all sinners saved by God's grace. Unfortunately, it seems as if once we get in church, we begin to believe all the sinners are on the outside. We get comfortable sitting in those pews, and over time we convince ourselves that we are not the broken ones. We are not the Samaritan woman in need of grace and forgiveness. Those people are off somewhere else. But Jesus knows us intimately. He sees us right where we are with our brokenness, with the sin we can't seem to quit, and with the guilt and shame weighing us down. He sees us, and He doesn't condemn us. He is offering His forgiveness and His grace.

Scripture tells us, "God so loved *the world* [Your name] that he gave his one and only Son, that whoever believes in him shall not perish but have eternal life. For God did not send his Son into the world to condemn *the world* [Your name], but to save *the world* [Your name] through him" (John 3:16–17 NIV, emphasis added). God sees you where you are and is offering you the forgiveness He has already provided. It is a free gift. Take it. Embrace it as your own.

POINT OF FOCUS

If we confess our sins,
He is faithful and righteous to forgive us our sins
and to cleanse us from all unrighteousness.

1 John 1:9

Realize His Restoration

chapter ten

S HE STOOD OFF to the side as I greeted the people who had come to the front of the auditorium after my talk. She was a young woman, dark-haired, not very tall. Her eyes were sad and revealed unspeakable pain. As I spoke to the people in line, she waited, keeping her distance, quietly withdrawn. Once the others had finished, she approached me, whispering as she talked, afraid someone might overhear our conversation.

Sadly, her story was not all that unusual, and it had shattered her life. Her husband had had an affair. She was so humiliated and hurt and angry. She would show him! So she went out and had her own affair. Now she was being crushed under the load of guilt, regret, and remorse. Why had she done it? She wished she could go back and undo it. She desperately wanted her life back. What could she do to recover? She just wanted to feel normal again.

Living Forward

While normal can mean something different for everyone, we can intuit what this young woman meant. Her life had been wrecked. Her heart had been wrecked. She wanted the pieces put back together. She wanted wholeness. She wanted restoration.

Restoration is the process of being put right. The word *restoration* implies a return to the way things used to be, but it means something more. A restored work contains the original, but the original has been perfected, made better. When you restore an old house, you are not making it exactly what it used to be. That time is past. Many of those original materials have rotted or fallen into disrepair. But the house has good "bones," and the restoration workers build on what was there so that now the house is not only repaired but improved. The restored house is an updated version, a more workable version than the original—it is something that will be of good use now and in the future.

The woman who shared her story with me wanted to experience this kind of healing. She wanted to see restoration *realized* in her life. The word *realize* can suggest an awakening on our part, a new awareness. We observe changes, even subtle changes, in our lives, and we realize God is at work. We see the damaged places in our hearts healing up. Things that used to sting or wound don't seem to have the same effect they had when we were fresh in our brokenness. We see God renewing relationships and other aspects of our lives. We realize He is restoring us.

But *realize* can also suggest something we do. To realize means to accomplish. God restores us, but we realize His restoration—we demonstrate it—as we live it out. We do something with our healed lives. We embrace God's restorative work. We bear it out or manifest it as we live. You can restore an old house and let it sit there, or you can move in and inhabit that house. You can enjoy it. Live in it. Make it a home. Open it up to others. God restores us so that we can live out, or realize, our restoration from day to day. So that we can be of good use both now and in the future.

When you embrace God's forgiveness, you are freed to go forward, but when you realize His restoration, you are *living* forward. After I experienced the healing work of God's grace in church while staying with my parents in Montreat, I went back to Virginia to start living again. God worked in my life during those years to rebuild my emotional strength, to deepen my spiritual life, to teach me to love others with more compassion, to repair my confidence, and to show me what gifts and talents He had put in me. He gave me work. He gave me opportunities to help others. He strengthened my relationships. I worked through the process of counseling. I made more mistakes, sought God's forgiveness, and let Him restore me again. Restoration in my life has been an ongoing process. Not an easy process. But with every step I take, I am realizing God's restorative work. I am living it out as He continues to accomplish it in me.

At this time in my life, I can see the way God's restoration has carried me into the ministry I founded, Ruth Graham & Friends. God has taken my experiences, my failures, my sins, and the hurts I suffered, and He has transformed them into tools I can now use to help other people in a more concerted, focused way. Through conferences, our Ruth Graham & Friends team comes alongside churches and communities to make God relevant for real life. We address some of the tough, life-controlling issues that many churches do not have the resources to tackle, including divorce, loneliness, addiction, anger, depression, domestic abuse, abortion recovery, pornography, homosexuality, and body image. Our desire is to model transparency and to offer Scripture-based hope, ministering God's grace to every life.

God does not waste anything. His transformation of our hurts and failures into qualifications we can use to help other hurting people is the heart of His restoration. We are here to love God and to serve others. God makes our pain into something that works not just for our good but also for the good of those He uses us to help (Romans 8:28). I can now thank God for the way He uses my past hurts. Had I not suffered, I would not have the same heart for others who are suffering. I would not have been able to relate. I would not have known that people sit in the pew with a broken heart. I would have taken others' masks at face value. But I know firsthand about heartache and masks, and part of realizing my own restoration is letting God use me as part of His restoration process in someone else.

Remorse and Regret

As we realize God's restorative work in our lives, we should not be surprised to find ourselves in a battle. We already know we have an enemy who wants to keep us right where we are—broken, stuck, unable to move forward, hopeless about the future, resigned to living in the ruins. On top of that, while we can embrace God's forgiveness and experience the freedom of forgiveness, as God restores our lives and puts the pieces back together, we can also find ourselves getting trapped in remorse and regret. Have you known that experience? Remorse and regret are akin to our old companions, guilt and shame, and as with guilt and shame, we must learn how to win the battle with these so we can move forward into more of God's purpose.

What is the difference between remorse and regret? Merriam-Webster's defines *remorse* as "a gnawing distress arising from a sense of guilt for past wrongs."[1] *Regret* suggests sorrow and disappointment—more like grief. By these definitions, remorse seems to be the more penetrating emotion. Regret doesn't seem to have the same edge.

Remorse will eat us alive if we let it, but we don't have to do that. Remorse can be productive. It can be part of the conviction experience. We don't have to get stuck there; remorse can lead us to action—to repentance. If we are truly remorseful, we will want to change our behavior. Peter was remorseful after he denied Jesus. The Bible says, "He went out and wept bitterly" (Matthew 26:75). Afterward, as we will see later in this chapter, Peter accepted the leadership role Jesus gave to him, and he testified about Jesus for the rest of his life. Peter's remorse worked for him. It drove him to different behavior.

I remember a time when my brother made me angry. I strongly disagreed with what he was saying, and I thought he was being unreasonable and stubborn. I was tired, having just driven for several hours, and he was on my last nerve. We were on the phone, and finally my frustration reached its limit. I blew up, saying things I should not have said and in a way that was not Christlike. After I hung up, God began to speak to my heart. He convicted me about my harsh words and tone. Then remorse set in—a "gnawing distress"—and I realized I couldn't go on until I had contacted my brother to ask for his forgiveness. I didn't get stuck fretting. I let the remorse and the conviction drive me to act.

Regret, on the other hand, often hangs around in our hearts, becoming something we live with. If remorse gnaws at us, pressing us to act, then regret can hang over us like a fog whether we take action or not. One year I needed a new car. My husband gave me the choice between a common-variety station wagon and a luxury sedan with beautiful, navy blue leather seats. Oh, I wanted that luxury sedan and those navy blue leather seats! But we had just attended the Billy Graham Evangelistic Association sponsored conference in Amsterdam for itinerant evangelists. More than eight thousand itinerant evangelists from all over the globe had come. Some had walked for days to catch a bus or an airplane to the conference. Some had no shoes. Why did I think I needed a luxury sedan? The money could be used to help someone in need. I went back and forth for days with indecision, making my husband and the salesman crazy. In the end, I gave in to my own selfish desire. We bought the luxury sedan, and I regretted it as soon as we drove it away from the dealership. I never was comfortable driving that car. But I did live with it; I didn't take the car back. And the regret just sat there.

More serious regrets can keep us tied to the past and prevent us from experiencing the freedom of restoration. More than hang over our hearts, deep regret can shut us down. Regret can take us down a dead-end street into bitterness and despair. After he betrayed Jesus, Judas was full of regret. To find some relief from the burden, he tried to return the thirty pieces of silver he had been paid for Jesus' betrayal. But when that didn't bring relief, in a depth of regret that led to hopelessness, Judas—in contrast to Peter—went out and hanged himself. While not all deep regret leads to suicide, in regret we can start to believe that because of our sin or failing we will never know joy again. Never have hope. Never know balance. Never make any good memories. Life will be hollow. Hopeless. Broken. Loveless. That is where the woman I talked with at my speaking engagement seemed to be living. That is where I was when I went to my parents' home in Montreat after my personal failure. The pain can be profound.

We Don't Have to Live in Regret

Regret can make us feel worthless—we believe we proved our worthlessness in committing that sin. At the same time, regret can make us seek to blame others and to avoid responsibility for our sin. We want relief. We go around in circles—feeling worthless, blaming others—all the time growing more and more hopeless. We inhabit an emotional landscape that has little to no nourishment, no water in sight, and no life. Like Death Valley, this place is barren. If we stay here, we will wilt and shrivel to nothing. This is not what God wants for us. Regret is not where He wants us to live.

In God's eyes, we have infinite value. No matter how many times we fall, He will never see us as worthless. Scripture says, "But God demonstrates his own love for us in this: While we were still sinners, Christ died for us" (Romans 5:8 NJV). While we were still flawed, still in sin, still messed up, God gave all that He had because He loved us. He would never have given Himself to such a horrible death for worthless junk. He values us. The Bible says we are valued (Isaiah 43:4, 62:4; Matthew 6:26).

Overcoming the feelings of worthlessness that accompany regret is not easy, and Satan tries to hinder us in it. He wants us to believe that God can never use us again. He wants us to think we have outsinned God's love, grace, and forgiveness. He wants us trapped in regret and hopelessness. He wants us to believe our lives are too messed up to be restored. The enemy knows where we are vulnerable. He knows where we live. And he uses us against ourselves—in our thoughts, in our self-talk. He uses our negativity to play on our regrets.

What do you say to yourself in the shower? I do not usually tell myself that I did a wonderful job, that I looked beautiful today, or that I am such a good mother. I usually think that I messed up this task, that the wrinkles are winning, and that I have failed my children in some area. Negative self-talk takes a toll on us, and it isn't honoring to God. It keeps us stuck in the past—and in condemnation. Scripture tells us to think differently: "Finally, brothers, whatever is true, whatever is noble, whatever is right, whatever is pure, whatever is lovely, whatever is admirable—if anything is excellent or praiseworthy—think about such things" (Philippians 4:8 NIV).

Other people or the opinions of others can also keep us in regret. I remember sitting on an airplane some years ago. I was going to speak at a prayer rally and was reading the newest book by one of my favorite authors. As I was reading, I came to a passage quoting a letter the author had received. The writer of the letter explained that he had heard somewhere that Billy Graham and his wife had prayed for their daughter whose marriage was in trouble. The daughter got divorced anyway. If Billy Graham's prayers weren't answered, then why should he, this man, pray? What was the use? Well, you can imagine my shock: I was the daughter whom the letter referenced. I was stunned and hurt. Was I responsible for Billy Graham's prayers not being answered? Was I destined to live chained to my past?

What I learned from that moment, and from other moments in my life, is that I can either stay in regret, allowing my mistakes, sins, and wounds to define me, or I can move beyond them and let God define me. In his book *A Charge to Keep*, President George W. Bush wrote that one of the first political lessons he learned was to never let others define you.[2] That's a good political lesson, but it is also a very good life lesson. How many of us constantly worry about what other people think of us? Or about what they say of us? We let this concern for others' opinions dictate our actions and reactions, influence our decisions, interrupt our dreams, dash our hopes, and erase color from our lives.

Are you always trying to measure up to someone else's standards and ideals? Are you letting the opinions of others keep you tied to your past? I have come to understand that I have an audience of One. If I am trying to please God, if my heart is to trust and to obey Him, then I am right where I need to be. Let people say what they will. I used to think everyone was talking about me. The truth was they were too busy talking about themselves! Besides, when people talk about others' failures and mistakes, it is usually so they can feel better about their own. I have since learned to let God be my vindicator. The Bible says, "I [the Lord] choose the appointed time; it is I who judge uprightly" (Psalm 75:2 NIV).

God wants us to love ourselves. Not with arrogance or pride but with a confidence that we are valuable and loved. God loves us just as we are. He loves us unconditionally, without limits. I love my children. I am sure there are times when they have questioned my love, but I love them dearly. Did they disobey? Yes. Did they get on my nerves? Yes, they did. Did they mess up? Yes, again and again. Did I have to discipline them? Yes, and they will tell you that. Did I have to rein them in? Yes, lots of times. Was I always pleased with them? No. Sometimes I was very disappointed in them (as they have been in me at times). Did any of that change my love for them? No. Absolutely not.

I go back to my parenting analogy. Scripture teaches us that God is like a good parent. We read, "Just as a father has compassion on his children, so the Lord has compassion on those who fear Him" (Psalm 103:13). And: "The Spirit Himself testifies with our spirit that we are children of God" (Romans 8:16). God looks at you and me as a father watching His child struggling to choose right from wrong. God does not berate us. He doesn't stand on the sidelines waiting for us to fall flat. He doesn't turn His back. He is cheering us on. He is active on our behalf. When we do fall, He is standing there to help us up. He loves us regardless. We don't have to live in regret the rest of our lives. We don't have to let it shut us down. With God there is always a way back. He promises us "a future and a hope" (Jeremiah 29:11).

Moving Beyond Regret

We can move beyond feelings of regret and unworthiness with God's help through the Holy Spirit. When we become children of God through faith in Christ, God puts His Spirit within us to help us. The Holy Spirit teaches, guides, and comforts us. He does these things for us as we yield to Him and allow Him to do so. We can block Him with our stubbornness and disobedience, but as the Holy Spirit enables us to move beyond feelings of regret and unworthiness and as we respond, we disarm the past; and we give God's restorative work in our lives more room.

We looked earlier at the principle of embracing God's forgiveness. I believe one of the keys to moving beyond the feelings that chain us to the past is forgiving ourselves. When we release ourselves, the past and our regrets are stripped of their power. They can no longer hold us. We can move forward and realize God's restoration in a greater way.

Learning to forgive ourselves doesn't happen overnight. It is a process much like forgiving someone else can be a process. Releasing ourselves from past mistakes, failures, and sins takes time. It takes effort and God's help. We must renew our minds.

When I was in Montreat with my parents for those months dealing with the fallout of my damaging choices, I battled guilt, shame, and regret with every ounce of energy I had. I was not confident that God had forgiven me. As I shared, I felt unworthy—as if I were a disappointment not only to God but also to my whole family. In the process of dealing with my issues, I eventually embraced God's forgiveness, and I worked very hard to forgive those who had wounded me. But the last hurdle to freedom was forgiving myself.

One day it dawned on me that if the great, almighty God of the universe could forgive me, then who was I not to forgive myself? If the sacrifice He made on the cross is vastly, abundantly, and overwhelmingly able to wipe away the deepest and blackest sins, then what was I doing holding my sin against myself? It was plain arrogance refusing to release myself from the past when God had already done so. The thought actually caught my breath. Was that what I had been doing—placing myself above God? I asked God for His forgiveness for that, and I asked for His help in forgiving myself. As I said, this became a process.

The first step in forgiving yourself is realizing that you are forgiven. If you struggle with this, then I suggest you go back to the previous chapter and spend as much time as you need meditating on what it means to embrace God's forgiveness. God has forgiven every wrong you have ever done, and He provides forgiveness for every wrong you ever will do. As we have discussed, God's forgiveness came at a high price, the life of His only Son. Jesus was betrayed, mocked, falsely accused in an unfair trial with witnesses stacked against him, abandoned by his friends, beaten, scourged, nailed to the cross and left there, bleeding, naked, humiliated, and suffocating—all for you.

If God has given all that to forgive you, then you can forgive yourself. You can choose to do that. That is the next step. You make the decision and say the words, "I choose to forgive myself." Once you make that choice, God by the Holy Spirit inhabits your choice and helps you to live it out. Begin the process of renewing your mind with the Scriptures. Remember, the Bible tells us that we can be transformed by the renewing of our minds (Romans 12:2). We have talked about personalizing Bible verses by inserting our names in them. Study what God says about you. Meditate on verses that tell of His love, His care, His joy, His delight in you. He created you and said it was good. Write your name into those verses and memorize them. Go to verses that affirm God's forgiveness and then tell yourself as many times as necessary that you too forgive you. Ask the Holy Spirit to help you grow in your faith in these truths. Ask Him to lead you out of regret. It can be done with His help!

Cracks and All

God is a restorer—He specializes in restoration. The Bible says He looks with compassion on our ruins. He makes our wastelands, our deserts, like Eden. He promises joy, gladness, thanksgiving, and the sound of singing will be found in us again (Isaiah 51:3). When we are at the bottom—reeling in regret, doubt, uncertainty, and feelings of unworthiness—restoration looks completely out of reach. We know restoration is healthy. We know it is what we need. But we think it is impossible to obtain. We feel God has already written us off, and we are ready to do the same. Think about the Samaritan woman who met Jesus at the well. She had gone through marriage after marriage until finally she reached a point where she no longer even cared if the man she lived with was her husband. She thought she was beyond restoring. But Jesus thought differently. When He looked at her, He saw the work already done.

When the year 2000 came around, I decided to have a millennium party and invited several close friends over for dinner to celebrate the New Year. On my sideboard in the dining room, I had two tall, blue-and-white porcelain Chinese temple jars. As I got up to clear the dinner table, an item on the sideboard somehow was knocked over, and it hit one of the temple jars, cracking it, breaking the rim, and chipping the porcelain glaze completely down the side.

When I tried to pick up the pieces, I cut my hand on the sharp, broken glaze. It was a mess, and though I assured everyone that I was okay and that the jar was okay, inside I felt sick. I had found one of the jars at a local flower store—not the usual place for a blue-and-white Chinese temple jar. Then a few weeks later, when I returned to the flower store, there was another. Not an exact match but close. I was delighted to have a pair. I used them at my older daughter's wedding as vases for flowers in the church, so these jars had great sentimental value to me.

Now I had one perfect, beautiful vase and a partner that was quite the opposite. The break was obvious. It wasn't something I could just turn around to the back and hide. A few weeks later, I was at a brunch conversing with a woman who worked at a local museum. I just happened to ask her if she knew of anyone who repaired porcelain. She did. He was in Richmond. I made an appointment and drove the jar and all the broken pieces to him.

The restorer examined the jar. He said it could be restored but that it would not be exactly as it once was. "I can restore it, but you will still see the cracks," I remember him saying. I told him I understood and left the jar in his masterful hands. A few weeks later, he called to say that it was ready. Eagerly, I drove back to Richmond to pick it up. My once-broken temple jar was now restored, not quite back to its former condition—if you looked very closely, you could make out the cracks—but it was even more beautiful to me.

I thought about what the jar had looked like when it was broken. Many people would have thrown up their hands, believing it had lost its value. It looked ruined, impossible to fix. But because the jar had value to me, I had willingly paid the price to have it restored. I wanted to restore its beauty and function. That is what God does when He redeems us. He sent His Son to pay the price for our restoration because He values us and wants us to be as He sees us: Healed. Whole. Like the restorer who examined my broken temple jar, God looks at us and sees the work completed.

But what about our "cracks" or scars? We can still see them. Does that mean God has somehow done an imperfect job restoring us? Are we damaged? God never does imperfect work in our lives. His work is always the best work. Our cracks are not a liability. They have purpose. They remind us of where we've been and of how far we've come. They also remind us of the pain and warn us against starting down those old paths again. When our faith starts to weaken, when we find ourselves facing tomorrow with fear and uncertainty, our cracks can help us remember God's faithfulness, His ability, His constancy, and His love.

Our cracks are also our testimony for other people. Others need to know what God has done for us. Our cracks can be a sign of hope. They say that we have a story to tell. They make things more interesting. When you see a man with a scar on his face, you may wonder what happened. Our cracks or scars don't have to be menacing and off-putting. God can use them to draw others to us. God weaves those scars into new patterns in our lives for the sake of His purpose, and that purpose involves others. He doesn't restore us just to leave us where we are. He wants to use our lives, cracks and all.

Peter's Restoration

Many of us love and identify with the apostle Peter. We can relate especially to his brashness and impulsivity, but Peter was a multifaceted man of depth who knew Jesus intimately. He walked with the Lord and listened to His teaching. He fished with the Lord. He celebrated and relaxed with Him. Peter was part of Jesus' inner circle. He was with Jesus during the transfiguration and heard God announce that Jesus was His Son with whom He was "well-pleased" (Matthew 17:5).

Peter was the one who declared Jesus to be the Son of God, who passionately declared he loved Jesus so much he would die with Him. Peter was in the garden of Gethsemane with Jesus when Judas betrayed Him. Peter tried to defend Jesus, cutting off the high priest's servant's ear with a sword, and then he looked on as Jesus healed that servant. The other disciples fled and abandoned Jesus after His arrest. Peter and John, at least, followed from a distance.

But then Peter lost his footing. When the pressure was on and his fear got the best of him, he denied Jesus, not once, but three times. Not only did Peter deny Jesus, but sitting around a fire with strangers, he used foul language to swear he didn't know Him. This disciple who had seen so much; who knew who Jesus was, the Son of God; who loved Jesus passionately; who had given up everything to follow Him; who was one of Jesus' trusted confidants—this man still denied Him. The cock crowed three times. And then, the Bible tells us, Jesus looked at Peter.

What must that look have been like? What did it do to Peter? At that point, Peter didn't understand that Jesus would be raised from the dead. Peter must've feared that look would be the last Jesus saw of him—and He would see him as a denier. Surely, Peter feared he would never have the opportunity to tell Jesus how broken he was over what he had done, how devastated, how sorry.

What did Jesus' face reveal? Disappointment? Hurt? Anger? I think He wore a look of tenderness. A look of understanding and grace. A look that said, "Peter, I know you are weak. I love you anyway. I am going through this for your sake, and I am going to use you mightily." Jesus saw what Peter was going to become.

Peter, though, had no way of knowing what the future would hold. He must have been tormented over having no way to repent to Jesus. Talk about remorse and regret! As we learned earlier, Peter went out and wept bitterly. After that, what did he do? What *could* he do? Did he tell the other disciples? Did he cover it up? Did he beat himself up? Did he go into a deep depression? We are not given the details.

We know that after the resurrection, an angel instructs the women who have come to the tomb to go tell the disciples—and Peter—that Jesus will meet them in Galilee. Peter is mentioned specifically. He is singled out. What a reunion that must have been! To come face-to-face with the resurrected Jesus, knowing that He knew it all—the cursing denials. We do not know exactly what happened at that meeting, but we can imagine. Was Peter fearful? Anxious? Surely he repented in brokenness and humility. Surely the Lord's forgiveness relieved Peter's fear and healed his brokenness.

But then what? Jesus had plans for Peter about which Peter had no clue, yet Jesus, as we have discussed, was not living with the disciples in the same way now. He was resurrected. He appeared to them only on occasion. Peter was trying to find his footing in this new, uncertain reality, so he went back to what he knew. Fishing. His comfort zone.

In an earlier chapter, we followed the story of Jesus breakfasting with the disciples after the resurrection, but now I want us to look at the rest of the story in John 21. Let's pick up after Peter and the disciples have eaten their fresh-caught-fish breakfast with Jesus on the beach. The men are fed and satisfied. We can only imagine the depth of wonder and joy they must have felt sitting with Jesus. They are relaxed, tired, and comfortable, sitting around the fire.

Jesus turns to Peter and asks him a question. "Simon, son of John, do you love Me more than these?" (John 21:15).

Here Jesus uses the word *agapao*, meaning a Godlike, self-sacrificial love. *Do you love me with a Godlike love more than these?* Jesus wants Peter's love, his total devotion. But what does He mean by "more than these"? More than the other disciples? More than comforts? Fishing? Nourishment? Activity? Security? The old days? The memories of everything they've done together as a group? *Peter, do you love me more than these?*

Peter answers Him, "Yes, Lord; You know that I love you." Peter does not use the word *agapao* but *phileo*. He is saying, "Yes, you know that I have affection for you like a brother. I've traveled with you for more than three years. I've eaten with you. I've listened to you. I've followed you. Yes, I love you." But Peter is not using *agapao*. He does not claim to have that Godlike, self-sacrificing love. Why? Perhaps Peter changes the word because he knows he cannot do what Jesus is asking. Peter betrayed Jesus. He has proven that his love is not self-sacrificing. Perhaps in an earlier time he would have blurted out, "Yes! I love you with a Godlike love!" Now, in his brokenness, Peter does not presume. His answer is affirmative but not boastful.

Jesus tells him—He commissions him—"Tend My lambs." *Take care of those weaker than you. Watch over them. You now know what it is to be bruised and broken. Take care of the weak, the tender ones.*

What is Jesus doing? He is giving Peter work to do. That is part of

Peter's restoration. Jesus doesn't give us permission to sit out or to let ourselves stay stuck in our regret and remorse. We are not to give up. God won't let us get away with that. After our repentance, He asks us to get right back in the game. He wants us to take that first step forward. He doesn't disqualify Peter because of his failure. He gives him an assignment: "Tend My lambs."

Again Jesus asks, "Peter, do you love me with a Godlike love?" Again Peter replies that he loves Jesus like a brother—he has affection for Him. Jesus tells him, "Shepherd My sheep." *Be a guide. Protect. Guard. Pastor. Care for My sheep. They are precious to Me. I gave My very life's blood for them.* By giving Peter this work, Jesus knows that Peter will have to stay close and dependent on the Holy Spirit.

Then Jesus asks a third time, but this time, He uses Peter's word. *Peter, do you love me like a brother?* Peter is saddened that Jesus seems to feel He must ask a third time, but Jesus is calling Peter back to the place where he went wrong—the place of denial—and giving Peter a chance to affirm his love. It is painful, no doubt, for Peter. He must feel the weight of his failure. He knows himself better now. He knows that he can't love Jesus with a pure, Godlike love.

Peter responds, "Lord, You know all things; You know I love You like a brother, that I have affection for you." I feel a sense of surrender in Peter. This is a confession. *Lord, you know how I bragged that I would die with you. You know how I denied you, not once, but three times. You know I cursed and swore that I didn't know you. You know I'm a coward at heart. When the going got tough, I failed. You know my inability to love you with a pure love. You know my weaknesses, failures, and shortcomings. Lord, you know it all.*

Jesus tells Peter, "Tend My sheep." *Step into your calling. Take care of those I love.*

Jesus is restoring Peter in a way that Peter can understand. By an open fire with strangers, Peter denied Jesus three times. By an open fire with friends, he now has to affirm his love for Jesus three times. Perhaps there on the beach Peter better grasped the depth of his sins. Not just the denials. But the willfulness. The anger. The lies. The misguided passion. He had thought, perhaps, that he could just forget the betrayal, cover it up, and get back to fishing. But Jesus wanted Peter to see where he went wrong. Jesus called him back to face his sin, and Peter seemed willing to surrender.

God Sees Value in Our Brokenness

After denying Jesus, Peter had a wounded heart and spirit, but Jesus saw the value of his brokenness. Jesus knew that Peter was useful in a different way now that he had been broken. Oh, sure, Peter always had natural gifts. He had leadership skills. He could speak in front of a crowd. He was outspoken and knew how to cut to the chase. He could organize a group. He initiated activity. But those things were not what Jesus was after. Jesus was looking for humility. Contriteness. Dependence on Him. Surrender (Psalm 51:17, Isaiah 57:15). Peter's failure did not disqualify him from serving. In God's hands, Peter's brokenness became an asset.

Peter allowed his failures to make him humble and repentant. He was transparent with Jesus and with others. He was surrendered. After all, how did the gospel writers know that Peter had denied the Lord? They weren't there with Peter—the disciples had fled. I think Peter told others himself. He came clean. He confessed and was transparent. He came to know himself, his limitations, and how desperately he needed God. Jesus makes that kind of awareness a qualification for leadership. Peter was going to have to take care of sinful, broken people who had failed and made mistakes.

Jesus was saying to Peter, "Yes, you failed. But I believe in you. I know you love me. I know you're dependent on me. Not only can I restore you to where you used to be, but I can take you further. You will do even more." That is restoration. Jesus met Peter where he was, and He took Peter forward. Jesus wants to do the same with us. We come to him broken. He sees in us what He wants us to become. And He moves us there, cracks and all.

Peter went on to be the first to preach the gospel publicly. He was the mouthpiece for the new Christian community. The disciple whom Jesus called "the rock" was one of the first to endure hostility for the cause of Christ. Peter was the first to declare the gospel to the Gentiles. He was one of the first to be told he would be martyred for Christ. The ministry Jesus gave to Peter must have reached far beyond what Peter expected or dreamed. Remember, he had settled for going back to fishing. But God had something in mind for which Peter had no frame of reference. Peter realized, in both senses of the word, his restoration.

God Makes Beauty Out of Our Broken Pieces

Jesus is comfortable with broken people. If we are honest, we all experience brokenness in life. When we first come to faith in Christ by repentance and confession of faith in Him, we are acknowledging our own brokenness by sin. We cannot fix ourselves. We are all broken—all sinners saved by His grace. As we journey in our faith walk, we make mistakes, fail, and sin. We are broken by life, by the choices of others, and by our own failures. That does not disqualify us from service to God. We tend to think that it does, but failure only underscores our need for God. I think we often lose sight of that. We judge people for their wrongs and then pronounce them unfit. Thankfully, God's qualifications are different than ours. When we have experienced brokenness, we can either hide behind our masks, or we can choose to move forward in dependence on God, which brings Him the glory.

I believe brokenness is a desirable attribute for one who ministers to others. Someone once said, "Don't trust a pastor who doesn't limp." I know I cannot relate to those who tell me they are always victorious, always happy, always in step with God. I don't live there! I know I am flawed. I know God continues to work on me. I don't seek to minister out of perfection but out of my human imperfection. That is where God's strength can be found—in my weakness. I know He has used my broken places to enable me to better relate to people—and them to me—and to bring Him glory. He uses our brokenness as we give it over to Him in dependence and surrender.

A. W. Tozer wrote, "It is doubtful that God can use a man greatly until He has hurt him deeply."[3] Many people have not failed as I have—willfully sinning, altering my life. They are blessed. But more and more, I believe that brokenness, however we each experience it, is God's requirement for our being used in effective ministry and for His purpose.

Moses was raised in Pharaoh's palace. He was politically savvy. He had connections, power, and respect throughout the land. Surely, he was qualified to lead the nation of Israel out of bondage. But Moses murdered an Egyptian, and God sidelined him. Instead of placing Moses at the head of the chariots, God put him on the back side of the desert to tend sheep. Moses was broken. A has-been. He stayed that way until he was eighty years old. He must have believed he had been disqualified forever, but that was not at all what God intended. In Moses' brokenness and humility, God had been forging him into the leader who would change the history of the world.[4]

Perhaps you have experienced brokenness in life that has left you feeling like a has-been. Perhaps you feel like Moses, living on the back side of the desert. Perhaps you've resigned yourself to staying there. You can't imagine God ever wanting to do anything beautiful through your broken life. I want to encourage you to open your heart and ask the Holy Spirit to help you hope again. God has good plans for you. Plans to give you a future and a hope. Remember—God doesn't waste anything.

In his book *Reaching for the Invisible God*, Philip Yancey tells the story of the west window of Winchester Cathedral in England.[5] I have often used my own folksy version as an illustration. As the story goes, during England's Civil War in the 1600s, Oliver Cromwell's soldiers broke the cathedral's gorgeous stained-glass windows. The cathedral was the center of the town's civic, social, and spiritual life. It was the heart of the community. When the soldiers came storming through and smashed the windows to bits, the townspeople fled in fear. Once the soldiers had gone, the people crept out to see what had happened and found their beautiful cathedral ruined. The life had gone out of the town.

But not exactly. The people of Winchester surveyed the damage and began to pick up the pieces of what was left of their precious windows. Broken bits and pieces. Shattered hopes and dreams. Maybe one little lady gathered some of the broken glass from the windows and put it under her bed. Maybe a farmer picked some up and stored it in his barn. They saved what they could, not necessarily because they could envision a use for it, but as a reminder of what used to be.

Years later, enough money was collected to repair the windows. An artisan was hired, and he arrived with his plans and drawings and set to work. Then one day he had an idea. He stopped and asked whether anyone had some of the glass from the broken windows. The farmer said he had some in his barn. The little old lady said she had some under her bed. The artisan asked them to bring the pieces to him. Townspeople came streaming in with their sacks of glass, and the artisan used what they brought to do the work of restoration.

When you look at the cathedral's west window today, you can see it looks remarkably modern and abstract. You can't make out a pattern in the colored glass. No saints or Bible stories are depicted. The window is a mosaic of fragments, beautiful and distinctive. When the sun shines through, it reveals a kaleidoscope of color.

This is what God does with our broken lives—He restores them. He has done it for me, and He will do it for you. Bring Him your broken pieces, whatever they are. He will take them and create something beautiful and distinctive that He can use for His glory. Our restoration is just that—that He uses us. We come to Him in pieces. He crafts something beautiful. And He uses that beauty to heal a broken world.

POINT OF FOCUS

"For I know the plans that I have for you,"
declares the Lord, "plans for welfare and not
for calamity to give you a future and a hope."
Jeremiah 29:11

Enjoy His Affirmation

chapter eleven

IN THE FALL of 1994, I traveled with Samaritan's Purse to Kenya, Zaire, and Rwanda. The trip came some months after my transformative experience of God's grace in Montreat. I had now returned to Virginia to rebuild my life. I had reenrolled in college to finish my undergraduate degree. I was working with a counselor. And I had taken a job as a donor-relations coordinator with Samaritan's Purse, the international Christian relief organization my brother Franklin serves as president. The trip to Africa was meant to be a look-see so that I could better explain to donors what the organization was doing in Central Africa, but mainly in Rwanda, which had just seen the end of its bloody civil war between Hutus and Tutsis. I was scheduled to spend ten days there and then go on safari.

Once we arrived in Kigali, Rwanda's devastated capital, however, we learned that the timetable for relocating a group of orphans to a former agricultural school campus had been accelerated. The school campus had been the site of slaughter during the war, and evidence of genocide was still in plain view. I realized there was no way I could leave the Samaritan's Purse staff doing such critical work and go on safari. The staff readily accepted my offer to stay and lend a hand. They needed all the help they could get to clean up the gore. Bone fragments were scattered in the yard. A skull was in view as I looked out the kitchen window. Blood stained the walls of the buildings. We learned that the house where we were staying had contained rotting corpses, and the smell of death still lingered. It was a mess.

Every morning before setting out to perform our sometimes grisly duties, the team held devotions around the dining-room table. One evening I was asked if I would lead devotions the following morning. I was anxious—I didn't want to lead devotions. I wasn't an official member of the team. I was still recovering from brokenness in my personal life. I didn't believe I had anything to offer. What would I say? I believed they had asked me because I was Franklin's sister and Billy Graham's daughter. Perhaps they thought it would be natural for me to lead devotions. They didn't realize the idea struck fear in my heart. I had to rise to the occasion, and I didn't feel that I had anything to rise with.

But that morning as I was having my private time with the Lord, He gave me a verse to share from Genesis: "After these things the word of the Lord came to Abram in a vision, saying, 'Do not be afraid, Abram. I am your shield, your exceedingly great reward'" (Genesis 15:1 NKJV). This verse begins God's covenant promise to Abram (Abraham) to give him a son and to make him the father of innumerable descendants. Step by step I walked with the team through the verse.

Do not be afraid. Though we were not working in a necessarily dangerous situation, we were working in what I might call a tense situation. There was an uncertainty about the day as we all scattered to do our different tasks. Violence was still occurring in the countryside. The peace was shaky at best, and we were ever mindful that this was not by any means a settled situation. Some of our teammates had been detained at gunpoint for several hours. And yet, what did we hear God saying through this verse from Scripture? He was saying, "Fear not."

I am your shield. Here God was giving us the reason we were not to be afraid. He was with us. He was our shield. He would protect us.

I am your exceedingly great reward. We were not serving for a reward, and yet God promised us one. What was that reward? The Rwandan people could not reward us for what we were doing. We were not being greatly rewarded by anyone financially. Our reward for the work we performed was going to come from God Himself. God Himself *was* our reward. He was our refuge, strength, peace, wisdom, and guide.

Reward would also come in knowing that we had made a difference in people's lives—people who at that point were helpless and in desperate need of everything we could name. We were there as Jesus' ambassadors not only to clean and to scrub but also to lend hope, courage, and all the things a relief organization offers. We were doing eternal work. That did not mean each day was a spiritual high. I was not aware of any personal spiritual growth at the time. I was just putting one foot in front of the other, trying to be helpful and expecting God to show me what to do next. But as I look back, I can see how God was rewarding me with a deeper understanding of how He works through other people in the face of incredible need and how serving others encourages personal healing.

Abram goes on to say, "Lord God, what will You give me, seeing I go childless?" (Genesis 15:2 NJKV). Abram knew he didn't have it in himself to make God's promise for his life and his posterity come to pass. He was old and childless. As a team, we did not have in ourselves what we needed, either. The work was physically, mentally, and emotionally exhausting. Our task seemed overwhelming. The needs were incredible. Death. Disease. A land raped and ruined. The lack of basic services. Destroyed homes and neighborhoods. Black-market goods at sky-high prices. The tales of horror were hard to comprehend as we listened to people tell of being maimed or of hiding for fear of their lives as neighbor turned against neighbor. Nothing, no one, was untouched by the violence. How could we hope to help in a lasting way? We knew it would have to be God's work, and we simply had to rely on His promise: He would be with us. He would strengthen us. He would help us.

When I had finished sharing, I felt great peace. I realized God had given me the opportunity to lead devotions in order to reveal more of Himself to me. He had called me to lead in my inadequacy so that He could be adequate. The message was coherent and spoke so directly to what we were doing that I knew it had to have come from Him. It was relevant. And it encouraged us. It encouraged me. I realized that in stretching me to serve the team, God had affirmed me. He had affirmed *Himself* in me. At a time when I felt like a bruised reed who, though recovering, was still weak, God affirmed me by choosing to use me in that small way. He was letting me know I was valuable to Him—not only by giving me the chance to lead devotions but also by allowing me to be part of the team there in Kigali, making a difference.

God's Affirmation

The way God affirms us can be very different from what we expect. We expect pats on the back or encouraging words from others, but God will turn around and say, "I am going to use you more." He affirms us as He uses us.

Often after I finish with a speaking engagement, I am encouraged by affirmation from people. God certainly uses people to affirm us—the words of others can be of great value in spurring us on. So can our accomplishments; they can make us feel competent and give us a sense of worth. But affirmation from people and from our achievements can have a relatively short "shelf life." People can die. They can change. They can betray or reject us. Achievements can fade—you have to keep producing in order to stay ahead. To the world, an author is only as good as her latest book or an actor as great as his latest movie. It is when God chooses to use me again that I experience a lasting affirmation.

As I get ready to speak at events, I ask God to flow through me. I pray, "Lord, I empty myself, and I ask You to fill me with Your Holy Spirit. Please minister Your grace to those here." I often feel so inadequate in these moments—I do not have it in me to do what God needs me to do. "Please do it again," I ask Him. And He does. God does His work, and He chooses to take me along for the ride. What incredible affirmation! When Solomon was preparing to build the temple, he declared God's greatness and said, "Who am I then, that I should build Him a temple, except to burn sacrifice before Him?" (2 Chronicles 2:6 NKJV). That is how I feel about being a small part of what God is doing in the lives of others.

If we let it, our sense of inadequacy can hold us back from saying yes to God and experiencing the affirmation that comes in partnering with Him. As I have already mentioned, the messages we receive on a daily basis do not affirm us. The subliminal messages of advertisers tell us that unless we use their products, we are falling short. Our self-talk can belittle us. Our enemy accuses us and reminds us of our failures. On balance, we can feel as if we have a deficit of affirmation.

As a result, we develop feelings of inadequacy—or *greater* feelings of inadequacy. We worry that we won't measure up to the standards that we, or others, have set. Were the folks in Kigali expecting a profound message from me due to my family affiliation? Was my fear of taking on the challenge based on what I believed they expected? We may try to convince ourselves that we are not inadequate. We may try to pretend that we can do it all. But inside, we may be trembling, afraid, and anxious—as I was in Kigali—that our inadequacy will be discovered.

That persistent feeling of inadequacy can prevent us from moving forward with God. It can cause us to shrink back. This is one of Satan's tricks. He cons us into thinking we are inadequate for the task so that we don't take it on. Or so that we quit before we really get started. I could have easily declined the offer by the Samaritan's Purse team to lead devotions. But I would have missed God's affirmation.

As it was, God stretched me beyond my comfort zone and asked me to push through my sense of inadequacy. I could only move forward by relying on Him to use me for His purpose that morning. He taught me His sufficiency. I experienced it for myself. I learned that it didn't have to come *from* me but *through* me. As I said, God affirmed me. He affirmed Himself in me.

Can you see why it is so important that we constantly renew our minds with the Scriptures? God has written us a letter of affirmation. He tells us what He thinks of us. We need that truth to seep down into our souls so that it has more influence over us than any other messages. I don't want fear and inadequacy holding me back from all that God has for me. I want to be able to stand on His truth about me and rise to the occasion when He calls me—to step out in trust and participate in His work, whatever it may be.

There is an energy, a joy, that comes with being used by God to serve other people. When I am traveling to our Ruth Graham & Friends conferences, I often find I am weary before I get there. My mind is cluttered. I don't feel focused. But once I arrive and step into the work, I feel an energy kick in. It is not an adrenaline rush. It is an energy that comes from God—and from knowing that God is using me to minister to others through the gifts He has given me. I love what the runner Eric Liddell says of God in the film *Chariots of Fire*: "When I run I feel His pleasure." When I am exercising my God-given gifts and talents in the service of God and others, I find an energy and a delight that carry me forward. Once I finish, I am drained and need to rest. But in those moments when I step out to be used by God, He honors my willingness and enables me to accomplish what He has given me to do. The experience is fulfilling and satisfying like nothing else.

How many of us wonder, "What is my purpose? What am I supposed to be doing?" God answers those questions when He places responsibility in our hands and empowers us to fulfill it. He invites us to participate, if we will only say yes. We read about Jesus inviting Peter and the other disciples to breakfast, saying, "Go get some of the fish *you* caught." Jesus called the disciples to participate. He was the one who enabled them to catch the fish—He told them to put the net on the other side of the boat. But the disciples got to partner with Him in it.

They said yes. They obeyed and moved the net. They hauled the fish to the beach. They contributed to the breakfast. In doing these things, they were experiencing God's affirmation. They had stepped into the flow of what Jesus wanted them to do. Were they tired from having been out fishing all night? I would imagine so. But I would also bet they came alive when they recognized Jesus and began to partner with Him. Joy comes that way. When we recognize God's affirmation and step into it, we discover His joy.

Participating in the Miracle

By the time of that breakfast on the beach, the disciples were old hands when it came to partnering with Jesus. They'd had plenty of practice. He had been asking them to participate from the beginning. Let's take an example from the middle of Jesus' ministry. Jesus has already met the Samaritan woman at the well, calmed the storm, healed the woman with the issue of blood, and worked many other miracles. The disciples have witnessed it all, and now they are being sent out to minister themselves.

In Luke 9, we find that the disciples have just come back from a trip. Jesus sent them out, and as far as we know, they did a good job. They traveled through villages and towns, preaching and healing the sick. When they got back to Jesus, they reported to Him what they had seen and done. No doubt they were on a spiritual high—elated at having witnessed God at work through them. But surely they were also very tired. As I have shared, ministering to people is a high privilege for which God gives us the energy, but serving can also be extremely draining. My father has shared about preaching involving a spiritual battle. He would come home from his crusades totally exhausted and often ill. During his 1957 crusade in New York alone, he lost some twenty pounds.[1] Once you are finished pouring out, you need rest.

The disciples were probably in need of time to recover and regroup, and Jesus gave it to them. The Bible says, "Then he took them with him and they withdrew by themselves to a town called Bethsaida" (Luke 9:10 NIV). But the retreat didn't last long. Jesus' popularity was likely at its height by this time, and the crowds started following Him.

How must the disciples have felt when they saw the crowds? Overwhelmed? Discouraged? Jesus too was in need of rest. It hadn't been long since His cousin, John the Baptist, had been beheaded, and Jesus had just heard the news. I can imagine He would have been longing for solitude, quiet, and time to grieve the loss of His beloved cousin. He wanted to talk with His Father. But here came the crowds.

As with Jesus and the disciples, our plans don't always work out as we expect or desire. I might have resented such an intrusion by the people. But not Jesus. He sees them as sheep without a shepherd (Mark 6:34). The Bible says He welcomed them. He had compassion for the people's needs, and He began teaching and healing the sick.

This is the way Jesus works—He is always available. He doesn't leave early or quit on the job. He isn't selfish with His time. We know ministry took something from Him. When the woman with the issue of blood touched His garment, Jesus stopped, saying, "I know that power has gone out from me" (Luke 8:46 NIV). In His humanity, Jesus at times needed to get away. The Bible tells us that He took time alone to pray, to commune with His Father, and to refresh Himself so that He was able to make Himself available to those around Him. But Jesus did not miss opportunities to touch people's lives. He saw interruptions as opportunities. In His willingness, He is picturing God for us. We don't have to make an appointment with God. The Lord extends His invitation to us at all times: "Come."

We read that Jesus continues to minister to the crowd until late in the day. The people have stayed with him all afternoon, listening attentively. Like the disciples, they are no doubt hot, tired, and by now hungry. Right on point, the disciples diagnose the problem. They see the need, perhaps prompted by their own growling stomachs, and they tell

Jesus their solution: "Send the crowd away so they can go to the surrounding villages and countryside and find food and lodging, because we are in a remote place here."

How often I do just what the disciples did in this situation! I tell Jesus my problem. Then I say, "This is the way I think you ought to handle it." Jesus knows the need of the people in that crowd better than anyone, but the disciples jump in and tell Jesus—they don't even ask, they tell Him—what He should do. They think they have things figured out. We're the same way. We get out in front. We rush ahead of God with our ideas. Meanwhile, Jesus has a better plan, and He wants to include us in it.

Jesus turns the tables on the disciples. They say, "Send the people away." Jesus says, "You give them something to eat." *You do it. You take on that job.*

That response must have astonished the disciples. I can imagine the looks on their faces. *You have got to be kidding!* Certainly, they have been learning how to partner with Jesus, but this is a huge crowd of people—five thousand men, plus women and children. Is Jesus really saying, "You do it"? It hadn't even occurred to the disciples that they would have the responsibility here. Their solution was to put the onus on Jesus to deal with the crowd. But what is Jesus doing in shifting responsibility back to the disciples? He is giving the disciples an opportunity to participate in a miracle and thereby affirming them. He is saying, "You can do it." The men don't see it yet, but God doesn't always clue us in ahead of time. He wants us to trust Him.

I can imagine how the disciples must have felt as they stood there looking at the thousands of people. Feeding them must have seemed impossible, and it was impossible. Even if they had gone to a nearby town and spent all the money they had, there would have been no way to provide for all those people. The disciples promptly point out to Jesus that all they have in their hands are five barley loaves of bread and two fish. A crowd of thousands and only five loaves of bread and two fish? A riot could break out!

We limit God in so many ways. Like the disciples, we say, "We can't." Or, "We only have . . ." We only have this much money or this little bit of food in the fridge or this much gas in the car. We are only young people. We are only insignificant folks. *We only have this much, Jesus. What do You expect us to do?* But God is not looking at our "only." God calls us in our inadequacy so He can expand our capacity for ministry. Our "only" gives Him the chance to step in and be more than enough so He can get the glory. Jesus wants the disciples to experience that kind of partnership with Him, but they have their eyes on the circumstances: "Either we give the crowd this little bit of food, or we try to buy some, which really isn't an option." They have no other scenarios in mind. Jesus wants to expand them for ministry. He wants to raise their sights.

Notice that Jesus doesn't even answer the disciples' concern about how little food they have. He doesn't address it. He already knows what He is going to do. Remember the way He handled the Pharisees when they brought Him the woman caught in adultery? Jesus knew what He was going to do then. He knew who He was. He didn't bother responding to the Pharisees' questions. He wrote in the dirt. Here too Jesus knows who He is, and He is preparing for what He will do.

He starts by giving the disciples a task: "Have them sit down in groups of about fifty each." Jesus tells the disciples to organize the crowd. Without some plan of organization, a riot could indeed have broken out. God is a God of order, not of chaos or confusion. What is amazing is that all these people obey. The Bible says, "The disciples did so, and everybody sat down." It is spring time, and I can imagine it was a beautiful day. Mark's account tells us the grass is green (Mark 6:39). Imagine the sight of all those people organizing themselves and sitting calmly on the green grass in their colorful robes and dresses. By this time, they would have been expectant, craning their necks to see what was going to happen.

Then the disciples hand the loaves and fish over to Jesus. I am sure the men were more than a little curious to see what Jesus would do.

The situation seemed fraught with inadequacies and impossibilities. The fish and loaves were peasant food, simple food from a child (John 6:9). The loaves were made from barley grain used to feed animals; the fish were small and dried or salted. But Jesus takes what the disciples give Him. God takes the simple things we offer Him—things deemed insignificant by others—and He uses them. Nothing we put in His hands is too small.

Jesus takes the fish and loaves, and He gives thanks. For the food? For the unselfishness of the one who originally provided it? For what was about to happen? For what the people would learn? For the way God was going to demonstrate His abundance? Surely, Jesus was thanking God for all the above. He lived with grateful heart. He saw God's hand in and behind everything.

Giving thanks is a habit we need to cultivate ourselves. I am fortunate to have grown up in a home of prayer. We never let a morning or evening go by without gathering for prayer. We never ate, even in public, without giving thanks—nothing long or fancy, just an acknowledgement of the good provision from God's hand. I am so grateful for my parents' example, but whatever our background, we can develop grateful hearts. We can imitate Jesus. In giving thanks, we are recognizing our dependence on God for all things.

Once He blesses the food, Jesus gives it to the disciples to distribute to the people. He is using the disciples to meet the needs of others. They are participating with Him. They are the link between Jesus and the crowd. Jesus could have fed the people Himself. He could take care of some of our problems directly too if He wished. But He chooses to use us in the process, if we will let Him. God is extraordinarily gracious to give us a part. If He did it all without us, then we would be unnecessary. God's way is to involve us. He is constantly inviting and including us. As we are learning, He *looks* for ways to include us. Inclusion is His affirmation.

Notice that Jesus is patient with the disciples as He teaches them with practical experience. Their solution was not what God had in mind, but Jesus didn't criticize them. These men had seen the people's need, and they had brought it right to Jesus. How many of us turn to Jesus first when we see a need? Then the disciples were honest as they considered solutions—they acknowledged they did not have enough to meet the need themselves. Neither do we—we are inadequate. Can we admit it? The disciples gave to Jesus what they had in their hands. They did not hold back or try to keep something for themselves "just in case." They released their resources—all they had. This is important. When we are fearful about tomorrow, we have a hard time hearing God, obeying Him, and letting go of what we have—whatever that might be. We struggle to trust. But for all their foibles, look at how far the disciples had come. They might have been weary. They might have doubted. They might have proposed the wrong solution. But they obeyed. They gave Jesus what they had. They trusted Him.

As the disciples trusted, Jesus affirmed them not just by using them but also by giving incredible results. The Greek verb implies that Jesus gave out the food and kept on giving. The disciples would hand out their pieces of fish and bread and then come back to Jesus for a fresh supply. Not until every single person was fed and satisfied did Jesus stop. That was more than five thousand people! All fed. All satisfied. The people ate and their need was met fully, not partway.

Afterward, Jesus instructed the disciples to collect the leftovers. Again, He invited them into the process of a miracle—they picked up twelve baskets of leftover food! I believe Jesus wanted to illustrate that God's supply is abundant. God is not stingy. The disciples filled twelve baskets, one for each of them. As we make our gifts and talents available to God for His use, He provides enough not just to satisfy those He sends us to help, but also to take care of us in the process.

Expanded for Ministry

When God challenges us to serve out of our inadequacy, He is giving us an opportunity to be expanded for ministry. As we come to Him in our weakness, we give Him room to do His work in and through us. He has more room to work. We are not in the way. He can affirm Himself in us. When Jesus told the disciples, "You feed them," they were forced to admit their inability to do it. They were right where Jesus wanted them. Their inadequacy spotlighted His adequacy and caused them to depend on Him. In dependence, the disciples' capacity to help others was expanded—they could meet the need through Jesus' power and sufficiency. The disciples were just servants. That is our role too. As God affirms us and invites us to participate, we give out of the supply that He gives us: an expanding, abundant supply.

Years ago, I went to see my father one Valentine's Day. He was in Charlotte, North Carolina, at the time. I wanted to deliver my Valentine card personally, but even more important, I needed to talk with him. I was struggling in an area I had discussed with him before. He had given me wise counsel years earlier, but now I was back again in the same place. My life had taken another painful turn.

I was very nervous to tell my father, and as I drove, fear began to shake my determination. I felt like such a failure. How could I burden my father again with this issue? How would he react seeing that I had not learned from his wise counsel? All the way, a two-hour drive, I renewed my mind with a verse from Isaiah: "And the crooked shall be made straight, and the rough places plain" (Isaiah 40:4 KJV). I trusted that God was going to prepare the way for me.

When I arrived, my father greeted me warmly. As I told him my difficult news, he listened carefully, and when I was finished, he patiently gave me the same wise advice. He then asked me to come sit beside him. He put his arms around me, held me close, and began to pray for me. He released me to God's loving care, and he asked that God would expand my ministry to others who were hurting. I did not know what that might look like. I had no vision for the future. At the time, I was just trying to survive.

Some time later, a thought came into my mind as I was pulling out of a parking lot. I had been speaking at various events, and yet I believed there were many broken people out there whose issues still needed addressing. I thought, "I need to hold a conference that addresses the difficult issues hurting people face."

It is interesting the way major life decisions can hang on something as seemingly insignificant as an idea in a parking lot. I did not know it, but the work I envisioned in that moment was going to be the river of God's purpose for me. His plan to use my broken life was far bigger than I could have imagined.

As I began to think about the idea of the ministry that became Ruth Graham & Friends, I looked back at my experience of God's grace those years ago in Montreat. At the time, I thought God was making me whole just so I would be whole. After what I had gone through, that would have been plenty. But looking back, I now saw that God had been making me whole the way He made Peter whole as they sat by that fire on the beach. God was restoring me so I would be able to reach others. He was going to redeem my life for His purpose. Even then He was expanding me for ministry. What unfathomable affirmation! That God would redeem me after so many failures. That He would pause that Montreat church service to touch my life and prepare me for His use. That He would continue to redeem me in the years that followed as I continued to make mistakes and fail. As I have shared, God gives amazing, outrageous grace. That is what His affirmation is—it is a grace.

I began to see that my father's "Welcome home" and the grace he showed me during that same period had planted the seeds for the work I now wanted to do. Once I experienced that depth of grace, I wanted to pass it on. Our experience of brokenness is what opens the door for God's grace, and when we have known grace ourselves, we want to give it to others. So many of my wounds had come as a result of my own choices, but God was making those wounds into something useful for other people. I never dreamed I would later start a ministry. The thought didn't cross my mind. My personality didn't fit with that plan. I was the middle child in our family. I was used to blending in to the background. I wouldn't have wanted to start a ministry. After all my mistakes, I would have felt disqualified, utterly inadequate. But through my failures God expanded my capacity for ministry. In my weakness, He had plenty of room to work.

Over time, as I prayed and talked with friends, the idea of the ministry evolved, and eventually we formed Ruth Graham & Friends. Through the ministry, we wanted to create an environment in which hurting people would feel safe dealing honestly with their issues. So many people live with fear, guilt, and shame, just as I have, and we wanted to address difficult issues in a biblical way that would be non-threatening. We wanted the people leading our workshops both to be qualified and to have had experience with the issues, so they could say, "I was here. Now I'm here. This is how God brought me out. This is what I learned. Here are some practical steps."

We sought not just to help the hurting but also to give helping, practical tools to the people around them, those sitting in the pews. As I remember evangelist James Robison once phrasing it in a conversation with me, our desire was to "free the captive and equip the compassionate." So often you or I might know someone who is hurting, but we don't know how to help that person. Either we don't do anything or we do the wrong thing. Our team's goal was to come alongside local church communities and equip them to address the life-controlling issues of our day. Often churches just don't know where to start and don't have the resources. A church staff cannot do it all. The laity needs to be trained and equipped. Later we would include an ongoing follow-up program so that people who attended the conference would have a way to continue to grow when the conference ended.

I remember as I left for our first event in Tacoma, Washington, I was full of anticipation. The feelings of inadequacy and fear were behind me. It was too late—I had jumped out of the boat, and I was very excited to see what God would do. I knew whatever good that happened would be His work; the task was way beyond my own ability. The event was small, but those who attended gave us great feedback and shared testimonies, affirming for me what we were doing. We still had challenges and growing pains ahead of us, but I knew we were on the right track.

We grow in our faith when we see God using us in our weakness. When we look at our meager resources and see God use them effectively, we are emboldened to step out and trust Him again. Our capacity to minister to others *in the future* is expanded. This is what happened for me after those early ministry events. We had stepped out in faith. We did not do everything perfectly, but perhaps if I had spent too much time thinking at the beginning, I might never have gotten off the ground. I might have let fear and feelings of inadequacy hold me back. We stepped out in our weakness. God met us. He ministered to people through us with His sufficiency, and in doing so, He let us know that He is trustworthy, building our faith for the future.

At one event, a woman attending an exhibition in the same building decided to attend our meetings. Afterward she told us, "I came in here and found the answer I needed." That is why we exist as a ministry. Whether a person's issue is anger, loneliness, divorce, abuse, depression, addiction, pornography, or any other of the issues we try to address, we want to love that person, provide practical tools, and invite God to do His work. We are trying to follow Jesus' example and meet people where they are in order to help them take the next steps. Isn't that our calling as followers of Christ? As we are discovering, Jesus met people in whatever condition they happened to be. He didn't try to get them to clean up or say the right words or go down the sawdust trail to get their theology straight. He met them, and He helped them to move forward.

Enjoying His Affirmation

The work God does is all His doing. So often I come away from a conference asking the question Solomon asked: *Who am I that you would choose me to be a part of your work?* (2 Chronicles 2:6) I take the time to acknowledge God's affirmation and to thank Him for it. One of our soloists sings a song called "I Was in the Room": "And I am so overwhelmed how your Spirit moved I am just glad I was in the room."[2] That is the way I feel—I am glad to be in the room when God shows up and does His work. I *enjoy* watching God work through my inadequacy. We are appreciating Him as we enjoy whatever it is He gives us to do.

How do you see God working through your life right now? How is He using you to touch others? How is He using you to touch your family, your children? I encourage you to take the time to recognize what He is doing in and through you and then to enjoy the ways He is using you. His work through you is His affirmation. Be purposeful about enjoying it. Be present. Live in the awareness of His affirmation. At our conferences, I enjoy seeing people use their gifts to minister to people and to serve God's church. I enjoy seeing people respond to the teaching. After all my mistakes, it is wonderful to see God using my life in this way. It doesn't mean I don't face enormous challenges, struggles, exhaustion, and my own shortcomings. But the joy is greater and more lasting. I purposely tap into that joy—the joy of being used by the God of the universe. And so can you!

Perhaps you are experiencing deep feelings of inadequacy and unworthiness in your life at this time. You may feel you have outsinned God's grace. You don't believe God wants to use you. You may have resigned yourself to hiding behind your failure. You may believe it is too late for your gifts, your desires, your dreams. God may have a purpose for other people, but you don't believe He would ever want to work through you. That kind of affirmation seems beyond reach.

Let me encourage you. God sees you where you are. He is a God of grace. He has plans for you that far exceed what you can imagine. The

Bible says He has good plans for us—plans to give us a future and a hope (Jeremiah 29:11). What's more, there are broken people in this world who need what you have. You have walked a road and learned things that God wants to use to help others. He has given you gifts and talents He wants to use for His glory. God not only wants to affirm you, He wants to affirm Himself through you so that others will see who He is. In affirming you, He is revealing Himself to others. That is His desire.

If you do not have a sense of God's purpose in your life, begin to pray that He will show you, that He will begin to move you in the right direction. Be open to the guidance of His Spirit. Ask Him to help you see what He is doing through your life right now—begin to pay attention to ways God is already using you to help others. Be aware of those experiences. Journal them for a record that you can review. Ask God to reveal more of what He wants to do through you. I was in my fifties when God showed me this part of His purpose for my life. Moses was in his eighties. God isn't in a hurry, and He taps us at just the right moment.

Is God asking you to give Him something? Is He asking you to put something in His hands? The disciples didn't hesitate to give God those few fish and loaves. Don't be afraid of your inadequacy—through it God has room for more of Himself. Give God what you have and ask Him to multiply it. Ask Him to make your small gift a part of whatever He is doing.

If you just can't see how God would ever want to affirm you or use your life, let me assure you that God does want to do those things. He does want to use you. He is a restorer. He is a redeemer. He is a grace giver. That is who He is, and you are not exempt. His good plans include you. He may not lead you in the direction you expect. His plans may not be what you think. We look at it from our point of view. God calls us to look at things differently—He calls us to a broader perspective. Ask Him to help you see and enjoy the ways He is affirming you even right now. Ask Him to help you see what He sees: Your ruins restored. Your fish and loaves turned into a banquet.

POINT OF FOCUS

After these things the word of the Lord
came to Abram in a vision, saying,
"Do not be afraid, Abram. I am your shield,
your exceedingly great reward."

Genesis 15:1 NKJV

Grasp His Hope

chapter twelve

A COUPLE OF YEARS ago I had the privilege of speaking in Scotland, the home of my father's ancestors. It was my first trip there, and I fell in love with the country. The people we met were lovely. I was particularly impressed by the number of young people in the audiences—by their attentiveness and excitement about God. We had wonderful times of fellowship. We were also able to do a little sightseeing.

One day we took a bus into Edinburgh and walked up to Edinburgh Castle. It is such an imposing structure. Perched high atop a volcanic rock formed millions of years ago, the castle seems to be a small city of its own. Castle Rock, as it is called, is steep and high. When you stand at the base looking up, you really have to crane your neck. You look straight up the massive rock to a huge, foreboding stone edifice. The scene is inhospitable, repellent. The castle was a fortress, after all. It was meant to keep people away.

But then, as you stand there looking up at the rock and the castle, trying to take it all in, you notice that in cracks and crevices in the rock, pretty little wildflowers are growing. They are just little glimpses of flowers scattered without rhyme or reason. No one planted them; they have sprung up out of what would seem an impossible situation. Those I saw were delicate. I remember seeing blue, some green, a little bit of white, and maybe a yellow. You have to get close to see the blooms because they are so dainty—just little outcroppings of plants every once in a while on this harsh, austere rock—but they are flourishing.

God's Life Is Our Hope

In the most inhospitable, difficult, bleak, barren places, God plants His beauty. He plants his nature. Whatever we are facing, however dark and foreboding, God can plant His nature in it. And that is our hope. When we were dead in sin, God planted His nature in us. He made us alive in Christ. Paul wrote, "Christ in you, the hope of glory" (Colossians 1:27).

God is a life-giver. Life is God's nature. Jesus said, "I am the resurrection and the life" (John 11:25). Resurrection and eternal life, of course, are our ultimate hope. God has promised them to us, and they are ours in Jesus. Our very faith depends on Jesus' resurrection. If Jesus had not been raised from the dead, the Bible says, then our faith would be futile (1 Corinthians 15:13–14). Jesus' resurrection is what secures our hope of eternal life.

In this life, too, Jesus is the resurrection and the life. Our hope is seeing His life defeat the many everyday deaths we suffer. As we are learning, death in our lives must give way in the presence of Jesus. God stands at our tombs and raises what is dead. He plants His life in our ruins (Isaiah 51:3). He makes rivers run in our deserts (Isaiah 43:19). He brings good from our heartache. His promise is life. And that is our hope.

Consider Joseph in the Old Testament. Joseph is an almost perfect character in the Bible, although he seemed to be a pretty bratty teenager! When he is young, Joseph's jealous brothers sell him into slavery. He is taken to Egypt and sold to Potiphar, for whom he works faithfully, becoming the head of Potiphar's household. Then Potiphar's wife becomes attracted to this handsome slave, and when Joseph resists her efforts to seduce him, she falsely accuses him of trying to seduce her. Potiphar gets angry and has Joseph put in jail, where, eventually, he is put in charge of the other prisoners. He makes two friends and interprets their dreams for them. He tells them, "When you get out of jail, please remember me." But they promptly forget him, and Joseph languishes in prison. Talk about somebody who could've built up a head of steam of anger, bitterness, and resentment!

Some time later, Pharaoh has a troubling dream, and no one can tell him what it means. Finally, one of the two former prisoners remembers that Joseph can interpret dreams. Joseph is sent for, and he interprets the dream for Pharaoh. Pharaoh is so impressed with Joseph that he places him as second in command of all of Egypt. God had revealed through Pharaoh's dream that there was going to be a famine in the land, and Joseph begins to prepare the country. Then the famine hits and spreads. The brothers who sold Joseph into slavery come all the way from Canaan to Egypt to find food. They have no idea who Joseph is, but he recognizes them. He could've killed them on the spot and no one would've questioned him. He had every right; he was second in command. But Joseph is not out for revenge. When he finally reveals himself to his terrified brothers, he says, "Do not be distressed and do not be angry with yourselves for selling me here, because it was to save lives that God sent me ahead of you" (Genesis 45:5 NIV). Later he tells them, "You meant evil against me, but God meant it for good" (Genesis 50:20). That is a declaration of the hope Joseph clung to all those many years. It is our hope too.

Joseph's hope was that through all he suffered and experienced, God was still at work. God did not cause the evil, but He took Joseph's trials and transformed them for good, bringing life out of those situations. When Joseph was a slave and then a prisoner, God was using Joseph's circumstances to mold him into the man He could use to change the course of history. Joseph could've rebelled and said, "God, I'm not going to be your man in this place. I'm going to live like I want to live. I'm going to sleep with Potiphar's wife and get ahead the best way I know how." But he didn't respond that way. Joseph let God have His way, and he left the results to God. Now we can see that God used Joseph's painful circumstances to make him into a picture of Christ. Isn't that the hope that we have? When we are experiencing life's hardships, we have the hope that God is at work in us, forming us to be more like Jesus.

Being more like Jesus really is our goal—we want to have the attitude of Jesus in the end. That is God's goal for us too. It gives me hope to know that God uses what I go through to make me more like Jesus. Just to know that it's not wasted. Despite the suffering and difficulties, God's purpose in my life is marching forward. He is working on me. He hasn't given up on me. I am an ongoing, unfinished project. He is going to use whatever I have in order to make me what He wants me to be. He isn't finished. That is my hope. That is our hope.

Hope in God

There is something in our hearts that compels us to hope. We are born with hope; it is part of our spiritual DNA. We hold on to hope even in the face of overwhelming odds. Hoping is like peering over the edge of a hill to see what's on the other side. It is standing on tiptoe. It is looking for the sunrise or expecting a rainbow to appear through a rain shower. The word *hope* is pregnant with desire for a future and the expectation of fulfillment. Hope is what keeps us going. It gets us up in the mornings. Without hope life is not worth living.

Hoping is different from wishing. We wish for a million dollars, for a new house or a new car, for a better score in the game, for a perfect ending. A wish can be flimsy and farfetched. Hope, on the other hand, comes out of the depth of the heart. We hope for a fulfilled life, for peaceful days, for the well-being of our children and loved ones. When we hope, we aren't dreaming or living in a fantasy world; we are expressing our hearts' desires. We may toss the word *hope* around in superficial ways, but true hope has substance. The Bible says, "And now these three remain: faith, hope and love" (1 Corinthians 13:13 niv).

Hope can certainly be dimmed by life experiences. Any number of things can dim hope. A diagnosis of cancer or of another devastating illness. The loss of a job and no responses to résumés sent out.

Rejection. A child bent on self-destruction. An abusive marriage. An addiction that takes over your life. Living under stress for long periods of time. A long battle with degenerative disease. In light of all that happens to undermine hope, we wonder, is the statement "Fear not tomorrow, God is already there" a platitude? After all, beyond what we go through personally, there is a lot to fear these days. We read the news reports, and things just seem to be getting worse. A struggling economy, terrorism, ongoing wars and threats of wars to come. It can be easy to perceive our circumstances as hopeless and to throw up our hands in surrender to fear, pessimism, or cynicism. We can't see God. We can't feel Him. Is God really there in our tomorrow?

That is a critical question, and as we are discovering, it can be answered with a resounding "Yes!" Remember, Scripture promises that God is with us. He will never leave us. In Jeremiah we read, "They will fight against you, but they will not overcome you, for I am with you to deliver you" (Jeremiah 1:19). God knows things will come against us and try to rob us of our hope. But He promises those things will not overcome us, because He is with us. Our hope isn't a whistling in the dark. It isn't pie in the sky. Our hope is based on God Himself. His presence is real.

Job is one of the oldest stories in the Bible. As Donald Miller points out in his book *Searching for God Knows What*, the first message God wanted to tell us was "life is hard, and there is pain, great pain in life, and yet the answer to this pain, or the cure for this pain, is not given in explanation; rather, God offers to this pain, or this life experience, Himself. Not steps, not an understanding, not a philosophy, but Himself. . . . And so from the beginning, . . . God presents life, as it is, without escape, with only Himself to cling to."[1]

Our ability to maintain hope in difficult times depends on what or whom we put our hope in. So often we put our hope in things that can't deliver. The Israelites put hope in the golden calf they created at the bottom of Mount Sinai. They got tired of waiting on God and turned to an idol, hoping that somehow it would do something for them. The Pharisees put hope in their legalism. They thought keeping rules and laws could earn them favor with God. We put our hope in so much that is temporal—in money, in people, in our plans working out. These things cannot sustain hope. The despairing psalmist encouraged himself, saying, "Hope in God" (Psalm 42:11). That is what we must do. When we look to God, we put our hope in the only reliable One.

When my parents built our log-cabin home in Montreat on the side of a mountain, they made sure to drill pilings into the mountain's bedrock. Some years ago, a hurricane dumped over ten inches of rain on the mountains of North Carolina. There were huge landslides as the ground gave way. One part of our mountain, along with its age-old poplar and oak trees, slid away. Had the house not been secured on bedrock, it would have suffered massive damage. But the house was grounded on something reliable—something that would hold.

When we drill down to the bedrock of God's character, we can withstand the damage that life storms bring. We may feel and hear the fierce winds howl, be drenched by rain, and be stung by pelting hail, but we can stand because our foundation is secure. God will not fail us. His character does not change. I think of the words of the famous hymn: "My hope is built on nothing less Than Jesus' blood and righteousness; . . . . On Christ, the solid Rock, I stand—All other ground is sinking sand, All other ground is sinking sand."[2]

Grasping God's Hope

The word *grasping* suggests urgency. It suggests intensity. Grasping is more than holding. It involves reaching out, taking hold, and clasping tightly. That is what we must do with God's hope—we must seize it and refuse to let go. I wonder if that is what Jesus is talking about when He refers to people grasping for the kingdom of heaven, saying, "Forceful men lay hold of it" (Matthew 11:12 NIV).

There is a battle for our hope. Not only does life take a toll on it, but we also have an enemy out to destroy it. If Satan can kill our hope, then we spiral downward, and thoughts of suicide begin to haunt our minds. As I shared earlier, without hope, life no longer seems worth living. But even if the enemy can just dim our hope, we suffer. When hope fades, life becomes gray; there is no color to it. If the enemy can keep us discouraged and hopeless, then we won't be able to live from the heart. We won't have the boldness to step out and try things. We won't be able to love fully. We won't have energy or vision. You can't step boldly into God's purpose without hope. Without hope, the future holds no promise.

I think about the prophet Jeremiah and all that came against his hope. He preached God's message for so long, and no one believed him. He was persecuted for what he preached. He himself grieved over what he preached—the nation's overthrow, exile, and captivity in Babylon. Imagine carrying that grim message around for decades. Jeremiah could've easily lost hope, but he did not. He wept. He is called "the weeping prophet." But he was obedient and faithful to his calling until finally God's Word came to pass. Judah was captured and taken into exile in Babylon, at which time Jeremiah needed hope all the more.

What kept Jeremiah going? Beyond his obedience to God, I believe Jeremiah endured because he fundamentally embraced the hope that God was going to fulfill the other half of the message. Yes, God would exile the people. But He would one day bring them back. He would restore them to their land. That was the hope. God told Jeremiah, "Go buy a piece of property. Your people are going to come back here. That land will be your sign. When you all are in Babylon, build houses, have children, plant gardens, live. But believe what I say: You will come back." Right here in the narrative is where we find that great promise: "For I know the plans that I have for you, . . . plans for welfare and not for calamity to give you a future and a hope" (Jeremiah 29:11). Jeremiah grasped that hope—God's promise of restoration. How? By believing that God could be trusted. By drilling down to the bedrock of God's character.

In the midst of our impossible circumstances, God extends His hope to us. The hope of a future. The hope of restoration. The hope of life in the midst of our ruins. The hope of our ruins being used for our good. No matter how impossible the situation, no matter how hopeless it may seem, no matter how grim the prospects, God can transform it for good. When I saw the repercussions of some of my mistakes and sins in my children's lives, I wept. I had failed myself and them miserably. But I remember telling God, "If you can ever use this mess, Lord, then it is yours." I had no way of knowing what God had in store for me—that I would stand before people each year to tell my story and give hope to others who may feel as I once did. God transformed my mess into something for His glory. He continues to transform it. And as He does, He is fulfilling my hope for restoration, redemption, and resurrection—the promises we have in Christ Jesus.

Part of grasping God's hope is grasping the life that He gives us. The good and the bad. The beautiful and the ugly. Leaning into the pain. Embracing life with the understanding that whatever we face today God can use to build a good tomorrow. We can choose to do what Job's wife suggested when Job lost everything. She said, "Curse God and die." Or we can stand up, take hold of God's hope, and say, "God is with me, and I want to see what's on the other side of this mountain." I remember telling God after I had messed up my life that I still wanted everything He had for me, everything He wanted to teach me through my circumstances. Somehow in my despair, I was able to grasp God's hope for my tomorrow. I wanted to come out looking more like Jesus.

Today as you read this, if you are feeling discouraged, if you are feeling broken, battered, or just simply hopeless, I want to encourage you. God has not left you or forgotten about you. He has planted His hope within you. You can hope again. Bill and Gloria Gaither wrote a wonderful song that I used to play for my children and that they now play for their children. The words are "I am a promise, I am a possibility."[3] Every morning, you wake up to a new day with new potential, new possibilities, new ways to experience God's character, and new opportunities to enjoy this gift God has given you called life! Yesterday's challenges may change into today's promises fulfilled. There is still hope!

Holding On in the Dark

When we endure prolonged challenges, holding on to hope can be extremely difficult. I think of a friend who is battling cancer. Or of family members supporting their loved one in long-term illness. We struggle in the waiting. The Bible says, "Hope deferred makes the heart sick" (Proverbs 13:12). One thing I suffered through the experience of divorce was the pain of having the process go on for so long. The longevity of the hurt is what threatened to suck me under. We can find ourselves struggling for such a long time that we become resigned to it. Hope fades. Expectation fades. The hymn writer Frederick William Faber expressed it this way: "O Lord! I live always in pain, / My life's sad under-song,— / Pain in itself not hard to bear, / But hard to bear so long."[4]

How do we keep hope alive in a protracted struggle? How do we hold on in the dark? It is hard. It takes faith. We have to keep going back to God's character. When there are no answers, we just go back to His character and determine to trust. After all, we do not know what God is doing.

Joseph did not give up all those years while lying in a pit, being sold into slavery, and waiting in a cell. Though no doubt feeling moments of intense despair, he did not choose to let despair overtake him. The prophet Daniel waited twenty-one days for an answer to his prayer—not until three weeks after he started fasting did the angel arrive with a message. Daniel trusted God in the waiting. He wasn't going to give up. My friends prayed for months that their sick granddaughter would survive after birth. When the baby died just a few hours after delivery, I did not know how to console them. What could I write to them to bring some measure of comfort? I wrote to them of God's character. He is wise, loving, kind, and merciful. He knew what He was doing, though I did not understand.

During a challenging period of my life, I beat myself up relentlessly, questioning every action, decision, and choice. As far as I could see, the future held no real promise, nothing but sustained darkness. Still, I kept turning back to God's character, trying to hold on in hope. The process was not easy. It took time. It took the prayers of family and friends. Often I didn't have the strength to pray for myself. When you are hopeless, it is hard to pray. My prayers were faltering at best. But that is when the Holy Spirit intercedes for us with "groanings too deep for words" (Romans 8:26). There are times when I simply groaned. I just trusted the Holy Spirit was praying for me.

How do we hold on to God's character and His love when life storms are blowing all around us? The process requires support. It is important that we surround ourselves with people who will cheer us on and help us. When we are feeling despair, sometimes we have to borrow another's hope. We cannot see the future, so we ask friends to see it for us. They have hope on our behalf, and that keeps our hope alive. Godly friends are a vital ingredient in our walk with Christ, and I am grateful for those who have hoped for me when I couldn't do it for myself. Those friends held up a picture of God's character. They were with me. They were for me. Their presence gave me strength.

It is also important to keep remembering what God has done for us in former days. We have talked about the value of journaling as a way to reinforce our faith. That practice can also help us grasp God's hope. When I was going through hard times, I could not see God's hand. But I would go back to my journals and remember how He had helped me before. When we can see God's hand in our past experiences, we are better equipped to hope for our tomorrows. We grasp God's hope when we refocus our thoughts from what can go wrong to the fact that He can transform our troubles and turn our problems around. We focus not on our mistakes but on His promise to give us a future and a hope.

I once read that one of the biblical words for the verb *to wait* means "to cling" or "to wrap" as a vine might wrap around a tree. Sometimes that is what grasping God's hope becomes—a clinging, a wrapping. And when we are too tired to do even that, we have the promise that "underneath are the everlasting arms" (Deuteronomy 33:27 NKJV). When we finally can't hold on to hope any longer, God Himself holds us.

Many of us live as if we have to earn God's love and support. If we can just do the things that we think will please Him, then He will be somehow duty bound to help us. He will rescue us from bad times. He will fulfill our hope. If we can just do enough for God, then He will be obligated to us. But we don't have to earn God's involvement or His love. God is all-loving and all-gracious. We are in a relationship with One who loves us desperately.

This great God to whom we cling has said He never leaves nor forsakes us. I love His emphatic, resounding promise in Hebrews in the Amplified Bible: "I will not in any way fail you nor give you up nor leave you without support. [I will] not, [I will] not, [I will] not in any degree leave you helpless nor forsake nor let [you] down (relax My hold on you)! [Assuredly not!]" (Hebrews 13:5). We also have the assurance that God does not change—His character does not change. The Bible tells us that the Father "does not change like shifting shadows" (James 1:17 NIV). The basis for our hope is secure.

Even as we reach out to grasp hope, it is important to understand that God sustains our hope. Paul wrote to the Romans, "Now may the God of hope fill you with all joy and peace in believing, so that you will abound in hope by the power of the Holy Spirit" (Romans 15:13). God's character is infused with hope—Paul calls Him the "God of hope." God's will is that we not just survive but that we "abound in hope." I return to what my friend in England said: "God doesn't know how to fill a cup. It always overflows." By the power of the Holy Spirit, God causes hope to overflow in our lives. Though we can cultivate hope, we cannot work up hope. We ask God for it. We ask Him to restore it in us. He is the source of hope, and we receive it from Him. We make the choice to reach for it—to grasp it—and we trust in Him to keep our hope alive.

My mother, who was very artistic, once drew me a pen sketch of an old stump. On first glance, the stump looked dead. But on closer examination, you could see a small sprout beginning to grow out of the stump. She called her pen sketch *Hope*. We are back to the lesson of the Edinburgh Castle Rock. God's life springs up in ways we do not expect. In our dark times, in our drawn-out, demanding struggles, God promises us hope. He does not leave us on our own. Paul writes, "We also rejoice in our sufferings, because we know that suffering produces perseverance; perseverance, character; and character, hope. And hope does not disappoint us, because God has poured out his love into our hearts by the Holy Spirit, whom he has given us" (Romans 5:3–5 NIV). We have Someone with us at all times who can give us the hope for which we yearn. Let us ask the Holy Spirit to help us drill down to the bedrock of God's character and grasp His hope.

A Hope and a Future

I have often wondered how Mary Magdalene felt when she took that long walk to the tomb after Jesus was crucified. It had been three days. Had the grief subsided, or was it even deeper? Each morning when she awakened, was it as if He had died all over again? Was she despairing? No doubt she was confused, as were the others. I am sure the grief was unspeakable. From the time Jesus died on Friday, Mary had been waiting to make this journey. Saturday, the Sabbath, when Jewish law forbids any work, must have seemed a hundred years long. Now it was Sunday morning, and she had gotten up before dark. She went as soon as she could, desperately making her way to the tomb.

Mary had known Jesus and loved Him. She had seen Him nailed to the cross and had watched Him die. Can you imagine watching anyone be crucified, much less your dearest friend? The movie *The Passion of the Christ* gives us a glimpse of the horror of crucifixion. Many people criticized the film because it was so graphic and gory, but Pope John Paul II was reported to have said, "It is as it was."[5] Loving Jesus as she did, Mary watched that horrible scene. I cannot imagine the depth of her despair. She had been helpless. Now she was hopeless.

As Mary walked to the tomb, I imagine her mind was clouded and dulled by her grief. She could not foresee the resurrection. Why was she going to the tomb? Maybe she went to try to sort out her feelings and mourn. Soon after my mother died, I visited her grave on several occasions. It helped to sit there under the trees, listening to birds sing and to the hymns playing softly on the grounds. I am not sure what I expected. I needed a private time of closure. I thought of Mother, my last days with her, and the events that had occurred since then. I thought of things I would love to discuss with her, questions I wanted to ask her. I turned my back to others who were visiting her grave—I tuned them out; they didn't know who I was—and I wept.

Perhaps Mary too went to the tomb seeking some sort of closure. Had her hopes and dreams died with Jesus? Could she even see a future without Him? She was the one who had anointed Jesus' feet with costly perfume, washing His feet with her tears and drying them with her hair. She used to sit at His feet just listening to Him. Adoring Him. Jesus had changed her life—cast seven demons out of her—and given her a new beginning. A new life. Perhaps Mary went to the tomb cling-ing to the memories of what used to be. Just to weep. To feel her grief. To lean into her pain. Maybe she thought being there would make it hurt less.

But when Mary arrived at the tomb, she was shocked to discover that the heavy stone sealing His grave had been moved away from the entrance and that Jesus' body was gone! Immediately, Mary went to those who had been close to Jesus—those who had loved Him and who shared her grief. They would know what to do. When we are grieving, we turn to those who share in our loss. Mary ran to Peter and John, saying, "They have taken the Lord out of the tomb, and we don't know where they have put him!" (John 20:2 NIV)

Hearing this, Peter and John took off running to see for themselves. John got to the tomb first. Perhaps timid and afraid, he only bent down and peered inside. But arriving just behind him, Peter went right in. What the men saw was confusing. The linen grave clothes were lying there as if the body had simply vanished, and the head cloth was off to the side. What in the world? If others had stolen the body, surely they would not have taken the time and effort to remove the burial clothes! What was going on?

Something began to gel in John's heart. He entered the tomb be-hind Peter, and the Bible says, "He saw and believed." What exactly did John believe? We are told the disciples still did not understand about the resurrection, but John believed something. Perhaps all that Jesus had said about rising from the dead began to stir under the surface of John's thoughts. There inside the empty tomb, he stared at the grave clothes, and hope in his heart was born.

We are told that after they looked in the tomb, Peter and John went back to where they were staying. They went home. That is amazing to me. Were they afraid of the Romans? Were they just mystified? Clearly, something important was happening, and yet they left the scene. In-credible.

Mary, however, stayed at the tomb weeping. Not only was Jesus dead, but now there was no body. She just didn't know what to do. Jesus' body was all she had left. His body had been so brutalized and abused—all she wanted was to treat it with respect and tenderness. When you lose a loved one, the body is the visible part of that person. It is what you have left to love. Tending to my mother's body after she had gone to be with the Lord was a sacred, loving act, and I thank God I had that opportunity. Those who have lost a loved one without being able to recover the body can understand better than any of us the horrible emptiness Mary must have felt realizing Jesus was gone. Now she had nothing. No hope at all.

We are told Mary bent over to look inside the tomb. Maybe in her grief, she just couldn't register the reality of its being empty and so she looked again. Maybe something inside the tomb stirred and caught her attention. Whatever prompted her to look, this time she saw something: two angels dressed in white, seated where the body had lain— one angel at the head and one at the foot. Was this a figment of her imagination? Was her mind playing tricks on her?

"Woman," they asked her. "Why are you crying?"

Mary was confused. Her eyes were filled with tears. Her heart was breaking. She answered the angels without seeming to take notice of who they were, telling them what she had told Peter and John—someone had taken Jesus' body, and she did not know where it was. So great was her sorrow that apparently she didn't realize she was conversing with angels. When angels appear in Scripture, they usually greet people, saying, "Fear not." Angels in the Bible are often a fearsome and awesome sight. These angels dressed in white must have been dazzlingly bright, large, and powerful, but all was lost on Mary. She was absolutely overcome with grief. None of this was computing. Her brain had shut down. She just wanted Jesus.

Then Mary turned around and saw Jesus Himself standing there. Her eyes were so full of tears and swollen from crying and she was so overwhelmed with grief that she didn't recognize Him. Try to imagine her state of mind. She had witnessed Jesus' crucifixion. She had seen her dearest, closest friend murdered in the most brutal and vicious way. She saw Him die. He was dead. He had been buried. Now even the body was gone, and she would not have closure. She was undone.

Jesus in His gentle way asked Mary the same thing the angels had asked her: "Woman, why are you crying? Who is it you are looking for?" Her sobs must have kept her from recognizing Jesus' voice. Mary assumed she was talking to the gardener come to tend the garden and check on the new tomb. She blurted out, "Sir, if you have carried him away, tell me where you have put him, and I will get him." What could she have been thinking? How would a woman have been able to retrieve a body? Where would she have put it? Mary was speaking out of raw emotion. She was so absorbed in her loss that everything else was out of focus. She couldn't see the mystery of the grave clothes. She couldn't see the angels for who they were. She couldn't see Jesus or recognize His voice. She didn't seem to remember His words about being resurrected on the third day. Her mind was numb.

Jesus, of course, knew why Mary was weeping. He asked her the question so she could articulate what was happening and what she wanted. Jesus was meeting her where she was—in her deepest grief, in her hopelessness. But He wasn't going to let her stay there. He called her by name: "Mary."

Ah! What a moment! It was His voice. The gentleness. The love. The tenderness. The Bible says Mary turned to Him and cried out, "Rabboni! Teacher!" William Barclay references this as one of the greatest recognitions in all of literature.[6] Maybe it was the way Jesus said her name—in a voice revealing intimate knowledge and lovingkindness. Maybe her sobs had subsided, and she was a little steadier. However the recognition happened, Mary suddenly saw that this was her Lord, her Friend. She had come to the tomb utterly hopeless, and she had met Hope head-on.

Immediately, Jesus addressed her issue. He said, "Do not hold on to me." Mary was grasping for the Jesus she had known when He walked among them. She wanted to cling to the relationship she had experienced in the past. Perhaps that was part of her longing to be near the body; she didn't want to let go. But now everything had changed. Mary's hope was not going to be found in the past. Jesus had plans for Mary and for the other disciples. They would turn the world upside down. Jesus wanted to enlarge Mary's perspective and move her forward—to give her not just a hope but a future.

Jesus told her, "Do not hold on to me. . . . Go instead to my brothers and tell them, 'I am returning to My Father.'" He pointed Mary to the larger picture. He was saying, "You are focused on the wrong thing. We have work to do. I will be with you, but I am going on to my Father. Go tell the others." Do you see what Jesus did? He gave Mary an assignment. He redirected her focus. He said, "Don't focus on your sorrow or on what used to be. Focus on Me, and let Me lead you from here." He was allowing her to participate in His work, to partner with Him. He affirmed her, giving her a mission.

Seeing Jesus

Mary had met Jesus, taken hold of His hope, and now she had a story to tell. She left the tomb with hope in her heart and went to give the disciples the news: "I have seen the Lord!" Isn't that our greatest desire when we are desperate for hope? We want to see God at work. We want to know He is there. Once Mary took her eyes off the tomb, she could see Jesus. She encountered the living Christ. She arrived at the tomb with no hope for tomorrow, and she met Jesus, who said, "Not only is there going to be a tomorrow, but you are going to be part of it!"

We can take hold of that same hope. God has a tomorrow for us. He has work for us to do, and He is going to be there in it with us. So often we don't see Him for who He is because, in our human weakness, we are overwhelmed by our pain. But if we can take our eyes off the problem, off the crisis, if we can come up out of our grief and focus on the character of God, then we will see Him. We need to ask the Holy Spirit to help us do that—to help us shift our focus and see God. He will show us His life—those little flowers—springing up in the barren, rocky soil of our lives. We will see Him in what we thought was the tomb of our situation. We will see Him, and our hope will grow. Grasp His hope. He invites you. It is yours for the taking.

You may be reading this and realize that you do not have an intimate relationship with God. Maybe you don't have a personal history with Him. You've been reading in these pages about focusing on God's character and learning to trust Him, but you may never have made the decision to give your life to Him. Maybe now you are feeling curious. You want the assurance of a future and a hope. Perhaps you've tried other things with no success, and now you're willing to consider God. If you would like to know more about how to begin the process of a new life with God, I want to encourage you to turn to the R.S.V.P. at the back of this book. Take advantage of His invitation. Make a decision for your future. Grasp His hope.

POINT OF FOCUS

Why are you in despair, O my soul?
And why have you become disturbed within me?
Hope in God, for I shall yet praise Him,
The help of my countenance and my God.

Psalm 42:11

Anticipate His Plans

chapter thirteen

MOST OF US know what it is like to anticipate something. I would venture that most children old enough to remember a Christmas or a birthday understand what it is like to anticipate! A bride and groom anticipate their wedding and their future together. Perhaps they anticipate a first child or a first house. A student may anticipate graduation. When we anticipate something, we look forward to it with expectation.

When I anticipate my children coming for a visit, I begin making preparations early. I plan their favorite meals. I bake their favorite cake. I talk to my friends and family about their coming. I even talk with strangers about the approaching visit. I get their rooms clean and put fresh flowers beside the beds. I make sure I am home at the time they plan to arrive, and I wait with eagerness and excitement. I am confident they will come. I am expecting them.

Our Creator made us to anticipate. The act of anticipation is hardwired into the universe and into us. To anticipate is to look forward, not backward. Sometimes we need to look back in order to become emotionally healthy. As we have learned, God calls us to remember. We review the past to glean wisdom and understanding. We remember what God has done in our lives so we can move forward with more confidence. When we recall that our last step out on the ice held, we can find the courage to take another step. But while examining the past is important, we cannot stay there. We must learn to cultivate anticipation. We must be forward thinking. As the saying goes, you cannot steer a car if you are looking in the rearview mirror.

Jesus' invitation, "Come," is a call to move forward. As we have seen, Jesus meets people where they are and moves them ahead. He doesn't leave people in their condition. You can see the forward-moving activity of Jesus all through the Gospels. He anticipates the cross. He sets his face toward Jerusalem. He has a goal, a mission. His life moves in a forward direction. He says, "My food is to do the will of Him who sent Me and to accomplish His work" (John 4:34). Jesus lives in a state of anticipation. With Jesus, God's plans are always in view.

When we anticipate God's plans, what exactly are we anticipating? After all, we do not often know with certainty God's plans. We may have a sense of direction. An impression. We may have an idea of where we are supposed to go. We may feel God leading us to make a certain decision. There are times in life when we may have a very specific promise from God about something. But as long as we are living on earth, the Bible says, we "know in part" (1 Corinthians 13:12). In heaven, all will be made clear, but for now we live in a fallen world. We don't often know exactly what to expect.

When we anticipate God's plans, we are anticipating His activity in our lives, in the lives of others, and in the world. We are expecting God to show up in our tomorrow, whatever it holds, and to do His work. We are counting on Him to be there as He promised. Can you see how anticipating God's plans is tied to trust? If we do not trust God, how can we depend on Him to be with us in the future? The future seems uncertain and random when we don't trust God. Anything can happen. Any misfortune or disaster can befall us and make us its victims. But when we know God's character, when we've drilled down to the bedrock of His nature, when we believe what Scripture says about who God is, then we can anticipate His plans with greater peace. We know He is in control. We know He is sovereign. Misfortune may come, but we believe that God will be with us; that His plans are not to harm us but to build us up; that in all the uncertainty, messiness, and tension of life, His plans for us are good (Jeremiah 29:11).

Living in Tension

Anticipation doesn't necessarily involve joy. We might not always be smiling at the future (Proverbs 31:25). The Bible says Jesus endured the cross "for the joy set before Him," but it also tells us that before His crucifixion, Jesus struggled intensely in the garden of Gethsemane, praying, "Father, if you are willing, take this cup from me; yet not my will, but yours be done" (Luke 22:42 NIV). Jesus was always submitted to God's plans, yet He anticipated His destiny with a range of emotions. Often we do too, and we should not feel condemned about that. We can look to Jesus.

Once my mother and father were preparing for a vacation with friends. Daddy's schedule had been particularly heavy, and he was exhausted. He needed the vacation, but he had quite a few things to do before he could go. As he and Mother made plans, he said to her, "I dread looking forward to it." Our family has always gotten a chuckle out of that statement, perhaps because we can relate.

We need to know that it is okay to be human. I like the title of a book by Mike Yaconelli: *Messy Spirituality.* Life is not tidy. Very little, if anything, is neat. We live with unanswered questions. We live in a tug-of-war between fear and trust, joy and dread. As long as we are alive, we live in tension. And it can be uncomfortable. Many of us fight to get out of that tension. Some of us develop addictions or turn to other coping mechanisms. A world of unanswered questions is not an easy place to be. And yet it is where we live.

Having conflict in our hearts does not mean that we are failing. Our hearts will never be perfect. We may have some fear about tomorrow—does that mean we don't trust God? No. I think of the father in Mark who asked Jesus to heal his son and said, "I do believe; help my unbelief" (Mark 9:24). That man was living in the tension between trust and doubt, and Jesus was okay with it. We can be a "new creation" in Christ and still have issues to address (2 Corinthians 5:17).

Somehow, we must be willing to anticipate God's plans and to look forward with expectation in spite of the tension we feel. This is not always easy. There is no formula for it. We live in a relationship with God, and we learn how to walk by relating to Him. I am grieved that as believers we often treat God like a vending machine. Somehow we think that if we put in A, B, and C, then all of a sudden, we will get D. For a long time I lived this way, practicing the steps and anticipating the desired result, but I learned God is much bigger than our formulas. We can do A, B, and C, and God may do D—but He may not. He may do something entirely different. Or He may take His time. This does not mean God is capricious. God does not think or operate as we do (Isaiah 55:8). He sees the big picture, the long view. While we do not always understand His ways, God's love for us is sure, and His character unchanging. These are the certainties we have while living in tension.

Trusting God's Process

Anticipating God's plans can be particularly difficult when we are submerged in the challenges and issues of the moment. People often tell me, "God is always on time." I reply, "Yes, but sometimes He cuts it pretty close!" We can get completely consumed in the now. We see only today or the day after, and we lose sight of the big picture. We get frustrated and impatient. We take matters into our own hands, often making decisions and judgments based on our limited perspective, and then we're thrown off balance when something happens for which we aren't prepared. We end up bewildered and mystified at the circumstances in which we find ourselves.

When Abraham was old and childless, God promised him a son, an heir. In the face of human impossibility, Abraham trusted God to fulfill that promise. We read, "Without becoming weak in faith he [Abraham] contemplated his own body, now as good as dead since he was about a hundred years old, and the deadness of Sarah's womb; yet, with respect to the promise of God, he did not waver in unbelief but grew strong in faith, giving glory to God, and being fully assured that what God had promised, He was able also to perform" (Romans 4:19–21). What was Abraham doing? He was anticipating God's plans.

Then trouble came: Time passed. Sarah especially became impatient, and I can understand why. When a woman who has longed for a child all her life and who has given up hope is now told she is going to have one, she wants that baby sooner rather than later! I am sure Abraham and Sarah were very excited and eager to see how God would fulfill His promise. They must have talked about it many times over dinner. If they were like many couples today, they picked out names for the baby. Planned a nursery. But as years went by and nothing seemed to happen, anticipating God's plans became tougher. Sarah might have begun to question. To doubt. Even to whine. Was this promise real? Had Abraham heard God correctly? Perhaps Abraham tried to reason with Sarah, telling her she needed to be patient and to trust. But when you feel you are at the end of hope, words of encouragement are difficult to hear and receive.

At a certain point, Sarah fell back on her own understanding. She convinced Abraham that God surely could not have meant a child would come from the two of them. She began to devise her own plan by which God could fulfill His promise—her way. Abraham would have a child by her much younger maidservant. That made more sense. A baby conceived that way with Abraham as the father could just as well be the promised heir. Abraham, we are told, agreed with the plan and went through with it. Turmoil, jealousy, anger, abuse, and heartache were the result. Yes, Abraham and Sarah had anticipated God's plans, but when the waiting started to get wearisome, they took matters into their own hands. They did not leave the timing and manner of the promise's fulfillment to God.

Anticipating God's plans requires a willingness to embrace the way those plans are played out. I know I am often impatient with God's process in my life. I don't want to go through the ordeal of planting a garden. I just want the garden. I don't want to practice a consistent exercise regimen. I just want the toned body and the healthy heart. But the journey—the process—is just as important as the goal, and maybe more so. W. Glyn Evans writes in his devotional book *Daily with the King*, "God's purpose is process, not destiny."[1] Like Sarah, we want to see the promise or plan fulfilled. We want to reach the goal. But when the goal becomes our focus and trust takes a backseat, we are in danger of making unwise decisions and getting in the way of God's plans.

God's ultimate goal for us is holiness—that we look like Jesus— and He asks us to trust the process. A friend of mine often tells me to be patient and "trust the process" in my own life. As we anticipate what God has planned, we must allow Him to do things His way. His process is what prepares us for His plans. So much of the growth in my life has been birthed in failure and difficulty. Struggle enlarged my capacity for ministry. God often uses the hard things in life to make us grow deeper. Did I like the process? No. But I do know that the deeper things of God are often learned during our times of struggle and pain. A guitar string needs tension to make beautiful music. A seed has to be scarified with well-placed incisions in its seed coat in order to germinate. In *Ruthless Trust*, Brennan Manning writes, "Trust must be purified in the crucible of trial."[2]

But what about enjoyment? At a certain point, aren't we also supposed to enjoy God's process in our lives? How do we enjoy the process when we live in tension, when we struggle with discouragement and unanswered questions, when it hurts? How do we learn from Abraham and Sarah's mistake and *keep* ourselves in the process, let alone enjoy it?

I don't think *enjoy* is a term that would describe how we feel in the process all the time, but we do enjoy it in the sense that we know that God is at work. That He has a plan. That it's not all up to us to make that plan happen. We are gratified in the fact that we're part of a larger picture and that we're not just out there on our own. You may not enjoy the way the process is being worked out in your life, but if you can look at the overarching picture and say, "Yes, Lord, I trust you," then peace and a deeper contentment can at times be experienced.

After his brothers sold him into slavery and Potiphar's wife accused him, Joseph probably didn't enjoy being in prison, but he seemed to be aware that God was in charge. He trusted God's process and disciplined himself, doing his "homework" and faithfully serving where he was placed, so that when the time came for God's plans, whatever they were, to further unfold, he was prepared. I am also reminded of Shadrach, Meshach, and Abed-nego, who, before being thrown into the blazing furnace, said, "Our God whom we serve is able to deliver us. . . . But even if He does not, let it be known to you, O king, that we are not going to serve your gods" (Daniel 3:17–18). Like Joseph, these men were going to remain faithful and trust God's process.

Recognizing God's Plan

Simeon was an old man now. He had lived a long, full life. I can imagine his parents had raised him in the synagogue and taught him all that the prophets had foretold about the coming Messiah. Simeon loved to hear the stories. No doubt they were shared around the dinner table. We are told that Simeon was a devout and righteous man who in his old age was waiting for the Messiah "to come and rescue Israel" (Luke 2:25 NLT). There wasn't anything extraordinary about Simeon except that he believed the promise of God. Prompted by the Holy Spirit, Simeon had cherished in his heart the hope that before he died, he would see the Messiah. He not only hoped, but he anticipated that moment. And he waited year after year.

What made Simeon think that God was about to fulfill the words of the prophets, words that had ceased 400 years before? Did Simeon really think this moment in history was the time for the Messiah? Surely many people in previous generations had hoped theirs would be the moment. Why here? Why now? But Simeon wasn't moved by circumstances or events. W. Glyn Evans writes, "Faith cannot tell time very well."[3] Simeon simply kept on trusting God to keep His promise. He had faith in God's character, and he looked to the future with expectation and hope.

We do not know when the Holy Spirit gave Simeon his promise about seeing the Messiah, but certainly Simeon had been maintaining his sense of expectancy for a long time. How did he do it? How did he keep his anticipation alive? He did it by maintaining a daily relationship with God. Simeon's preparation was not elaborate, but it was consistent. I'm sure not every day of his life was exceptional. Nonetheless, day by day Simeon put one foot in front of the other, fulfilling his devotion to God and trusting that God's timing was better than his own. I wonder how many faces Simeon studied as he walked to the temple each day. Could that be the Messiah? Could that man be the one? Is this the day? I would have given up hope, but Simeon stayed faithful, cultivating his relationship with the Lord and keeping watch for the promise that had been given to him. Simeon did his part. Now God was about to do His.

Imagine with me the scene at the temple the day that Jesus, likely still an infant, is brought for dedication to the Lord. It is an ordinary day. People are coming and going. Rituals are being observed. There are no signs to indicate anything special is about to happen. The temple officials and priests go about their many tasks. Worshippers fulfill their ritual obligations. Then a young couple enters the temple court, carrying their infant son to present him to the Lord and to offer the required sacrifice. The couple is very poor, only able to offer two turtledoves as prescribed by the Law.

Prompted by the Spirit, Simeon is in the temple that day, and he notices the young couple. He sees them. He sees their baby. There is a moment of recognition. By the Holy Spirit, Simeon knows this child is the One he has anticipated all these years. But wasn't the Messiah supposed to come on a white steed to conquer Rome and set Israel free? Wasn't He going to come with power and authority and free the captives? Surely not a baby, a helpless infant? But perhaps Simeon would not have been surprised. He would have known the messianic prophecies, including Isaiah's: "Behold, the virgin shall conceive and bear a Son" (Isaiah 7:14 NKJV).

Whatever might have been in his heart, Simeon allows God to be

God. He looks at the baby and he knows: *This is the Christ, the Messiah!* His heart must have quickened inside of him much as Elizabeth's baby leapt in her womb when Mary arrived at her home, pregnant with Jesus. What were Simeon's thoughts? We can only imagine the joy. Wonder. Awe. Relief. I wonder if he clapped his hands and laughed. I am sure he was itching to get his hands on that child. Any grandparent knows the feeling!

I can see Simeon approaching the couple slowly, reverently. His eyes see so much. Not only the little family but the future. Was he afraid? Certainly he trusted God and His character. Imagine the awe he must have felt. He doesn't yell out and say, "Look here, people! This is the Messiah come to rescue us! Stop what you are doing. God has come as He promised." He doesn't draw attention to himself. Nor does he rush God's process of revelation. Simeon is discreet. He is a man who walks in step with the Lord. He is tuned in to what God is doing. He exercises wisdom, allowing God to unfold His plans in His own way.

Simeon approaches gently and holds out his arms, asking permission to hold the child. He holds the baby close. Smells His baby smell. Looks into those eternal eyes and knows he holds the Savior of the world to his heart. What must he have felt? What were his emotions? Inexplicable joy. Gratitude. Praise. Tears must have coursed down that old weathered face. At that moment, the hope of his life is being fulfilled! Not necessarily as he expected. Or when he expected. But God has fulfilled the long-awaited hope.

Simeon acknowledges God's sovereignty and His promise fulfilled not only for the Jewish people but for the whole world. We are told that Simeon praises God, saying, "Sovereign Lord, as you have promised, you now dismiss your servant in peace" (Luke 2:29 NIV). I love that! Simeon calls himself a servant. What humility. It is as if he is telling God, "I'm just here, Lord, at your bidding, and now that you've fulfilled your promise to me, I am ready to go." It is a sweet moment. Simeon is seeing the fulfillment of what he anticipated. He is experiencing the capstone of his life and work. He has been faithful, waiting for the Messiah. Now he is holding the Messiah in his arms, and he knows that his purpose is accomplished. The servant has seen his Master, and it is enough. Perhaps Simeon was born for this moment—to recognize Jesus, to talk to Mary, to praise God at this moment, to bless the child. He is an old man, and here he is at the pinnacle of his life.

As he is speaking, we read, Mary and Joseph are listening in amazement, marveling at what Simeon is saying about the child. Surely, they are surprised that a stranger has such deep insight into the destiny of the baby entrusted to them. As far as they are aware, outside of the shepherds, and perhaps some family, the child's identity mostly remains unknown.

Simeon blesses Mary and Joseph. Then he turns to Mary and speaks to her prophetically. He tells her the child will be the rise and fall of many people, and that ultimately, He would give His life in order to reveal the thoughts of many hearts. "A sword will pierce even your own soul," Simeon tells her.

We do not know if Mary understood everything this old man was saying to her. On some level, his words must have been frightening. Mary was still just a young teenager. Yet she and Joseph had already come through so much uncertainty, so many unusual events. What we know of Mary is that she, like Simeon, is discreet; she is thoughtful. When the shepherds came to Bethlehem after Jesus' birth, having been directed by angels, the Bible tells us Mary listened to what the shepherds related about the child and "treasured all these things, pondering them in her heart" (Luke 2:19). She took it all in and kept quiet. Here too, standing with Simeon, Mary doesn't seem to be fretting or fearing the future—we sense more that she is taking in the prophecy as part of God's plan for her life, pondering it, listening to the words. She and Joseph had trusted God this far, and they knew He was trustworthy. They would continue to trust Him for their tomorrows.

At this moment, a prophetess named Anna approaches. Anna, too, has waited for the Messiah with anticipation. We are told she is "advanced in years," eighty-four, and has been widowed since she was a young married woman. Old. Bent. Gnarled. Alone. At this point, Anna has every reason to retire from service, but she does not wallow in self-pity. Quite the opposite, she serves continually in the temple. In the loss of human companionship, she has chosen God to be her daily, lifelong companion. She loves God's house and God's people. She worships with prayer and fasting. As Simeon ends his prophecy over the baby, Anna walks up and begins to give God thanks—she thanks Him out of the overflow of her heart! Afterward, she continues to talk about the child to others who, like her, are waiting for Jerusalem's redemption. Anna becomes the first woman to preach the gospel!

It is interesting to note that God chooses two elderly people, one of them a woman, to recognize and acknowledge His Son. As far as we can see, Simeon and Anna's only qualifications for this honor are their devotion to God and their anticipation of His plans. God's plan of salvation is their cherished hope. They are not focused on their age or on the delay in their hope being fulfilled. They are looking to God and His promise. God's promises are living and active—not stale or dead (Hebrews 4:12). God's promise is what sustains them.

Simeon and Anna's consistent focus on God and His plan is what prepares them to recognize the Savior. Mary Magdalene at the empty tomb was too absorbed in her grief to recognize Jesus. The disciples on the road to Emmaus were caught up in confusion and hopelessness and didn't recognize Him. But Simeon and Anna, who had their eyes constantly on God, saw the baby and, prompted by the Spirit, knew.

God breaks into history as a baby, and only two people notice. The religious people are too busy fulfilling their rituals to recognize that what they have been waiting and looking for is now a reality. They are not wrong to be busy, but they have let routine and everyday life erase their anticipation. We have to be careful of that as well. Like Simeon and Anna, we must be diligent in keeping our focus rightly placed. We want to recognize Jesus in our lives! We want to recognize His work, His activity. The Holy Spirit helps us to see and understand—He reveals truth to us. But Simeon and Anna prepared themselves by faithfully nourishing their relationship with the Lord and cultivating anticipation. That is what we must do.

Cultivating Anticipation

Maybe we need a new language for anticipating God's plans. A "problem" becomes an "opportunity" to see God work. A "doubt" becomes a "chance" to grow into His plan for us. "Discouragement" becomes a "challenge" to trust God in a deeper way. A "struggle" becomes an "adventure" in our relationship with Him. How do we cultivate anticipation? We change our language. We change our focus.

I was in the midst of a very difficult situation in my life, and it consumed much of my thought and energy. I kept thinking that if I could just maneuver around it, go over it, dig under it, or get it out of the way, then things would run smoothly and I would be much more peaceful. I was focused on finding a way out. One day it dawned on me that God was using this problem to make me more like Jesus, which is what I ultimately want. God changed my perspective. I began to praise Him for the situation because He was using it to accomplish His work in me. My language about the situation changed—the problem became an opportunity. My focus also changed, and I could now anticipate God's plans.

We have certainly seen ways in which the Lord helped people in the Bible to change their focus. Mary's husband Joseph's focus shifted from his uncertainty about the future to God's trustworthiness. The woman taken in adultery—from judgment to grace in Jesus' presence. Mary and Martha—from death to resurrection. The disciples in the boat—from the storm to God's power. The woman with the issue of blood was so focused on Jesus she found help. The two disciples on the road to Emmaus—from disappointment to peace. The disciples out fishing all night—from their own efforts to His invitation. The woman at the well—from rejection to acceptance. Peter—from a broken past to future ministry. The disciples in the crowd of five thousand—from their inadequacy to Jesus' affirmation and sufficiency. Mary Magdalene— from the empty tomb to the risen Lord. And Simeon and Anna, of course, had it right. Their focus was consistently on God, His promise, and His plans.

One way we can adjust our focus is by talking about what we are anticipating. We can build anticipation. We can create a buzz. Consider some of the ways we often encourage children to anticipate Christmas. We talk about Christmas. We ask the children what gifts they would like to see under the tree. We may tantalize them as did my father when he would say to us with eyes dancing, "I know what you're getting for Christmas, but I'm not telling!" We decorate the house. We bake cookies and special treats. We have parties and family gatherings. We attend the church's Christmas pageant. We play Christmas carols and read the Christmas story. On top of that, our society underscores the secular aspects of Christmas with advertising, television specials, and any number of means. By the time Christmas Eve comes, children are at a fever pitch. They can't go to sleep because of the anticipation!

Sadly, the anticipation often creates an unrealistic expectation, and as Christmas Day draws to a close, disappointment sets in. The artificially created reality doesn't meet the children's expectations, and life moves on. We adults know what this kind of disappointment feels like. We too put our faith in artificially created realities. The family vacation we carefully planned and anticipated didn't meet our expectations. The new car we saved for is replaced by another new and improved model. The new house has plumbing problems. And on it goes.

But this sort of letdown is not what we experience when we cultivate our anticipation of God's plans. God's reality is far above anything we can imagine. The Bible says, "No eye has seen, no ear has heard, no mind has conceived what God has prepared for those who love him" (1 Corinthians 2:9 NIV). When my mother was near the end, she was anticipating heaven, and we constantly talked to her about it. We talked about the freedom from the pain. We talked about the new body she was going to get in exchange for the worn-out body. We talked about the friends and family she would see in heaven. Not to mention she would be in the very presence of Jesus!

Do you think Abraham and Sarah were disappointed when Isaac was finally born and they held him in their arms? The fulfillment of God's plans far exceeded what they had anticipated. Do you think Simeon and Anna were disappointed when they beheld the Messiah? They were filled with wonder and joy. God does things far better than we could ever dream. He gives more, so much more. As Paul wrote, He can do "exceedingly abundantly above all that we ask or think" (Ephesians 3:20 NKJV).

Anticipating the Savior

The man who perhaps epitomizes anticipation in Scripture is John the Baptist. His life's purpose was anticipation. Before John was conceived, an angel appeared to his father, Zacharias, and told him, "It is he [John] who will go as a forerunner before Him in the spirit and power of Elijah, to turn the hearts of the fathers back to the children, and the disobedient to the attitude of the righteous, so as to make ready a people prepared for the Lord" (Luke 1:17). John was born to literally anticipate the Messiah's coming.

John's mother, Elizabeth, was probably Mary's cousin. When the angel appeared to Mary to tell her she would bear a child named Jesus who would be the Son of the Most High, the angel also told her that Elizabeth in her old age was expecting. Mary went to visit Elizabeth, and as Mary greeted her, we read, "the baby [John] leaped in her womb; and Elizabeth was filled with the Holy Spirit" (Luke 1:41). Even before he was born, John was anticipating his Savior!

I can only imagine what it was like for Zacharias and Elizabeth. Not only did they finally have a child after a lifetime of barrenness, but the child would play a part in the fulfillment of prophecy given from Genesis on through the history of their people. They knew the Scriptures—Zacharias was a priest; Elizabeth was descended from priests—and they would have taught their son line by line about the coming Messiah. I imagine that as a child, John was told about his purpose as foretold by the angel. The story of the angel's visit might have been told and retold at bedtime. No doubt Zacharias and Elizabeth shared with John what the Messiah's coming would mean to the Jewish people, who had waited for so long in anticipation. John would be the first prophet in four hundred years—since Malachi. The parents' excitement would have been contagious for their little son.

Once John began his public ministry, his sole purpose was to bear witness of Jesus. When the Jewish leaders asked who he was, John did not grab attention for himself. Certainly, he was an attention-drawing prophet, dressed as he was in camel hair and living in the desert. John was a popular figure. He had his own disciples. He drew large crowds and preached powerfully. But he knew his purpose was not to build his own ministry and following, and he never even seemed tempted to do so.

John knew his purpose and was not shy about declaring it to all who asked, even the priests and the Levites. He told them flat out, "I am not the Christ. . . . I am a voice of one crying in the wilderness, 'Make straight the way of the Lord'" (John 1:20, 23). When the priests continued to press him, John said of the Messiah, "It is He who comes after me, the thong of whose sandal I am not worthy to untie" (John 1:27). John made it clear that his purpose was to prepare the people to anticipate Jesus' arrival. He said, "He who comes after me has surpassed me because he was before me" (John 1:15 NIV).

Perhaps you have known the experience of introducing two of your friends who do not know each other. You want them to like each other. You are the link between them, so you begin the process by talking to each of them about the other, describing the other one, telling of the other's personality, interests, and hobbies. You talk about each of their families and backgrounds. You talk of their work and the interesting things they have done. You tell of your experiences with them. You prepare the way for the introduction. You anticipate that moment, and you draw each of them into the anticipation.

That is what John did in preparing the world for Jesus. He anticipated the coming of Jesus, and he worked to help others also look forward to it. He talked about the time when Jesus would be revealed. Perhaps he illustrated his sermons with stories of their childhood, talking of days when they played together as boys. John planned for Jesus' appearance. He wasn't looking to institute something for himself—he didn't build the First Baptist Church. He was a signpost pointing to another. When some of his own disciples left to follow Jesus, John did not get upset or feel threatened. He wanted to work himself out of a job.

One day, as John was preaching at the Jordan River, Jesus came, asking to be baptized. In humility, John refused, saying it was he who needed to be baptized by Jesus. Did they argue good-naturedly like cousins would? I imagine John could be stubborn! In the end, as Jesus explained the higher purpose, John relented. The Lord had already told John he would recognize the Messiah when he saw the Spirit descending from heaven on Him. As Jesus was coming up out of the water, Scripture says, "The heavens were opened, and he saw the Spirit of God descending as a dove and lighting on Him, and behold, a voice out of the heavens said, 'This is My beloved Son, in whom I am well-pleased'" (Matthew 3:16–17). Wow! Can you imagine John's experience standing there? Being able to see the heavens open and hear God's own voice confirm the fulfillment of his expectation? In that moment, John's anticipation was fulfilled.

As Jesus took His place on center stage, John moved off the scene somewhat. He didn't quit his ministry. He was thrown in prison for condemning Herod's illicit relationship with Herodias, his sister-in-law. Still uncompromising, still faithful, John was eventually beheaded at the request of the same woman he had accused. When Jesus heard of John's death, He withdrew to be by Himself. Surely, He was deeply grieved, wanting to remember John and honor his memory. But Jesus also knew things were coming to a climax. The forerunner was gone. The one who had understood Him and His purpose perhaps better than anyone other than His mother was gone. John's purpose to anticipate was now fulfilled, and he was waiting in heaven for that great act of redemption and victory for the world—the cross and the resurrection.

Standing on Tiptoe

We lived in the Philadelphia area when my oldest child, Noelle, was a toddler. Her father commuted each day into the city and back home again at about six o'clock in the evening, depending on traffic. Each night, as the time for her father's arrival drew near, little Noelle would go stand inside the storm door and wait for him, watching each car as it approached. I have a clear picture in my mind of her standing patiently by the door with "blankey" clutched in her hand and her thumb in her mouth, anticipating her daddy's homecoming. When she finally saw him, she squealed, anxious for him to open the door and scoop her into his arms. God wants us to be like that, standing as if on tiptoe in anticipation of the good things He has for us.

As we have learned, we can "stand on tiptoe" by walking consistently in our relationship with God, by keeping our focus on Him, and by looking toward the future with the expectation that He will be there. But like Simeon, Anna, Mary and Joseph, and John the Baptist, we also anticipate the future by doing what is in front of us. We stay faithful in the now. Jesus lived anticipating the cross, but he also said, "We must work the works of Him who sent Me as long as it is day" (John 9:4). God does not expect us to wait passively. Simeon and Anna served the Lord faithfully in the temple. Mary and Joseph brought up Jesus. John the Baptist prepared the people. There is work to be done.

When Jesus was twelve years old, He told His mother, "I must be about My Father's business" (Luke 2:49 NKJV). So must we. Life with God is not a spectator sport. We don't sit on the sidelines waiting for things to happen. The Christian life is an active relationship! No relationship is static. As I shared, if I anticipate my children coming home, I am going to prepare. That is true in our walk with God. He has commissioned us to go and make disciples of all nations (Matthew 28:19–20). He has invited us to participate in His work. While it is our choice whether we engage, it is important to realize that God's expectation is that we be active. We partner in His present activity even as we anticipate His future activity.

We can be faithful in what we are called to do, even into old age. As I have said, it took me more than fifty years to step into what I believe is now God's calling for my life. Moses was eighty before he started leading the children of Israel. It's never too late, no matter our calling—whether we're a mom, an executive, a farmer, a custodian, a pastor, a musician, or anything else. People often tell me they believe my father's reward in heaven will be great. I assume their view is based on the largeness of his ministry and the numbers of people who have come to Christ because of it. I am not sure what my father's reward will be in heaven nor how big it will be. I believe God rewards faithfulness, not numbers. We get wrapped up in numbers, bigness, and celebrity. God does not. My father has been faithful to his call, and so have countless others who faithfully do what God has called them to do. That is our job—faithfulness. Whether we are raising our children, writing a book, mowing the lawn, going to work every day, serving our families or others, we have work to do as we anticipate the work God is doing in us.

Ultimately, we anticipate the culmination of history. Our greatest anticipation is that Jesus is coming again! When Jesus left this earth, the angels told the disciples, "This Jesus, who has been taken up from you into heaven, will come in just the same way as you have watched Him go into heaven" (Acts 1:11). He is coming back! What we watch on the television or read in the news is not all there is. There is more, so much more. We live in the light of eternity.

The Bible tells us we are "to live sensibly, righteously and godly in the present age, looking for the blessed hope and the appearing of the glory of our great God and Savior, Christ Jesus" (Titus 2:12–13). We've talked about living in tension, about looking forward with joy and dread, about the struggle to trust and not to fear as we are confronted with life's issues. When Jesus comes back, our issues will all be made right. There will be a new world, a new life. We will be reunited with Jesus, and everything will be made just. I remember my mother saying, "When we get to heaven, all the questions and answers become one." She now knows that relief.

Our struggle is that here on earth we live with unanswered questions. We are asked to follow God in the dark. We don't know what to do, so we are afraid. When Jesus returns, we will know. All will be clear. As Paul wrote, "Now I know in part, but then I shall know just as I also am known" (1 Corinthians 13:12 NKJV). That is something to anticipate! As believers, we can live always in anticipation, ever standing on tiptoe, watching for the return of our Lord. "And it will be said in that day, 'Behold, this is our God for whom we have waited'" (Isaiah 25:9).

Fear not tomorrow—God is already there! Hallelujah!

POINT OF FOCUS

No eye has seen,
no ear has heard,
no mind has conceived
what God has prepared for those who love him.

1 Corinthians 2:9 NIV

R.S.V.P.

I DON'T KNOW WHERE you are in these uncertain times. Perhaps your tomorrow holds no bright promise. You are feeling insecure and inadequate to face tomorrow—afraid of what it will bring. You have done all you know to do. Others are depending on you, and yet you have run out of your last bit of hope. You do not have any strength left. Perhaps you have blown it—big-time—and you wonder if you can ever begin again. You want out. You need peace and rest. You need help. You need to regain some measure of hope. You are desperate.

I am glad you are here. It is no accident that you are holding this book and reading this page. God wants you to know that He is already in your tomorrow.

Perhaps as you have been reading, a longing has developed in your heart, a longing to be in relationship with God—to know Him as a loving, personal friend. You can have such a friendship. God wants to be your friend. His invitation is "Come."

God has already prepared the way for you to respond by sending Jesus to die on the cross for you. He loves you that much. He invites you into an intimate relationship. He is everything you need to face tomorrow. He wants to give you all that He is in exchange for all that you are not. God will meet you where you are and take you where He wants you to be. He enfolds you into His heart. Forever. You need not be afraid.

Right now you can open your heart and tell God that you want to be in relationship with Him. That you need Him. That you are sorry for your sins and want to begin again. You can tell Him that you believe Jesus died on the cross and rose from the dead for you. You can ask Him to take up residence in your heart and life as Savior and Lord. The moment you ask, God responds—He is in you. He loves you unconditionally and accepts you as you are. You don't have to understand it all right now, but you can take the first step. If you would like, you can pray the prayer below. The words are not as important as the sincerity of your heart.

> God, I read in this book that You do not want me to fear tomorrow, because You are with me. You invite me into a close relationship with You. I want that. I want to know You in a personal way so that I don't have to be afraid of the uncertainty of life. I want to trust You with my tomorrows. I need You. I believe Jesus died on the cross and rose again for me. Please forgive my sins, and come into my heart and life. I receive You as Lord and Savior. I believe, but help me in the areas of my unbelief. Amen.

If you prayed that prayer just now, then you have begun a personal relationship with God. You have given your life to Him, and He accepts you. I am excited for you! You have entered the most fulfilling relationship ever. Now I would like to encourage you in some areas that will help you grow in your relationship with God.

- Tell someone about your decision. That will help confirm it in your own mind.
- Get a Bible and begin to read it. Get a version that is easy to read and understand. Set aside some time every day to read and study it. John's gospel in the New Testament is a good place to start. Read until you think God has spoken to you. Ask God to help you understand what you read.

- Pray every day. Talk to God like you would your best friend. Tell Him everything, and ask for His help throughout the day.
- Find a church that teaches and practices what the Bible says, and go there regularly. It is important to be around others who can encourage us in our faith walk.

If you would like more information about living your new relationship with God, or if you are thinking about beginning a relationship with God and want to learn more about what this means, you can visit www.billygraham.org and click on the "How to Know Jesus" link. If you do not have access to a computer, you can call toll-free at 1-877-247-2426 or write to the following address:

The Billy Graham Evangelistic Association
1 Billy Graham Parkway
Charlotte, NC 28201

In the meantime, may God continue to deepen your relationship with Him.

God bless you,
Ruth Graham

ABC Praise List

BELOW IS MY ABC list of God's attributes. I keep the list in the back of my Bible and use it as a tool in prayer—as a starting point for praising God. As I move through the attributes, I think about each one and about how God may be demonstrating them in my life. I may thank God for being my encourager, my healer. I may praise Him for His peace and ask Him to calm my anxiety. I may praise Him for being mighty and pray for a friend who needs Him to demonstrate His might in her life. I keep adding to the list, and I encourage you to do the same. You can add words in the margins of this book, keep a copy in the back of your Bible, or start fresh and make a list of your own. God gave us creativity—we can give it back to Him as we use it in praise.

A   Almighty, anchor

B   Beautiful, bountiful, big

C   Compassionate, composer, covenant keeper, creator

D   Deliverer, dear, death defeater, divine

E   Eternal, embracer, encourager

F Faithful, friend

G Gracious, great, good, gentle

H Healer, hope, help

I Infinite, my inheritance, invincible

J Joy, just, jealous, justifier

K Knowable, kind, keeper

L Love, long-suffering, lovely

M Mighty, merciful

N Near, necessary

O Omnipresent, omniscient, owner

P Peace, protector, preeminent

Q Quick, quiet

R Redeemer, rest, refuge

S Savior, sustainer, strength

T Trustworthy, tender, treasure

U Understanding, utmost

V   Victor, valuable, vindicator

W   Wisdom, wonderful

X   Xenophile

Y   Yes

Z   Zealous, zenith

Reading Resources

M Y MOTHER USED to say that no one should claim to quote her, because nothing she said was original! My mother was actually a very quotable lady, as you may have noticed in this book. She was a great reader and note taker, and she loved to collect quotations that captured her mind.

I too read, take notes, and collect quotes. I take notes when someone is speaking or preaching. Unfortunately, I do not carefully mark down where all these insights or quotes come from. I have quotes on pieces of paper that are stuck in my Bible, in books, in my desk drawer, and in my filing cabinet. As you can imagine, this is a very haphazard system and one that becomes a burden when writing a book, which requires you to credit your sources.

Such was the case in putting together this book. Many people have informed my thinking and my interpretation of the Scriptures. While I trust I have given proper credit to sources, numerous others have influenced me, and I would be mortified if I mistakenly had failed to cite them.

Below is a list of reading resources that have been helpful to me, not only in the writing of this book, but also in my own walk with God. I thank all those who have added to my understanding of God and the Scriptures—His Word. This list is certainly not meant to be complete, but I trust you will find it a source of enrichment.

Barclay, William. *The Daily Study Bible.* Philadelphia: The Westminster Press, 1956.

Buechner, Frederick. *Listening to Your Life.* San Francisco: HarperSanFrancisco, 1992.

Edersheim, Alfred. *The Life and Times of Jesus the Messiah.* Peabody, Mass.: Hendrickson Publishers, 1993.

Exell, Joseph S. and H. D. M. Spence, ed. *The Pulpit Commentary.* Vol. 15–17. Grand Rapids: William B. Eerdmans Publishing Company, 1950.

Manning, Brennan. *Ruthless Trust: The Ragamuffin's Path to God.* San Francisco: HarperSanFrancisco, 2000.

Miller, Donald. *Searching for God Knows What.* Nashville: Nelson Books, 2004.

Nouwen, Henri J. M. *The Return of the Prodigal Son: A Story of Homecoming.* New York: Doubleday, 1994.

Scazzero, Peter. *Emotionally Healthy Spirituality: Unleashing the Power of Authentic Life in Christ.* Nashville: Integrity Publishers, 2006.

Stibbe, Mark. *The Father You've Been Waiting For: Portrait of a Perfect Dad.* Waynesboro, Ga.: Authentic Media, 2005.

Yaconelli, Michael. *Messy Spirituality.* Grand Rapids: Zondervan, 2002.

Young, P. William. *The Shack.* Los Angeles: Windblown Media, 2007.

Other Books by Ruth Graham

A Legacy of Faith: Things I Learned from My Father

A Legacy of Love: Things I Learned from My Mother

In Every Pew Sits a Broken Heart: Hope for the Hurting

Step into the Bible: 100 Bible Stories for Family Devotions

Notes

Chapter One: Trust at My Doorstep

1. Ruth Graham, *In Every Pew Sits a Broken Heart: Hope for the Hurting* (Grand Rapids: Zondervan, 2004), 23.

Chapter Three: Experience His Presence

1. Ruth Graham, *A Legacy of Faith: Things I Learned from My Father* (Grand Rapids: Inspirio, 2006), 175.

2. William Barclay, *The Gospel of John,* vol. 2, The Daily Study Bible Series (Philadelphia: The Westminster Press, 1975), 1–9.

3. Tommy Walker, "Lord I Believe in You" © 1996 Doulos Publishing/BMI (Administered by Music Services). All Rights Reserved. Used by permission.

4. Ruth Bell Graham, *Collected Poems* (Grand Rapids: Baker Books, 1998), 223.

Chapter Four: Know His Comfort

1. Samuel Bagster, *Daily Light on the Daily Path* (Leeds: Lowe & Brydone Printers Limited, 1981).

2. Thomas Ken, "The Doxology," Public domain.

Chapter Five: Encounter His Power

1. Helen H. Lemmel, "Turn Your Eyes upon Jesus," Public domain.

2. Brennan Manning, *Ruthless Trust: The Ragamuffin's Path to God* (San Francisco: HarperSanFrancisco, 2000), 3.

Chapter Seven: Rest in His Peace

1. F. W. de Klerk, "Acceptance and Nobel Lecture," 1993, Nobel Foundation, http://nobelprize.org/nobel_prizes/peace/laureates/1993/klerk-lecture.html (accessed January 27, 2009).

2. Ibid.

3. Ibid.

4. Frederick Buechner, *Wishful Thinking: A Theological ABC* (New York: Harper & Row, 1973) as quoted in *Listening to Your Life: Daily Mediations with Frederick Buechner*, compiled by George Conner (San Francisco: HarperSanFrancisco, 1992), 295.

5. J. Boyd Nicholson, as quoted in "Choice Gleanings." Permission granted by Gospel Folio Press.

Chapter Eight: Hear His Invitation

1. John Eldredge, *Wild at Heart* (Nashville: Thomas Nelson, 2001), 57.

2. Lysa TerKeurst, *What Happens When Women Say Yes to God* (Eugene: Harvest House Publishers, 2007), 9–12.

Chapter Nine: Embrace His Forgiveness

1. Mark Stibbe, *The Father You've Been Waiting For: Portrait of a Perfect Dad* (Waynesboro: Authentic Media, 2005), 59.

2. Ruth Graham, *In Every Pew Sits a Broken Heart: Hope for the Hurting* (Grand Rapids: Zondervan, 2004), 141–52.

3. Corrie ten Boom with Jamie Buckingham, *Tramp for the Lord*, Billy Graham Crusade Edition, Billy Graham Evangelisic Association (Fort Washington, PA, and Old Tappan, NJ: Christian Literature Crusade and Fleming Revell, 1974), 108.

Chapter Ten: Realize His Restoration

1. "remorse." *Merriam-Webster Online Dictionary*. 2009. Merriam-Webster Online. 17 January 2009, http://www.merriam-webster.com/dictionary/remorse.

2. George W. Bush, *A Charge to Keep: My Journey to the White House* (New York: Perennial, 2001), ix.

3. A. W. Tozer, *The Root of the Righteous,* "Praise God for the Furnace" (Harrisburg: Christian Publications, Inc., 1955), 137.

4. I draw my interpretation here from a sermon preached by Allan Meyer at Careforce Church in Mt. Evelyn, Victoria, Australia.

5. Philip Yancey, *Reaching for the Invisible God* (Grand Rapids: Zondervan Publishing House, 2000), 277.

Chapter Eleven: Enjoy His Affirmation

1. Billy Graham, *Just As I Am* (San Francisco: HarperSanFrancisco, Zondervan, 1997), 323–24.

2. Dave Clark, Don Koch, Tony Wood, "I Was in the Room" © New Spring, Inc./Callender Lane Music.

Chapter Twelve: Grasp His Hope

1. Donald Miller, *Searching for God Knows What,* (Nashville: Nelson Books, 2004), 216.

2. Edward Mote, "The Solid Rock," Public domain.

3. Bill and Gloria Gaither, "I Am a Promise." Used by permission.

4. Frederick William Faber, "The Thought of Thee," as quoted by A. W. Tozer, *The Christian Book of Mystical Verse*, (Harrisburg: Christian Publications, Inc., 1963), 13–14.

5. Peggy Noonan, "It Is as It Was: Mel Gibson's 'The Passion' gets a thumbs-up from the pope," *Wall Street Journal*, December 17, 2003.

6. William Barclay, *The Gospel of John*, vol. 2, The Daily Study Bible Series (Philadelphia: The Westminster Press, 1975), 268.

Chapter Thirteen: Anticipate His Plans

1. Evans, W. Glyn, *Daily with the King* (Chicago: Moody Press, 1979), 13.

2. Brennan Manning, *Ruthless Trust: The Ragamuffin's Path to God* (San Francisco: HarperSanFrancisco, 2000), 9.

3. Evans, W. Glyn, *Daily with the King* (Chicago: Moody Press, 1979), 48.